Israel, the Palestinians, and the West Bank

A Study in Intercommunal Conflict

Shmuel Sandler
Bar-Ilan University and
   The Jerusalem Center for
   Public Affairs
Hillel Frisch
The Jerusalem Center for
   Public Affairs

LexingtonBooks
D.C. Heath and Company
Lexington, Massachusetts
Toronto

Library of Congress Cataloging in Publication Data

Sandler, Shmuel.
　Israel, the Palestinians, and the West Bank.

　Bibliography: p.
　Includes index.
　1. Jewish-Arab relations. 2. Palestinian Arabs—Politics and government.
3. West Bank—Politics and government. I. Frisch, Hillel. II. Title.
DS119.7.S3386　　1983　　323.1'19275694　　82-49204
ISBN 0-669-06435-1

Published simultaneously in Canada

Printed in the United States of America

International Standard Book Number: 0-669-06435-1

Library of Congress Catalog Card Number: 82-49204

To Channa and Edna

Contents

Figure and Tables

Acknowledgments

This book grew out of research supported by a 1979 Ford Foundation grant received through the Israel Foundation's Trustees. Additional support was provided by Bar-Ilan University and by the Leonard David Institute for International Relations of the Hebrew University of Jerusalem.

The bulk of the research and writing was done at the Jerusalem Institute for Federal Studies of The Jerusalem Center for Public Affairs. We would like to thank the center for providing us access to its archival material, for helping to underwrite the cost of our research, and for generously supplying us with office support. Special thanks go to Daniel J. Elazar, president of The Jerusalem Center for Public Affairs, for both his spiritual and professional support. Dan Elazar is not only a great mind but also a good friend. We would like to express our gratitude to Dan Horowitz, chairman of the Leonard Davis Institute for International Relations, for his advice. Several of the ideas in this book were developed from his conceptual framework and from studies conducted by him and Shaul Mishal.

During the course of this work we were greatly aided by the staff of The Jerusalem Center for Public Affairs. Judy Cohen and Tzipi Stein, the center coordinators, and Randi J. Land were of special assistance. Our greatest debt is to Amy L. Lederhendler for her editorial expertise.

Despite all debts, we accept full responsibility for the final product. Finally, we thank our wives, Channa and Edna, for their endurance and moral support.

Note on Transliteration

To maintain the flow of the text, we have avoided using scientific transliteration from either Arabic or Hebrew. We have, though, adopted a number of simple rules to maintain consistency. For Arabic terms, we use the consonant *k* to designate consonants that appear in scientific transliteration as *q*. Names are spelled as the personalities themselves spell them or as they appear customarily in English-language newspapers. Definite articles appear uncapitalized except for newspapers. Duplication of the first consonants in the sun letters is avoided. We always write out the definite article *al* in full. Geographic names are written as they appear in the *Map of Settlement in Eretz Yisrael*, produced and drawn by The Survey of Israel, 1982.

We write Hebrew terms and names as they appear in the *Encyclopedia Judaica*, except in cases where the scientific transliteration may mislead the reader. Thus, for instance, *z* appears as *tz*, as in Eretz Yisrael. For Israeli personalities and geographic names we use the same criteria we use for Arabic.

Introduction

The Arab-Israeli conflict has long been considered primarily from an international perspective. The outbreak of four major wars, waged by several Middle Eastern states, that indirectly involved Europe and the superpowers suffices to explain the emphasis of this approach. The interest in the conflict shown by the United Nations, the Arab League, and other international organizations has only served to reinforce the perception of the conflict as an international issue.

The prominence of the international dimension has diverted attention from the fact that two of the communities in conflict (the Jewish and the Arab Palestinian) have lived side by side under the same governmental administration for decades. In fact since the beginning of the century, when both communities began to develop national aspirations, the majority of the Palestinian Arabs have lived separated from the Jews by national boundaries for only nineteen years. Israel's rule over the West Bank and the Gaza Strip, although radically different from the pre-1948 British mandate, has once again brought the two communities into confrontation within one governmental framework. Unlike the mandate period, however, one community controls the central government organs, and the relationship between the two communities is that of ruler and ruled.

To be sure, the communal dimension of the Arab-Israeli relationship has not totally escaped the attention of scholars. But the research that has been conducted so far has concentrated primarily on either the *Yishuv* period[1] (the preindependence Jewish community) or on the relationship between Jews and the Israeli Arabs.[2] While not underestimating the importance of the international dimension, we shall concentrate more on the relationship between the Israelis and the Arab inhabitants of the territories from a communal perspective, in the belief that a proper understanding of this intercommunal conflict may lead to a deeper appreciation of the problems facing both Jews and Arabs in the region.

The intercommunal nature of the conflict resurfaced in 1967 when Israel acquired a territory in which a separate populace dwelled. This populace, which never became totally integrated into the Hashemite Kingdom of Jordan between 1948 and 1967, had already existed as a separate public in the area before 1948. Though by 1948 the Palestinians had not succeeded in establishing a viable political community, their self-assertiveness was not crushed during the ensuing period (1948-1967) of Jordanian control.

Following the Six Day War a new process of Palestinian assertiveness started to emerge. This process evolved around two foci. One was the territorial unit that came to be identified with the West Bank—the largest territory

populated exclusively by Arab Palestinians. The second was the Palestine
Liberation Organization (PLO) which started to play a role on the interna-
tion scene in the early 1970s. The relationship between the PLO and the
West Bank was not a simple one and as a result the delineation of their roles
and responsibilities was not clear initially. To further complicate interrela-
tionships in the area, Jordan and Israel held some influence over the same
territory. It took several years for a discernible division of labor to emerge.
The growing influence of the PLO over the West Bank Arab population
would come to contribute to the intensification of the intercommunal conflict.

The intercommunal conflict was also influenced by the impact of the Six
Day War on Israel. Ten years after the war, the ruling Labor elite that
perceived the conflict and sought solutions from an interstate perspective
was replaced by a coalition that approached the West Bank as an integral
part of the Jewish state. The combination of developments in both the
Palestinian community and the Israeli polity served to intensify the struggle.
Even the names used to designate the area were laden with political
significance. The Jews would refer to the Land of Israel (Eretz Yisrael) to
indicate the territory which was known before 1948 as Palestine. The focus
of the struggle became the West Bank or Judea and Samaria, depending on
whether the intent was to link the area to the East Bank of the Jordan River
by association or to emphasize ties to the land from Biblical times.

Thus, the struggle between Palestinians and Jews was no longer confined
to the interstate setting but took place both outside and within the jurisdiction of Israeli authority. The peace treaty between Israel and Egypt contributed to the state of flux in the region by breaking down the traditional
framework of an Arab camp unified against the Jewish state. The inclusion
of the autonomy idea into the peace treaty also reflected an intercommunal
reality. The June 1982 war in Lebanon between Israel and the PLO was
another manifestation of an intercommunal struggle that was waged within
and beyond state boundaries. In this struggle not only sovereign states participated but also an organization which, though without territorial status,
came to play a role on the international scene.

The theoretical concepts of our analysis are introduced and examined in
the first chapter in which we introduce a frame of reference based on previously developed theories, adding our own modifications. Political scientists
are just beginning to develop the theoretical tools to deal with intercommunal phenomena; therefore, we have not attempted to present a comprehensive theoretical framework. It is our hope that one empirical case
study will contribute to the development of a broad, useful theory of intercommunal conflict.

The post-1967 pattern, which is the focus of this book, cannot entirely be
understood without examining the earlier periods—the period before 1948,

and the 1948-1967 years. The pre-1948 history explains the emergence of the main actors in the conflict and the institution of an interstate system in Palestine.[3] A key concept to be drawn from the earlier period is the territorialization process of diaspora-based communities. This concept is useful in understanding the policies developed by the two communities.

The period of Jordanian rule over the West Bank provides the opportunity to analyze the historical pattern of the West Bank as it lost ground to outside forces and to explain the peculiar structure that emerged during the 1970s in which one territorial population came to be dominated by several outside entities. Jordan's relationship with the West Bank before 1967 helps to explain both Jordan's role in the West Bank following separation and the subsequent reemergence of a Palestinian identity.

The economic and political development experienced in the territory during the first decade of the Israeli administration brought mixed results to the area. The local economy became dependent on Israel despite the economic growth that took place in the territory in those years. The political development in the West Bank strengthened Palestinian identity but never translated into territorial center building.

Center building in the Palestinian community was largely a diaspora event that produced the emergence of the PLO as a charismatic center and the subordination of the West Bank. This represented the PLO's chance for territorialization. But the important distinction remains between the Palestinian communal structure and the West Bank, which was the real loser in this development.

In the last part of this book we examine the impact of Israel's political transformation on its relations with the West Bank and the Palestinians. One manifestation of Israel's transformation was the massive settlement drive which began in the late 1970s.

The developments in both the Palestinian community and the Israeli polity culminated during the first year of the second Likud administration when intercommunal conflict turned into an intercommunal war conducted on two fronts: the West Bank and Lebanon. This war has demonstrated the validity of an intercommunal relationship, the limitations of the Palestinian communal enterprise, the limitations of Israel's capability to win conclusively the contest with the Palestinians over the West Bank. It is hoped that these realities will promote an atmosphere of compromise in both camps that will contribute to the resolution of the ongoing intercommunal conflict.

Notes

1. We refer to Dan Horowitz and Moshe Lissak, *MiYishuv LeMedina* (The Origins of the Israeli Polity), (Tel-Aviv: Am Oved, 1977) (Hebrew).

We use the Hebrew title in this case because there is a variation between the Hebrew title and the English one given in the book. There is also an English abbreviated version of the book, see Dan Horowitz and Moshe Lissak, *The Origins of the Israeli Polity: Palestine under the Mandate* (Chicago: The University of Chicago Press, 1978). We used the Hebrew version.

2. See, for instance, Ian Lustick, *Arabs in the Jewish State: Israel's Control of a National Minority* (Austin: University of Texas Press, 1980). See also Sammy Smooha, "Control of Minorities in Israel and Northern Ireland," *Comparative Studies in Society and History*, vol. 22, no. 4 (April 1980):256-280; and Sammy Smooha, "The Orientation and Politicization of the Arab Minority in Israel," *Occasional Papers on the Middle East* (New Series), no. 2 (Haifa: University of Haifa, 1980).

3. The development of the Palestinian national movement between the two World Wars was analyzed extensively in Yehoshua Porat, *The Emergence of the Palestinian-Arab National Movement, 1918-1929* (London: Frank Cass, 1974); and Yehoushua Porat, *The Palestinian Arab National Movement 1929-1939* (London: Frank Cass, 1978).

Part I
Some Theoretical and
Historical Introductions

1

Theories of Intercommunal Conflict

Approaches to Conflict in Deeply Divided Societies

The theory of plural societies recognizes three alternatives to problems of cohesion in deeply divided societies.[1] One alternative, national integration, can be achieved through assimilation, modernization, nation building, and other measures which are designed to supply society's factions with new identities and loyalty to a new center.[2] A second alternative could be a shared-rule arrangement. This approach accepts pluralism rather than national integration as the basis for building a stable regime. Stability under such conditions could be achieved either through power-sharing arrangements between the various elites representing the conflicting communities, that is consociationalism, or a territorial shared-rule arrangement.[3] The third solution is the opposite of the national-integration alternative. In this theory the plural society breaks down into separate political systems.[4] Ideally, this partition would result in homogenous units in which each contending community would be able to express its national identity.

In practice, the success of each approach has been hindered by various problems. In an age of rising communal assertiveness, national integration cannot guarantee to offer a viable solution. Even developed countries such as Canada and Britain are facing internal strife resulting from communal conflicts. Consociational systems have either been transformed into majority-minority systems of government or, like Lebanon and Cyprus, have collapsed.[5] In its turn, the partition solution has not always brought about stability. Continuing strife in what was the Habsburg empire before World War I, and in Palestine, Ireland, and India are all situations in which internal or international conflict continued to exist even after partition.

Growing awareness of communal conflict in the contemporary world has stimulated several contributions to the theory of divided societies. A by-product of this growing awareness is the mutual recognition by scholars from the consociational and federal schools that their theories are complementary. Arend Lijphart has described the relationship in these words: "Federalism can be viewed as a consociational device and consociationalism can be interpreted as a special form of federalism."[6] Federalist scholars such as Carl J. Friedrich and Daniel J. Elazar have also noted this relationship in their discussions of federal elements in systems that would otherwise be considered as unitary states.[7] Ivo D. Duchacek, who has emphasized the territorial dimension of federalism, recently stated that in a broader and less formal sense "federal practices and federal political culture may be found in many polyethnic states that in their constitutions claim to be unitary rather than federal."[8] The survival of consociationalism in Switzerland and Canada, which has been defined by Lijphart as semiconsociational, and the gradual shift of Belgium to federalism, demonstrates in practice the relationship between the two models and the support that federalism can provide for consociational arrangements.[9]

Another contribution to the theory of plural societies is the control model advanced by Ian Lustick. This model, which is largely based on the work of political sociologists Leo Kuper, M.G. Smith, and Pierre L. van den Berghe, explains political stability in deeply divided societies as resulting from the ability of one elite to dominate the central organs of power.[10] Like the consociational model, the control model applies to situations where national integration is inconceivable and plural structure therefore unavoidable. Unlike the former model, stability is not achieved through the mutual cooperation of subnational elites but is achieved through a relationship in which political action by the less-dominant elements of society are severely curtailed. In many situations, the theoreticians argue, control systems may be more realistic, if less desirable, than shared-rule or national-integration arrangements. When rival communities within one political system cannot reach a power-sharing arrangement and territorial partition is impossible, control may represent the only alternative to incessant turmoil. South Africa and Burundi are the ideal examples of this model.[11]

Edward Shils broke ground in the study of developing societies with his classic articles on center and periphery. More recently, the center-periphery framework has been applied to deeply divided societies where partition or incessant violence, not integration, seems to be the inevitable outcome. Because of its wide-ranging applicability, this model has served as a theoretical framework for our analysis.

According to Shils, the center embodies both a value system and the locus of institutional authority in society. Centers are imbued with an almost metaphysical aura; in Shils's words "they partake in the nature of the sacred."[12] The center's charisma heightens its institutional power, it sanctifies authority, and it legitimates the central institutional system. The periphery is composed of those segments of society that are removed from the aura of the center, and do not participate in the center's functions and institutions. Developed or integrated polities are, in Shils's view, those with a center that is all-embracing in at least two ways. First, such polities possess a center that integrates all cultural, religious, and professional value systems in one central zone.[13] Second, there must be a widespread acceptance of these values, stimulating widespread participation in the center.[14] The extent of such acceptance and participation, Shils suggests, is intimately tied with certain processes of modernization in the physical, economic, social, and cultural arenas. Once achieved, there emerges a mass society or civil "society with a wide diffusion of the virtues required for the effective role of citizenship."[15]

Developing societies lack these two characteristics. Any prospective central value system must compete with other autonomous and unintegrated value systems, and the central institutional system can hardly influence many segments of the polity. The center is neither embracing, comprehensive, nor effective. The necessary diffusion is hindered by tradition, inequality, and poor communications. Implicit in this analysis is the fact that the instability of many developing states can be explained by the lack of a comprehensive center. Notably absent in Shils's writings is the possibility of penetration by modern external centers into already weak state centers, which he described in theoretical terms.

Where Shils conceptualized nation building using a center-periphery model, his successors have increasingly employed this framework to analyze revolutionary changes in the third world and in deeply divided societies. They were influenced by disillusionment resulting from the experience of third-world states and by growing ethnic subnational conflict, often in states previously considered stable.[16] Instead of focussing on national integration, these scholars focussed on conflict-regulating mechanisms of ethnically diverse societies that were to a large extent unstable and prone to upheaval.

There can be no better illustration of this development than in S.N. Eisenstadt's treatment of center-periphery relations.[17] In a major book, *Revolution and the Transformation of Societies,* Eisenstadt identifies two historical categories of regimes typified by center-periphery relations—the imperial-feudal and the patrimonial. The latter is characterized by centers that do not attempt to alter the existing social structure of the periphery, or orient religious or political symbols toward the center. According to Eisenstadt, the most prevalent form of government in third-world polities retains the basic form of the patrimonial regime.[18] Their exposure to modernization, however, justifies describing them as neopatrimonial. Center-periphery analysis is turned into an effective explanatory tool for revolution and radical transformation of societies.

Eisenstadt concentrated on the crisis of government but others go a step further and employ the center-periphery framework in the analysis of deeply divided societies and state building under conditions of communal conflict. Focussing on Zionist center-building efforts in mandate Palestine, Dan Horowitz and Moshe Lissak describe a situation in which the creation of a single state center was never a realistic goal and two communal center prevailed.[19] Palestinian Jews succeeded in creating a center, composed of various subcenters, that radiated authority over its periphery while mobilizing support from the complementary diaspora center. Palestinian Arabs, in contrast, did not succeed in creating an equivalent center but were also assisted by external centers. Both the concept of multiple centers acting on one periphery and the relevance of external centers to the processes of conflict and cooperation are introduced by Horowitz and Lissak.[20]

Another study building on Shils's theoretical framework was that of Shaul Mishal on West Bank-East Bank relations between 1949 and 1967.[21] According to Mishal, Jordan attempted to be a comprehensive center for the West Bank. A comprehensive center provides a value system and a central institutional core, supported by the charisma of a nation-state. Annexation, however, did not result in the acceptance by Palestinians of Jordan as their comprehensive center.[22] Mishal applied Max Weber's dichotomy between charismatic and legal-institutional authority to the Jordanian-Palestinian standoff and concluded that Jordan was only able to be a legal-institutional authority and not a charismatic center embodying the community's value system. As Mishal viewed it, the limited legal-institutional authority Jordan commanded was based on its governance as an effective service state. Mishal introduced an important theoretical insight; that is the concept of division of labor between two centers radiating authority on one periphery.[23]

The scholars cited thus far have perceived center-periphery relations in terms of both power and charisma; however, a considerable body of literature exists in which center and periphery are viewed in economic terms.[24] Most of this literature focusses on the processes of neocolonialism or modern-day imperialism. Major stress is placed on analyzing the relations between external metropolitan centers, subcenter elites, and dependent state peripheries. The center-periphery concept has also been extensively employed by dependency theorists,[25] an offshoot of the imperialist school. Theorists of these schools have highlighted the element of subordination in the relationship between centers and peripheries, especially when centers maintain peripheries as part of their conscious design. In doing so, they have stressed the role of economic relations in system maintenance. They further use center and periphery to describe relations between states and within states.

In a recent study entitled "Dual Authority Polities," Horowitz developed a framework based on intercommunity conflict relations in four divided societies—Mandate Palestine, Cyprus after independence, Northern Ireland in the 1960s and 1970s, and Lebanon before the 1975 civil war.[26] Unlike the study on the Yishuv, this study concentrates on intercommunity conflict situations rather than conflict and accomodation between segments of one community. Horowitz bases his analysis on the assumption that members of a community may be attached to two or more centers.[27] He differentiates primarily between an inclusive and a primary center. The inclusive center exercises authority by providing the communities that comprise a polity with political and instrumental functions. The primary center radiates authority by providing members of the exclusive community with expressive functions such as symbols and values.[28] Both centers—the inclusive and the primary—may be situated within or outside the territory. When the inclusive center is outside it is usually a colonial regime. An outside primary center could be regarded as a diaspora center. On the basis of his distinction between these two types of centers, Horowitz delineates nine types of configurations. One of these nine configurations is particularly relevant to our study—the one in which the inclusive and primary centers are identical for one community in the polity while the rival community has its primary center outside. This disposition is relevant to the Jewish-Palestinian relationship since 1967.[29]

Intercommunal Conflict in the Arab-Israeli Context

The various approaches we have described are relevant to the Israeli-Palestinian context. Jewish-Palestinian relations in the mandate period represent one configuration of a dual-authority polity. Each rival community had its own primary center while the inclusive center was controlled by a third (colonial) power. This system broke down through partition and was replaced with an interstate conflict. At the same time, as we shall see in chapter 3, the relationship between Jordan and the Palestinians could be described as a combination of national integration and control. The consociational approach proves to be a useful tool for describing conflict and accomodation in the Israeli polity. But since 1967, a new configuration of the dual-authority polity has developed.

Horowitz's dual-authority-polity model is a useful refinement of center-periphery theory. We have continued to develop this line of thinking to analyze Israeli-Palestinian intercommunity conflict since 1967. One of Horowitz's main contributions was to break away from the conventional limitation of a political system to territoriality and citizenship, by including diasporas in the political structure of communities. His model, however, places little emphasis on the shift of centers from the diaspora to a territorial base and vice versa, a phenomenon pertinent to the conflict over Palestine. Our refinements concentrate on analyzing the dynamics of a diaspora center controlling a territorial unit that is subject to the control of another territorial entity. We also found it necessary to develop our own tools for examining a situation in which one community has more than one external center and both these centers lie outside of the jurisdiction of the inclusive center. This is the situation that has prevailed in the West Bank at least since the mid-1970s.

The most difficult problem facing researchers analyzing conflicts such as the Jewish-Palestinian conflict is the coexistence of interstate and intercommunal conflict. This problem is not effectively addressed by conventional political-science theory. The literature on communal conflict is generally confined to strife within one political system. To use Milton Esman's definition, " 'communalism' can be defined as competitive group solidarities within the same political system based on ethnic, linguistic, racial, or religious identities."[30] Most of the literature on conflict management does not make a distinction between purely internal conflicts and disputes that cross state borders. Similarly, international politics theory has centered around interstate conflict, thus focussing on balance of power and international integration as the main ways of conflict regulation.[31] Transnational relations theory, which fixes upon these limitations of the state-centric view, deals primarily with interaction between societies, states, and organizations functioning in stable environments. Moreover, it pays little attention to intercommunal conflict and interaction.[32] Linkage politics focusses on the nature of external and internal conflict on a purely theoretical level. Studies in this field tend to overlook the unique characteristics of communal conflict situations.[33]

To overcome these problems, we use the center-periphery framework but in a somewhat different manner. We differentiate between *diaspora-based* and *territorial-based* centers of communities with diasporas. A territorial-based center is the result of a territorialization process that involves the voluntary transfer, to a defined region, of most of the public resources of a movement whose wealth and members are based in the diaspora. This transfer is effectuated in such a manner that these resources provide the basis of power for the territorial leadership. This leadership eventually takes control of the movement as a whole. A diaspora movement is thus transformed into a territorial-center-diaspora-periphery movement. A diaspora center is a result of the subordination of a territorial population to an external leadership that expresses its particularistic identity. The territorial unit, despite its advantages in territory and sometimes in numbers, thus becomes a periphery to the outside leadership. The movement is thus transformed into a diaspora-center–territorial-periphery structure.

A comprehensive center fulfills three functions: charismatic leadership, legal-institutional authority, and command of resources. But in order to qualify as a center, it is sufficient that it fulfills just one function for one other component of the community. Thus the Israeli polity, though it holds no legal authority or control over diaspora community resources, could be perceived as a charismatic center for the world Jewish community. Jordan, although it aspired to be a comprehensive center for the West Bank, was only able to be a legal-institutional authority and not a charismatic center. Israel, as we shall see, radiated authority over the West Bank through the provision of resources, both coercive (armed forces, police) and utilitarian (employment, markets, welfare). Consequently, one component of a community may have more than one center, as Horowitz demonstrated in the four polities he analyzed. These centers may compete over functions and attempt to penetrate each other's jurisdiction. Each center may try to cooperate with another center against the third. Ultimately, however, the various centers would be constrained by their inherent characteristics. A diaspora center in order to become more than a spiritual center will have to territorialize. A territorial center, in order to establish a working relationship with a subordinate community that does not identify with the center, will either have to share powers through a consociational or a federal arrangement or maintain a control system as the Republic of South Africa has done.

Intercommunal relations are sometimes marked by contact between a territorial center of one community and a territorial periphery of another. In such an encounter, the territorial center enjoys the advantages of statehood—command of coercive and instrumental resources. This may result in a dependency relationship. The emergence of a diaspora center may only weaken the territorial periphery and may lead to what we call peripheralization of the territorial unit. The territorial periphery will lack leadership and its fate will depend on the status of its external center. This external center will be vulnerable because it lacks an independent territorial base.

We use the terms center and periphery in a way that is not affected by state boundaries and sovereignty. We adopted this approach because it is highly appropriate in this case in which the polities involved include sovereign states, national movements and organizations, and national communities—territorial and nonterritorial. The Palestinian community will be regarded as a distinct community even though its main components cross state borders. Similarly the June-August 1982 war in Lebanon is classified as an intercommunal war despite the fact that it involved the crossing of state borders.

This book is also an attempt to integrate three approaches to center-periphery theories. We adopt Shils's charismatic center as the repository of the sacrosanct. We also use Horowitz's classification of competing and complementary centers and their respective peripheries, and the ideas of theorists who perceive center-periphery relationships in terms of dependency and control. Rather than being opposing theories, each of them has validity in the different historical contexts they analyze.

In our analysis, three different foci of authority emerge in the peripheralization of one territory—the West Bank. The first is the charismatic. Centers of this type are common in the process of decolonization. This is the legitimate center. The second is the partially legitimate, legal-institutional center, characterized by neopatrimonial states. The third is the control center; it creates and maintains peripheries, not through a process of identification, but through coercion, co-optation, or economic pacification. The latter rarely aims at extending the center into the periphery and is thus devoid of integrationist tendencies.

Notes

1. The theoretical typology is based on several approaches. See Ian Lustick, "Stability in Deeply Divided Societies: Consociationalism vs. Control," *World Politics,* vol. 31, no. 3 (April 1979):325-344; Sammy Smooha, "Control of Minorities in Israel and Northern Ireland," *Comparative Studies in Society and History,* vol. 22, no. 4 (April 1980); Cynthia H. Enloe, "Internal Colonialism, Federalism, and Alternative State Development Strategies," *Publius,* vol. 7, no. 4 (Fall 1977):145-175; and Arend Lijphart, *Democracy in Plural Societies* (New Haven: Yale University Press, 1977), pp. 44-45.

2. On this alternative see Karl W. Deutsch and William Foltz, eds., *Nation Building* (Chicago: Aldine Atherton, 1966); S.N. Eisenstadt and Stein Rokkan, eds., *Building States and Nations* (Beverly Hills, Cal.: Sage Publications, 1973); and Philip E. Jacob and James V. Toscano, eds., *The Integration of Political Communities* (Philadelphia: Lippincott, 1964).

3. On consociationalism and other related theories see Arend Lijphart, *Democracy in Plural Societies*; Kenneth McRae, ed., *Consociational Democracy* (Toronto: McClelland and Stewart, 1974); Eric Nordlinger, *Conflict Regulation in Divided Societies* (Cambridge, Mass.: Harvard University Center for International Affairs, 1972); and Hans Daalder, "The Consociational Democracy Theme," *World Politics,* vol. 26, no. 4 (July 1974):604-621.

4. See Lijphart, *Democracy in Plural Societies,* p. 45.

5. Ibid., p. 25.

6. Arend Lijphart, "Federal, Confederal, and Consociational Options for the South African Plural Society," in Nic Rhoodie, ed., *Intergroup Accomodation in Plural Societies* (London: St. Martin's Press, 1979), p. 60.

7. Carl J. Friedrich, "Corporate Federalism and Linguistic Politics," (paper presented at the Ninth World Congress of the International Political Science Association, Montreal, 1973). See also Carl J. Friedrich, *Trends of Federalism in Theory and Practice* (New York: Praeger Publishers, 1968). For Elazar's concept see "The Role of Federalism in Political Integration," in Daniel J. Elazar, ed., *Federalism and Political Integration* (Ramat-Gan, Israel: Turtledove Publishing, 1979), pp. 13-57.

8. Ivo D. Duchacek, "Federalist Responses to Ethnic Demands," in Elazar, ed., *Federalism and Political Integration,* p. 68. For the territorial

1

dimension, see Ivo D. Duchacek, *Comparative Federalism: The Territorial Dimension of Politics* (New York: Holt, Rinehart and Winston, 1970).

9. Lijphart, "Federal, Confederal, and Consociational Options for the South African Plural Society," p. 63.

10. For control and domination theories see J.S. Furnivall, *Colonial Policy and Practice: A Comparative Study of Burma and Netherland India* (Cambridge, Eng.: Cambridge University Press, 1948); Leo Kuper and M.G. Smith, eds., *Pluralism in Africa* (Berkeley: University of California Press, 1969); Ian Lustick, "Stability in Deeply Divided Societies: Consociationalism vs. Control"; and Milton Esman, "The Management of Communal Conflict," *Public Policy,* vol. 21 (Winter 1973):49-78.

11. See Alvin Rabushka and Kenneth A. Shepsle, *Politics in Plural Societies: A Theory of Democratic Instability* (Columbus, Ohio: Charles E. Merrill, 1972), pp. 158-176.

12. Edward Shils, *Center and Periphery: Essays in Macrosociology* (Chicago: University of Chicago Press, 1978), p. 4.

13. Ibid., p. 5.

14. Ibid., p. 10.

15. Ibid., p. 46.

16. On the phenomenon of instability in third-world states and growing subnational ethnic conflict see Ivo D. Duchacek, "Antagonistic Cooperation: Territorial and Ethnic Communities," *Publius,* vol. 7, no. 4 (Fall 1973):3-29.

17. S.N. Eisenstadt, *Revolution and the Transformation of Societies* (New York: The Free Press, 1978).

18. Ibid., pp. 276-279; 282.

19. Horowitz and Lissak, *The Origins of the Israeli Polity,* ch. 2.

20. Ibid., chs. 1 and 2.

21. Shaul Mishal, "The Conflict between the West and the East Banks under Jordanian Rule and Its Impact on the Governmental and Administrative Patterns in the West Bank, 1949-1967," Ph.D. diss. (The Hebrew University of Jerusalem, 1974) (Hebrew).

22. Ibid., p. 17.

23. Ibid., pp. 17-18; 20.

24. For works employing center and periphery in an economic context see A.O. Hirschman, *The Strategy of Economic Development* (New Haven: Yale University Press, 1958); and Gunnar Myrdal, *Rich Lands and Poor* (New York: Harper and Row, 1957).

25. Two important works in this regard are Jagdish N. Bhagwatis, ed., *Economics and World Order* (New York: The Free Press, 1972); and Michael Barratt Brown, *The Economics of Imperialism* (New York: Penguin Books, 1974). For an analysis of the element of control in imperialist relations see John Galtung, "A Structural Theory of Imperialism,"

Journal of Peace Research, vol. 13, no. 2 (1971):81-118. Also see Stephen J. Rosen, James R. Kurth, and Karl W. Deutsch, eds., *Testing Theories of Economic Imperialism* (Lexington, Mass.: Lexington Books, D.C. Heath and Co., 1974). For a critical article on the dependency school see Tony Smith, "The Underdevelopment of Development Literature: The Case of Dependency Theory," *World Politics,* vol. 31, no. 2 (January 1979):247-280.

26. Dan Horowitz, "Dual Authority Polities," *Comparative Politics,* vol. 14, no. 3 (April 1982):330.

27. Ibid.:332.

28. Ibid.:333.

29. Ibid.:338.

30. Milton J. Esman, "The Management of Communal Conflict," p. 49.

31. The best book on the balance of power and international politics is Inis L. Claude, *Power and International Relations* (New York: Random House, 1962). See also, Ernest B. Haas, "The Balance of Power: Prescription, Concept, or Propaganda?" in *World Politics,* vol. 5, no. 4 (July 1953):422-477. For a good summary and analysis of the various approaches in international integration theory see Charles Pentland, *International Theory and European Integration* (London: Faber and Faber, 1973). See also Karl W. Deutsch, *The Analysis of International Relations* (Englewood Cliffs, N.J.: Prentice-Hall, 1972), ch. 18.

32. See particularly, Robert O. Keohane and Joseph S. Nye, Jr., eds., *Transnational Relations and World Politics* (Cambridge, Mass.: Harvard University Press, 1970); and by the same authors, *Power and Interdependence: World Politics in Transition* (Boston: Little, Brown, 1977).

33. Most of the pertinent articles on this subject can be found in Jonathan Wilkenfeld, ed., *Conflict Behavior and Linkage Politics* (New York: McKay, 1973). See also James N. Rosenau, ed., *Linkage Politics: Essays on the Convergence of National and International Systems* (New York: Free Press, 1969); and Richard L. Merritt and Stein Rokkan, eds., *Comparing Nations: The Use of Quantitative Data in Cross-National Research* (New Haven: Yale University Press, 1966).

Mandate Palestine: From Conflict to Partition

The Origins of the Conflict

Future historians will probably describe the Arab-Israeli conflict as the Hundred Years' War of the Middle East. The origins of the struggle over Palestine go back to the end of the nineteenth century. At that time, two powerful national movements were born—Zionism and Arab nationalism. Despite the fact that they were founded in different parts of the world, they were destined to cross each other because both focussed their attention on the same region. Although Zionism limited its demands to only a small portion of the region (Palestine), while Arab nationalism had larger regional ambitions, they were ultimately to confront one another.

As long as the Jews in Palestine did not present a potential threat and Arab nationalism was limited to small elites, there was no significant national dispute between Jews and Arabs. The actual conflict between Arabs and Jews emerged when the Zionist movement started to implement its design for establishing a Jewish state in Palestine. It was only on the eve of World War I, and particularly following the Balfour Declaration issued on November 2, 1917, that an active struggle against Zionism was put into motion. The recognition of Zionism by a global power, accompanied by disappointments with regard to promises given by Britain to the Arabs during the war, increased hostility toward both Britain and the Jewish national movement.

Nevertheless, the Arab attitude toward the Jews was not entirely consistent. On the one hand, the Palestinian Arabs, who were divided on various issues, were united in their objection to Zionism and particularly to the Balfour Declaration. In their struggle against the Jews, both the Moslems and the Christians of Palestine united in the foundation of the Moslem-Christian Association. Their general position was that there was no room for a Zionist political entity.

On the other hand, there were more moderate forces among the Arabs, represented by the Hashemite monarchs. Hussein Ibn Ali (sheriff of Mecca

The first and final sections of this chapter have been adapted from Shmuel Sandler, "Partition Versus Sharing in the Arab-Israeli Conflict," from *Governing Peoples and Territories*, edited by Daniel J. Elazar. Copyright 1982 by the Institute for the Study of Human Issues, Inc. (ISHI). Reprinted with permission of the Institute for the Study of Human Issues, Philadelphia, PA.

and later king of Hejaz), who was Britain's Middle East partner against the Ottomans, welcomed Jews to come and settle in Arab lands. His son, Emir Feisal (who was later nominated king of Syria), met with Dr. Chaim Weizmann, the leader of the Zionist movement, and also called for the immigration of Jews to Palestine in larger numbers.[1] In a memorandum dating from the first day of the peace conferences in January 1919, Emir Feisal made a friendly statement on Zionism and supported, in essence, the idea of a protectorate in Palestine in which Jews and Arabs could live peacefully.[2] To be sure, these proclamations did not support a Jewish state. Yet such attitudes were far from the positions held by the Arabs of Palestine demanding a halt to Jewish immigration and the abolition of the Balfour Declaration.

In the period immediately following World War I, both the Hashemites and the Palestine elites put their hopes in a plan to create a greater united Syria which would include Syria, Lebanon, and Palestine on both sides of the Jordan River. They expected that by the annexation of Palestine to Syria they would prevent the establishment of a Jewish state.[3] The creation of a greater Syria, however, was contrary to the wishes of Britain because, according to the Sykes-Picot Agreement, the area was to be divided between France and Britain, with Syria going to the former and Palestine to the latter.

This left the British with the problem of eastern Palestine. The territories east of the Jordan had been under Feisal's rule but with the British expelled from Syria, there was nobody to rule them. Historically, these territories were part of Palestine, and indeed they were included under the British Palestine mandate set up by the San Remo conference. Amir Abdullah, Feisal's brother, who came to eastern Palestine under the pretense of liberating Syria and restoring his brother's throne, solved the British problem. In a meeting between Winston Churchill, then Colonial Secretary, and Abdullah held in Jerusalem, the latter agreed to the British conditions—namely the acknowledgment of the British mandate in Transjordan (as eastern Palestine came to be known) and the abandonment of any war plans against France.[4]

The Zionist reaction to the partition of Palestine was mixed. It is true that there had been no Jewish settlement in Transjordan; however, the Balfour Declaration and the British mandate included both sides of the Jordan. Hence, the partition of Palestine and the establishment of an Arab government in eastern Palestine could have been considered as the first British violation of the Balfour Declaration. Moreover, the establishment of the Abdullah emirate closed the door to a compromise in which the Palestinians would have received the other side of the Jordan. The Zionist feeling of betrayal was further aroused when on September 16, 1922, the British government issued a memorandum declaring that Jews were forbidden to buy land in Transjordan.[5] This action amounted not only to the violation of the mandate but to religious discrimination as well. In any case, the first partition of Palestine, or Eretz Yisrael—the Land of Israel—as it was called by the Jews, crystallized the struggle between Palestinian Arabs and Jews over the western part of Palestine.

Although the reaction of the Palestinian Arabs to the partition was a positive one, since the ruler of that region was an Arab, this partition ultimately had a negative impact on them. With the collapse of the greater-Syria idea and the detachment of eastern Palestine, their nationalism was now expressed even more strongly against the Zionists and the British administration. It was at this time and under these circumstances that the leadership of the Palestinian Arabs shifted to Hajj Amin al-Husseini, the mufti of Jerusalem. Under his leadership, national feelings were interwoven with anti-Jewish feelings, not merely anti-Zionist. This new trend expressed itself in an outbreak of hostilities. In August 1929, a rumor was circulated throughout Palestine by the Supreme Moslem Council to the effect that the Jews planned to take over the holy sites in Jerusalem. The hostilities that began in Jerusalem spread to other cities such as Hebron and Safed. More than one hundred Jews were murdered and hundreds wounded.[6] At the same time, the new attitudes also prompted anti-British feelings, and the mufti preached the view that the foreign rulers were allies of the Jews and were therefore to be regarded as an enemy. Consequently, in October 1933 the first Arab uprising against the British took place—an event that was followed by the great Arab uprising in the years 1936 to 1939.

In contrast, Abdullah and tribal leaders from Transjordan met with Zionist leaders on several occasions to discuss Jewish settlement in these areas. Ultimately, these discussions failed to produce practical results because of threats from the Palestinian Arabs and the objection of the British government to Jewish immigration into Transjordan.[7]

The Territorialization of a Diaspora Movement

One of the outstanding developments of Mandate Palestine was the success of the Jewish community, the Yishuv, to accomplish most of its goals within thirty years. The Jewish community, numbering no more than 60,000 at the beginning of the mandate, faced an Arab-Palestinian population of 600,000 that was resolved to make the most of its plurality.[8] While the Jews were supported halfheartedly by the British mandate, the Arab Palestinians were surrounded by supportive Arab states, most of which objected to the Zionist enterprise. Yet, by the end of the mandate period, exactly thirty years after the British occupied Palestine, the extraterritorial movement had succeeded in creating a sovereign Jewish state. One of the greatest causal factors of this phenomenon was the territorialization of a diaspora movement. This process, as we shall see in later chapters, is very crucial in understanding the problems facing the Palestinian diaspora movement today.

In broad terms, the diaspora provided the Jewish community in Palestine with human and material resources that nourished its expansion. In its turn, the Yishuv within Palestine shaped the political, economic, and social institutions that constituted a nascent polity. This Yishuv created a de facto partition between the two communities well before the emergence of the State of Israel.

Territorialization involved substantial financial transfers from diaspora Jewry to the settlers in Palestine. The monies were collected by Jewish community organizations and distributed by the territorial arm of the Zionist movement, initially by the Zionist Executive in Jerusalem and later by its successor, the Jewish Agency. The funds collected for the express purpose of developing the national home were mostly channeled to territorial public institutions, primarily to those affiliated with the labor movement. These transfers often exceeded the amount spent by the mandate government in the Jewish sector and far exceeded the amount of funds at the disposal of political or quasi-political institutions in the Arab Palestine community.[9]

The territorialization of the diaspora movement involved much more than the transference of resources from the diaspora to Jewish Palestine. It involved a shift in the organizational focus from London to Jerusalem; a willingess to finance territorial institutions; and most important it meant a concession of leadership—a process in which the diaspora leaders of the World Zionist Movement in the 1920s were superseded by the leaders of the territorial institutions.

The origins of organizational territorialism can be traced back to the establishment of the Palestine office of the World Zionist Organization in 1907, when Palestine was part of the Ottoman Empire. The one-man operation in Jerusalem came to an abrupt end with the advent of World War I.[10] Its successor, the Zionist Commission of Delegates, dispatched by Chaim Weizmann in the aftermath of the war, represented the first serious attempt to create a territorial arm of the Zionist Movement in Palestine. Anxious to make the most of the Balfour Declaration, the commission made strenuous efforts to form a political community, to secure equal status for the Hebrew language, and to meet the serious problems of postwar physical reconstruction and large-scale Jewish emigration from Palestine.[11] In 1921, the commission was replaced by a higher-level Zionist Executive Jerusalem office, composed of members of the executive of the World Zionist Organization who moved to Palestine. Officially at least, the Zionist organization now bestowed equal status on both the London and Jerusalem offices.[12]

Organizational expansion in Palestine developed rapidly. Four offices were established: a political office, acting both as a representative of the

Jewish community to the British administration and as a watchdog for the London office; a department of immigration that maintained hostels to facilitate the absorption of immigrants; a department of colonization; and a department of labor. The latter worked in conjunction with the labor federation and the mandate authorities to secure employment for the young pioneers.[13]

This expansion continued in the thirties under new auspices. In 1929, a new organization coalescing Zionists and non-Zionists in the service of Jewish Palestine was created; the Jerusalem Executive was renamed the Jewish Agency for Palestine.[14] Though constrained by a smaller budget, a by-product of the world depression, the Jewish Agency compensated with growing efficiency. Expertise, both within the agency and amongst the various territorial movements in Palestine linked to the agency, meant that colonization efforts continued unimpeded. A major boost was also provided by a surge of German-Jewish immigration which doubled the Jewish population within three years.[15]

The Jewish Agency had to expand if it was to meet the needs of a larger and more affluent Jewish community. Departments from the 1920s were transformed into ministries in the succeeding decade. Moreover, the Jewish Agency's role was made greater through its official agreements with the German government on transferring Jewish capital to Palestine.

Control over the Jewish Agency by the Palestine Labor elite, a phenomenon we will explore later, also facilitated the shift from London to Jerusalem. For the first time, financial and administrative resources were in the hands of the group that had previously only implemented the projects the Zionist Movement financed. When David Ben-Gurion became the executive chairman of the Jewish Agency and the World Zionist Organization in 1935, and gained control over the financial resources of the agency, he did so as the uncontested leader of the most powerful sector of the Jewish Palestinian community, the Histadrut (the labor federation that comprised of over one hundred collective farms, labor unions and exchanges, cooperatives, and commercial companies).

The organizational territorialization of the Zionist Movement was complete once the Jewish Agency came under the control of an elite commanding the allegiance of the largest Zionist movement, both within and outside Palestine. Under Labor's direction the agency assumed an indisputable leadership role by taking responsibility for world Jewish concerns like the rescue of German Jewry.

An even more important aspect of territorialization lay in the willingness of the diaspora to finance territorial institutions and concede positions of worldwide Zionist leadership to the Zionist leadership in Palestine. Such was the relationship between the predominantly middle-class World Zionist Organization and the centrist Labor camp affiliated with the

Histadrut led by Ben-Gurion.[16] Not only did the World Zionist Organization finance most of the Histadrut and its affiliates, but the diaspora Zionists also gave a free hand to the labor camp to dispense the money as it wished. The availability of these funds enabled the Histadrut to continue its activities, and gave it the power to co-opt opponents and win over noncommitted laborers. By 1926, six years after its establishment, the Histadrut membership comprised 70 percent of the laborers in Palestine. By the late thirties, over one-fifth of the entire population was in some way affiliated with the labor federation.[17]

The terms of the alliance between the World Zionist Organization (WZO) and the Histadrut were worked out in a series of battles within the WZO. A foundation for the relationships was an almost universal agreement among Zionists that the socioeconomic infrastructure of the community had to be established before political goals could be achieved. The socialist pioneers enhanced the alliance with the romanticism of national rebirth which evoked great loyalty from a wide range of Zionists. Finally the relationship endured because of Labor's willingness to compromise in order to achieve long-term goals. There can be no doubt about the potency of the alliance in creating the Jewish national center in Palestine.

Just as diaspora support for territorial organizations was so crucial to center building in Palestine, the concession of leadership within the Zionist movement to the territorial leadership bestowed the center with power that far exceeded the physical resources of Jewish Palestine. The concession of leadership began with a series of election victories by the Labor camp at the Zionist Congresses. In 1925, the Labor section, which was already dominated by the territorial elements, polled 18 percent; in 1931, the figure increased to 29 percent, and in 1933 jumped to 44 percent. It was soon followed by a change of guard in the WZO; a transformation that involved not only personalities but roles. One need only compare the membership of the Jerusalem Zionist Executive with the four dominant personalities in the Jewish Agency in the thirties. The former group, mostly men associated with Weizmann, lacked any local power base; the latter group, which included Ben-Gurion, Moshe Shertok (Sharet), Chaim Arlozoroff, and Golda Meirson (Meir), were all leaders in the Histadrut.[19] These politicians were to play prominent roles in Israeli politics during the first two decades of statehood.

With the election of Ben-Gurion to the Zionist Executive chairmanship in 1935, the stage was set for the consolidation of the territorial-center-diaspora-periphery relationship. This was the mirror image of the Zionist communal structure at the outset of territorialization. Ben-Gurion was now able to transform the Jewish Agency, a creation of the diaspora center, into a government without sovereignty. He did this by uniting the financial resources of the agency with the local power he and his movement possessed. At the same time, he used the Jewish Agency-World Zionist Organization nexus and his own position as chairman of the movement to ensure that the diaspora continued to support the policies of the territorial center.

The Partition of Palestine

If the Zionists, in the period preceding the Balfour Declaration, did not fully realize the problems they would encounter in establishing a Jewish state in Palestine, in the 1920s these realities started to become obvious. The revolts of the Arab population and the British responses to them convinced many of the Jews that a purely Jewish solution was not practical. There were two main approaches in the Zionist camp. One was the moderate approach supported by Chaim Weismann, Chaim Arlozoroff, and David Ben-Gurion; and the other was maximalist Zionism (*Grosszionismus*), supported primarily by the Revisionists under the leadership of Vladimir Jabotinsky. The Revisionists demanded an immediate declaration that the final goal of the Zionists was the establishment of a Jewish state within the historical boundaries of Palestine, including Transjordan.

Within the moderate camp, there was no clear operational solution to the problem of the Arab population in Palestine. In general terms, however, the parity principle was dominant until 1937. Although most of the groups saw their final goal as achieving a Jewish majority, many of them perceived the goal as a joint state for Jews and Arabs as equal nations. In operational terms, this could be accomplished only through one of two ways—a binational state or cantonization.

The binational idea was supported primarily by two movements—Brit Shalom (Peace Union) and Ha-Shomer ha-Tzair (The Young Guard). The first group was composed chiefly of intellectuals at the center of the political spectrum, whereas the second was a leftist Zionist faction. Despite their differences on social issues, both movements supported the creation of an Arab-Jewish state. There were also supporters of the idea of binationalism among Ha-Poel ha-Tzair (The Young Worker) and Ahdut ha-Avodah (United Labor)—two socialist movements—but none of these parties had binational programs. Ben-Gurion, who saw the territorial issue as crucial, supported a federal solution based on cantonization.[20]

The foundations for the partition of Palestine were laid in 1937, when a British Royal Commission arrived in Palestine to investigate the disturbances caused by the Arab revolt of 1936. The Palestinian Arabs had called a general strike in order to demand a ban on Jewish immigration, the prohibition of land transfers from Arab to Jewish hands, and the establishment of an Arab national government in place of the British mandate. The strike was followed by a boycott of the Jews that gradually developed from sporadic acts of violence into open warfare against the Jews and the British administration. The rebellion failed and the Arabs suffered more from the disturbances than did the Yishuv. The government in London nominated a committee headed by Lord Peel to investigate the crisis and to recommend a solution to the Palestine problem.[21]

The proposals that were put before the commission followed along the ideological lines of the various camps. The Higher Committee, which represented the Palestinians, demanded that Palestine be established as an Arab state. The Revisionists urged the establishment of a Jewish state on both sides of the Jordan. The Jewish Agency submitted a parity proposal according to which a legislative council would be established with Jews and Arabs granted equal representation. Were this proposal to be accepted, the Zionists were prepared to commit themselves to maintaining this parity, "whatever the future ratio between Arab and Jewish populations might become."[22]

The Royal Commission rejected all these proposals on practical, moral, and political grounds, and instead recommended the partition of Palestine into sovereign Arab and Jewish states, and a British mandatory zone. The general outline of the partition was that the Jewish state would comprise the north and the coastal plain, while the remainder would go to the Arab state, which would be united with Transjordan. The British mandate would embrace the holy places (Jerusalem and Bethlehem) and a corridor linking them to the Mediterranean.[23]

The reaction to the partition plan among the Zionists was mixed. They were divided into two camps, for and against partition, independent of social and economic ideologies. The antipartition camp was composed of the leftist Ha-Shomer ha-Tzair, the religious Mizrachi movement, the conservative wing of the General Zionists (a free-trade and antisocialist party), and the nationalists of the Jewish State party. The propartition camp included parties from the moderate Left and the center, headed by Weizmann and Ben-Gurion. In the debate over partition, those in favor emerged victorious and the Zionist Congress accepted the principle of partition, with reservations as to the borders suggested by the Royal Commission.[24] In contrast, the Arabs rejected the partition plan outright. Not only was the plan rejected by the Palestinians, but all the Arab rulers except Abdullah came out against it.[25]

In the long run, the events of 1937 paved the way for the eventual partition of Palestine in 1947. Although the British government later withdrew its support for the establishment of two separate states, the plan reemerged after World War II. What was more significant was the fact that, on both sides—Zionist and Arab—the idea of partition was adopted by powerful leaders who controlled territorial communities. Ben-Gurion and Abdullah were ready to accept the partition for different reasons. Following the Arab revolt of 1936, the Zionists realized that a power-sharing arrangement in Palestine was inconceivable. Their primary goal of increasing the Jewish population in Palestine to a majority was unattainable as long as the Arabs objected to it and the British government was influenced by these objections. Thus, they preferred a compact Jewish state in which they would become a majority. Abdullah, who had detested the mufti, thought partition as a temporary solution could eventually serve his interests. Transjordan, in order to become a viable independent state, could not remain in its present form of a desert emirate. The establishment of a Palestinian state would have meant a total separation between his country and Palestine. In contrast, partition could result in the annexation of certain parts of the western side of the Jordan River. Thus, the Hashemite king, who had previously advocated cooperation with the Jews in order to improve the economic stituation of his country, was again the only partner in the Arab camp with whom the Labor-dominated Yishuv could negotiate. The forces of partition were thus born in 1937.

The events that took place between 1939 and 1945 demonstrated to the Zionists the urgent need for an independent Jewish state. The British White Paper of 1939, which put heavy restrictions on future Jewish immigration to Palestine, was published as a result of Arab pressure in Britain. The United Kingdom was now entering a struggle against Germany and needed all the support it could get in any part of the world, including the Middle East. It became clear to the Zionists that, despite their commitment to a Jewish national home, the British were ready to abandon their promises in the face of realpolitik. The new restrictions were fatal at a time when millions of Jews were being killed in Europe.

It was against this background that, in 1942, the Zionists openly requested the establishment of a Jewish state in Palestine. The Biltmore program (as the resolution came to be known) was then submitted to the Yishuv where it met with formidable opposition. While Ben-Gurion succeeded in obtaining the support of the parties of the Right and center, he encountered stiff resistance in his own party and among the binationalists. Despite this opposition, the statists, as they had became known, defeated the antipartition forces at both forums—the political institutions in Jerusalem and the Zionist organizations in New York. The Biltmore program was adopted.[26] The victory of the statists also represented the power of the territorial center and its leader Ben-Gurion, who now dominated the Zionist and the Jewish national institutions.

In 1947, the problem of Palestine came under the jurisdiction of the United Nations, which appointed an international investigating board—the United Nations Special Committee on Palestine (UNSCOP)—that advised the termination of the British mandate. After its study, the committee was divided between a majority recommending partition with economic union and a minority recommending the establishment of a federal government encompassing Arab and Jewish states, with Jerusalem as the capital.[27] The

Palestinians and the Arab states rejected both partition and federation, while the Zionists dismissed the federal proposal but accepted the partition plan. On November 29, 1947, the General Assembly endorsed the partition proposal by a vote of 33 to 13, thus giving it the necessary two-thirds majority.

Although on the surface the position of both sides seemed clear and consistent, internally the situation was still in flux. Abdullah, despite pledges to support the Arab cause, was striving for a partition of Palestine in which he would annex the new Arab state. In two meetings between Abdullah, Golda Meir, and Moshe Sharett in November 1947 and April 1948, it was agreed that the monarch would control the Arab portion of Palestine if he did not interfere with efforts to establish a Jewish state. Although Abdullah could not keep his promises, and under Arab pressure had to join in the war effort against the new Jewish state, he continued to try to reach an agreement with the Israeli leaders. In a series of secret meetings which took place in the second half of 1948 and early 1949, the two sides finally negotiated an agreement granting Transjordan those areas which later came to be known as the West Bank.[28] Another part of Palestine—the Gaza Strip—went to Egypt.

In the Jewish camp, too, the attitude toward partition was not unanimous; objections arose on both ends of the political spectrum. The Revisionists were willing to delay the establishment of the state in order to prevent partition. Ha-Shomer ha-Tzair objected to the resolution in accordance with its binationalist view of Arab-Jewish relations. The leaders of the leftist Ahdut ha-Avodah, who also objected to the partition of Palestine, supported the establishment of an international mandate that would encourage Jewish immigration to Palestine until Jews should constitute a majority, at which time a Jewish state would be established.[29]

Finally, while the Yishuv and Abdullah's emirate were consolidating their political power in the 1940s (the emirate acquired the status of a state in 1946), the Arab Palestinians were undergoing a different process. The most vehement force against partition, the Arab Palestinians were powerless to prevent it. When in 1946 the Palestinians finally succeeded in reunifying Arab Palestinian ranks and reviving the Higher Committee, the effort was too little and too late. The Arab League, constituting all the independent Arab states, had by then established a policy limiting Arab Palestinian autonomy within Palestine and neutralizing the influence of its exiled leader, the mufti. The transfer of the renascent political organ, the Higher Committee, from the territory in dispute to the diaspora was one more milestone in the Arab Palestinian community's final demise.

By the time the Arab states invaded the newly proclaimed State of Israel on May 15, 1948, it was no longer a conflict between two communities, it was a war between independent states. Similarly, the armistice bringing hostilities to an end dealt with problems between states. The Arab Palestinians were not partners, they were anguished onlookers.

Notes

1. Christopher Sykes, *Cross Roads to Israel* (London: The New English Library, 1965), p. 39.

2. Ibid., p. 40.

3. For an elaborate discussion of this subject see, Yehoshua Porat, *The Emergence of the Palestinian-Arab National Movement, 1918-1929*, ch. 2.

4. Sykes, *Cross Roads to Israel,* p. 56.

5. Robert John and Sami Hadawi, *The Palestine Diary* (New York: New World Press, 1972), p. 186.

6. Ibid., p. 207.

7. Amin Abdullah Mahmoud, "King Abdullah and Palestine." Diss., Georgetown University (Washington, D.C., 1972), pp. 46-53.

8. Noah Lucas, *The Modern History of Israel* (London: Weidenfeld and Nicholson, 1974), p. 97.

9. See Dan Horowitz and Moshe Lissak, *The Origins of the Israeli Polity,* table 2, p. 76; Jacob Metzer, "Fiscal Incidence and Resource Transfer between Jews and Arabs in Mandatory Palestine," The Maurice Falk Institute for Economic Research in Israel, Discussion Paper no. 8014 (Jerusalem, September 1980), table 8, p. 34; and Yehoshua Porat, *The Emergence of the Palestinian Arab National Movement 1918-1929,* p. 202; and Porat, *The Palestinian Arab National Movement 1929-1939,* append. A.

10. Walter Laqueur, *A History of Zionism* (New York: Schocken Books, 1976), p. 152.

11. Binyamin Eliav, ed., *The Jewish National Home* (Jerusalem: Keter, 1976), pp. 136-140 (Hebrew).

12. Ibid., p. 141.

13. Yonathan Shapiro, *The Formative Years of the Israeli Labour Party: The Organization of Power 1919-1930* (London: Sage Publications, 1976), pp. 24-25.

14. See Ernest Stock, "The Reconstitution of the Jewish Agency: A Political Analysis," in *American Jewish Year Book, 1972* (Philadelphia and New York: American Jewish Committee and Jewish Publication Society, 1973), pp. 178-180.

15. Roberto Bachi, *The Population of Israel* (Jerusalem: The Institute of Contemporary Jewry, The Hebrew University of Jerusalem, 1974), pp. 40-41 and 85.

16. For an extensive analysis of the relationship between the World Zionist Organization and the collective movement see Yonathan Shapiro, *The Formative Years of the Israeli Labour Party,* pp. 71-82.

17. Lucas, *The Modern History of Israel,* p. 122.

18. Shapiro, *The Formative Years of the Israeli Labour Party,* p. 240.

19. Eliav, ed., *The Jewish National Home,* pp. 142-143, 145.

20. For a broad analysis of the binational idea and its supporters see Susan Lee Hattis, *The Binational Idea in Palestine during Mandatory Times* (Tel-Aviv: Shikmona Publishing Co., 1970), pp. 38-77.

21. J.C. Hurewitz, *The Struggle for Palestine* (New York: Greenwood Press, 1968), pp. 67-72.

22. Ibid., pp. 73-74.

23. Ibid., p. 74.

24. Sykes, *Cross Roads to Israel,* pp. 184-186.

25. Mahmoud, *King Abdullah and Palestine,* p. 73.

26. Hurewitz, *The Struggle for Palestine,* pp. 162-163. See also Sykes, *Cross Roads to Palestine,* pp. 250-251.

27. Ibid., pp. 296-298.

28. For an examination of the negotiations between Abdullah and the Israelis, see Mahmoud, *King Abdullah and Palestine,* pp. 90-126.

29. David Ben-Gurion, *The Restored State of Israel* (Tel-Aviv: Am Oved, 1969), p. 73 (Hebrew). For the relationship between ideology and the political attitude of the various parties, see Dan Horowitz and Moshe Lissak, *The Origins of the Israeli Polity,* pp. 195-196. See also the reaction of the various party newspapers: the Revisionist *Ha-Mashqif* of September 2, 1947; and the binationalist *Mishmar,* same date. See also Hurewitz, *The Struggle for Palestine,* p. 359.

Part II
The West Bank and Its
Competing Centers

3

Jordan and the West Bank: The Politics of Integration and Control

When the first Arab-Israeli war ended in 1949, and the eastern part of Palestine was occupied by the Hashemite Kingdom of Jordan, Jordan acquired more than Arab territory; it acquired a community. Jordan's annexation of the West Bank came at a time when the kingdom could barely muster the resources required of a center; nor could the occupied territory and its inhabitants be regarded as a periphery. While the dominance of the center situated in Amman was indisputable by the 1960s, it was certainly not as clearly established at the outset. At the time of annexation, the Palestinians were not only more numerous and better educated than the Jordanians, but they were also more politicized and economically developed. The potential threat that this community posed to the Hashemite regime may explain why a center-periphery relationship rather than more equitable integration took place.

Jordan's ultimate goal for both sides of the Jordan River, including the Palestinian Arabs, was not dominance or control, but integration. Unlike other Arab states, Jordan offered citizenship to its new inhabitants and formally annexed the new areas in April 1950.[1] These steps were succeeded by a series of legal, constitutional, and administrative acts designed to achieve formal and actual integration.[2] From a sociopolitical perspective, however, its achievements were mixed. The Hashemites attempted to build a comprehensive center that would combine instrumental strength with legitimacy. A strong center and a relatively stable regime emerged, but the regime was never able to attain full legitimacy in the eyes of the West Bank inhabitants.

The period between 1948 and 1967 was characterized by a steady strengthening of the Amman center and a correlative weakening of the West Bank. By 1967, the formerly sophisticated Palestinians could no longer be considered on a comparable level to the East Bank elite. During the same period, the Palestinian opposition to the Amman regime gradually declined. When the Hashemites were challenged in the mid 1960s, it was by a combination of Palestinian groups abroad abetted by Arab regimes unfriendly to Jordan and, to a much lesser degree, by local Palestinians. The acquiescence of local Palestinians in 1966 presented a sharp contrast to Palestinian turbulence during the early years of the previous decade.

From the outset the Jordanian monarchy possessed three crucial assets. First, it monopolized the right to exercise force. The Arab Legion was the only Arab army that was effective in the war against Israel. The second asset was the friendship and support of the British, probably the source of both other assets. The third was a command of economic resources. Throughout the period, Jordan was able to spend far in excess of the revenues it commanded and spent increasingly more as the years progressed. This was of major importance as it allowed for the differential growth of the center without the need for severe extractive policies in the West Bank to finance it. The relentless modernization of the army was also largely financed by British subventions rather than by increased taxation or higher import duties. The subventions were large in comparison to the total economic resources of a very poor state and an even poorer citizenry. By relieving the regime of the need to finance the military, the Hashemites were able to expand the bureaucracy and to set up a rudimentary public-service system. The impact of these advances on a polity that was still overwhelmingly composed of peasantry was significant.

In contrast, the Palestinians suffered major drawbacks despite their advantage in terms of modernization. A series of blows to the community included a legacy of ineffective attempts at center building in Mandate Palestine; a defeat that dispersed the Palestinians and Palestinian talent over a wide area of the Arab and non-Arab world; and harassment in the host Arab states which led to disillusionment with the efficacy of political action. Their self-image as a public of refugees was increasingly internalized and repropagated. The modernizing characteristics that the Palestinians possessed proved insufficient when the Jordanian Palestinians needed the inner resources to create a local center. Ironically, these characteristics, which constituted a major problem to the monarchy in 1948, were transformed into a major asset to the regime. In a sense, the Palestinians were not so much depoliticized as bureaucratized in the service of the state.

In this chapter we analyze the processes of center building in the East Bank and the incipient peripheralization of the West Bank between 1948 and 1967. Our main task is to facilitate a better understanding of the processes that took place in the West Bank under Israeli rule and the concurrent changes in the Palestinian communal structure. In order to accomplish this we have differentiated between two processes of peripheralization—the economic and the political—that will later contribute to our analysis of the West Bank under Israeli rule. We also include a section that deals with the urban dimension of peripheralization which is an integral part of the process of domination.

At a time when state building was the preoccupation of the region, the Palestinian experience took a different course. An analysis of the West Bank's periphery status, which was established during the Jordanian state-building process, is essential to understand recent developments in the Palestinian communal structure.

The West Bank in an Emerging National Economy

It is by now a commonplace that the 1948 war produced two victors and one loser. As is often the case with wars, the outcome of the first round of the Arab-Israeli conflict bred new realities. For the Palestinian refugees it was a tragic and bitter episode. For the victorious states, Jordan and Israel, it proved only the beginning of a long series of trials and tribulations with which both states have coped rather successfully.

There is no doubt that Abdullah was politically and militarily the only victor in the Arab camp. Although he could negotiate with the Israelis from a position of relative strength, there were few regimes as ill equipped as his to handle the magnitude of political and economic problems that the armistice he later signed engendered.

The economic situation faced by Abdullah can be characterized by two prominent features. First, there was a positive correlation between geographic distance from the coast and economic modernization. Coastal regions were much more developed than the hinterland. The second feature, more imperfectly correlated, was the effect of altitude—the higher the altitude, the greater the likelihood of villages with more primitive autocratic economic structures. As a general rule, both variables were interrelated. To this we should add two more general observations: In the hinterland, the change was usually induced from the outside; and patterns of social modernization coincided with economic change.

How was this evidenced on the map of the region? Haifa, Palestine's largest port, emerged during World War II as a major regional transit center possessing a petrochemical refinery of regional importance and a nearby locus of related industrial activity. Tel-Aviv-Jaffa was the area's most important urban configuration; a major financial, institutional, and commercial center serving both the Jewish and Arab sectors, albeit clearly divided along communal lines. In time, both cities outstripped Jerusalem in population and at least toward the end of the mandate, challenged Jerusalem's political preeminence within the respective communities.[3]

The two cities, Haifa and Tel-Aviv, generated employment in their respective hinterlands and provided outlets for produce from the nearby rural areas. The first signs of urban development occurred immediately east of Tel Aviv, followed by a string of small, growing Arab towns situated along what later became the borders created by the armistice. Partial exceptions to the above rules of distance from the coast and altitude were evidenced in the string of towns on the Samarian ridges north of the West Bank, and Hebron and Bethlehem in the south.[4] Most of these towns, especially the latter two, were traditional urban settlements bearing traditional artisan industries.[5]

Clearly, the least-developed and most sparsely populated area under discussion was Transjordan. Beginning sixty miles inland from the Mediterranean Sea and situated on a high, relatively inaccessible plateau that slowly develops into desert, Transjordan's population barely exceeded 340,000 at the end of the 1948 war.[6] In the 1930s, Transjordan was mainly pastureland populated by *fellahinn* (peasants) and recently subdued *beduinn* (nomads). Though the boom witnessed in Palestine during World War II created a demand for the less-perishable vegetables grown in Transjordan and transformed Amman into a minor military and smuggling center, these were hardly the economic developments that could provide for Jordan's economic improvement.[7] The constitutional trappings that accompanied Transjordan's political ascendance from emirate to statehood could not belie the fact that the area continued to be ruled by a small coterie of the king's followers.

As was mentioned previously, the geography of social and political modernization followed similar lines. Again, the sharpest differences were to be found not within Palestine, but between Palestine and Transjordan. Although these differences have been discussed extensively elsewhere,[8] a number of important indices are worth noting. For example, 52 percent of Palestinian school-age children were enrolled in school, compared to 28 percent in Transjordan. In terms of political culture, the Palestinians in 1944 read three daily newspapers, ten weekly periodicals, and five monthly or quarterly journals. There was only one newspaper published in Transjordan at the same time.[9] A 1943 census shows that 47 percent of the population of Transjordan were either nomadic or seminomadic, and only 22 percent were classified as fully urban. By contrast, over one-third of the Palestinian Arab population lived in towns, which were for the most part larger and appreciably more modern than cities in Transjordan.[10] It is against this background that the events during and subsequent to the war should be gauged.

One of the most important developments of the 1948 war, at least as far as Jordan was concerned, was the massive influx of refugees into areas controlled by Jordanian forces. An estimated half-million Palestinian refugees, exceeding the entire population of Transjordan, poured into the West Bank in a period of less than one year.[11] These refugees, many of whom were educated, had to reestablish themselves in a less developed region.

With the paucity of resources at the disposal of the Hashemite regime, the absorption of these refugees faced additional obstacles. Of critical importance was the rudimentary state of the West Bank economy. It lacked a growing modern industrial base; its agricultural sector was already well endowed with working hands and made extensive use of existing cultivatable land.

There were few economic opportunities for the newcomers, especially because veteran West Bankers were also adversely affected by the war's outcome. Though the veterans did not suffer physical dislocation, many lost their livelihoods. Over one-fourth of the veteran population, composed mainly of farmers, lost access and then, as a result of the Rhodes armistice agreement, lost title to fertile land in the Sharon region.[12] Major transportation routes connecting the West Bank hinterland with the coastal region now terminated at dead-end border posts as the cease-fire and later the armistice agreement failed to ensure the free flow of laborers and goods across state borders.[13] At least one town, Qalqilya, lost its function as a minor transit center on the regional railroad network terminating in Haifa.

In the largest sense, the West Bank suffered major geoeconomic dislocation; it became a landlocked territory. Persistent tension along the newly formed borders transformed the area into an enclave threatened by a state that now surrounded it on three sides. While the State of Israel regarded itself as a polity fighting for survival with meager resources, the Palestinians regarded Israel as a potential occupier of the West Bank. The fact that the focal points of the West Bank faced major Israeli population centers added to feelings of Palestinian insecurity.[14]

Partition affected not only refugees and veteran inhabitants of the West Bank, but Jordan as a whole. Imports of basic materials and necessary foodstuffs that formerly flowed eastward from the coast had to be rerouted through Syria in the north.[15] This rendered Jordan much more vulnerable to Arab state pressures than in the past. Britain's shrinking presence in the Middle East was an additional contributing factor to an already deteriorating regional position. A notable lack of natural resources, a primitive agricultural sector exposed to the fluctuations of rainfall and erosion patterns, coupled with the gargantuan welfare task facing the government contributed to a grim situation. A World Bank mission visiting Jordan seven years after the war expressed pessimism regarding the state's economic future.[16]

Fortunately for Jordan, their assessment proved to be incorrect. Jordan succeeded in transferring major economic activities to the East Bank without compounding (and possibly even alleviating) the widespread problems facing the West Bank population. A modest but consistent improvement in social economic welfare resulted in an increase in area production. Disposable income rose largely without structural changes in the region's economy. Such changes occurred to a modest extent on the East Bank.[17] Thus Jordan was able to pacify the populace without initiating economic processes that could have undermined the new and growing Amman center.

Certainly those factors contributing to the simultaneous rise in well-being on the one hand, and the growing functional differentiation between the two banks, on the other hand, were not exclusively induced by government policy. In retrospect, though, Jordan must be credited with making the most of the relevant policy areas within its control. Two mechanisms were of great importance: subsidization and discriminatory investment policy. Jordan was one of the highest subsidy-per-capita states receiving foreign assistance, first from Britain and later from the United States.[18] This assistance, for the most part, came without strings attached, allowing the regime considerable latitude in its use of these funds for ultimately political ends. The activities of the United Nations Relief Work Agency (UNRWA) not only relieved the Jordanian government of a considerable financial burden, it also made possible the physical segregation of the most hard-pressed segment of the Palestinian refugee population.[19] Such physical segregation, encouraged by the refugees themselves, served to inhibit urbanization. Given the much higher politicization prevalent in West Bank towns, any developments that would tend to decrease the flow of refugees to these towns must have been welcome.

It is in the public-investment domain that Jordan's economic center-building efforts stand out. Probably as the result of deliberate policy, the link between solutions to Jordan's Palestinian problem and moves to consolidate the Hashemite center were made early on. Thus, Jordan's establishment of a communication and transportation network that would correspond with the new north-south economic situation involved the employment of Palestinian refugees in road construction in the East Bank.[20] Later the focus switched to the deepening and developing of Akaba, Jordan's only port. To gauge the importance of these undertakings we need note that these undertakings acounted for an estimated 28 percent of public investment even though the transportation sector was one of the smallest in Jordan's economy.[21] Another indication of governmental preference in developing the East Bank, as opposed to the West side of the Jordan river, is indicated by the state's equity participation in major capital projects during the 1950s. Only one of four such projects was located in the West Bank, accounting for only 5 percent of total government investment.[22]

Preferential treatment was not limited to these spheres. Jordan's major undertaking during this period, the East Ghor Canal project, was exclusively limited to the East Bank. By 1963, this project alone created an amount of irrigated land roughly equal to one-third of the irrigated land on the West Bank. The amount of irrigated land in the West Bank during these years remained almost constant.[23] A similar situation prevailed in the field of education; Jordan's first university was erected on the East Bank, far removed from the highly politicized urban areas of the West Bank.[24]

In 1952 the West Bank contained 60 percent of the population and approximately the same proportional share of gross national product, but by the time Jordanian rule came to an end in 1967, the situation was reversed.[25] More enlightening than the respective shares in the state's economy is a survey of what types of economic activities were located in these regions, which allows us to assess the extent of functional differentiation that emerged between the two banks.

Although no detailed breakdown of economic data was ever made in Jordan, the Gross National Product (GNP) shares for each of the banks and estimates of other pertinent data are available. An analysis of data relating to the size of sectors, the type of sector in question, and their growth rates and investment input, clearly reveal growing structural and functional differentiation between the two banks. One revealing example was the difference in industrial development. In 1965, industry accounted for only 5 percent of domestic regional product on the West Bank as compared to 10 percent on the East.[26] The highly capitalized mining sector was almost completely limited to the East Bank. A similar situation prevailed regarding modern infrastructural and service sectors such as banking, finance, and electricity. Value-added per capita in electricity and water supply, and banking and finance, two small but critical important sectors in economic modernization, stood at 63 percent. Moreover, progress on the East Ghor Canal project led to a reversal of traditional roles in agriculture, Jordan's largest sector.[27] In general, the fastest-growing and most modern sectors in the Jordanian economy were concentrated in the East Bank.[28]

Thus far we have emphasized those mechanisms exercised by the political center in consolidating its economic position. What were the ramifications of these policies for West Bank Palestinians? First and foremost, the process of center building on the East Bank drew from Palestinian human resources. Among the 150,000 Palestinians who left the West Bank were West Bank natives and refugees of war. These people were both Muslims and Christians.[29] The extent of the flight is indicative of the widespread feeling of unease in the area. Generally, these emigrants represented the young and the most highly trained and educated segments of the population; many emigrated abroad.[30] One important consequence of this exodus is obvious—it represented a brain drain both in the economic and political senses. The migration, however, had additional ramifications worth noting.

First, those that moved east were more likely to be absorbed into the bureaucracy. As emigrants they were more receptive to co-optation than to politicization. The opposite was the case with those who remained in the West Bank.[31] Second, emigration abroad proved to be more than just a safety valve for the regime involving the departure of students with little work opportunities at home. The remittances they sent home once they completed their studies were rarely if ever channeled into organizational endeavors that might have promoted Palestinian center building (along lines parallel to the Jewish communal experience). The effect of sending remittances back home to relatives helped to create prosperity without generating economic development. Thus, a study made of Nablus's development during this period reveals a phenomenon in which a decreasing population-growth rate coincided with increases in housing space (in large part attributable to real-estate investment by emigrés).[32]

The economic processes at work in the West Bank had a profound impact on politically modernizing institutions. Labor unions were almost nonexistent as was appropriate to the West Bank economy, especially the primitive state of its industrial sector. The importance of external transfers for the fast growth of the trade and services sector had deleterious effects on West Bank political development: effecting trade because it was the traditional economic power base of those conservative elements most supportive of the regime; and effecting the tourist-related sector because those involved in it were interested in preserving the status quo. Needless to say, both sectors were highly sensitive to administrative interference and as a result were vulnerable to government interference.

In sum, the rural West Bank, dominated by agriculture and trade, and having experienced a high level of emigration, was increasingly overshadowed by the Amman center rather than emerging as a center in its own right. This trend was further reinforced by urban developments.

Urban Development

Periphery, in location-analysis literature, is often coterminous with rural society. Indeed, many policy-oriented theories in this field perceive successful urbanization as the key to desirable growth.[33] The importance of urbanism and urban centers in the development of modern polities has not escaped the attention of political scientists. Lucian Pye, for example, views urbanism as an essential of the modern functioning polity.[34]

The retarded urbanization of the West Bank is not only a reflection of the growing periphery status of the region, it is very much at the root of the process. In a region that underwent intensive urbanization, the West Bank stands out as a sharp anomaly. In fact, during the nineteen years of Jordanian rule, the rural population-growth rate exceeded the urban (with the rural population growing to 70 percent of the total).[35] This anomalous situation coexisted with the larger phenomenon of being a periphery in a region characterized by intensive state building.

A comparison between Amman's and East Jerusalem's development during the period in question provides a vivid picture of the center-periphery relationship that characterized the two banks. Population estimates made by the mandate authorities reveal an almost equal number of inhabitants for both cities at the end of World War II. Twenty years later, Amman literally dwarfed its West Bank counterpart with a population almost five times greater than that of East Jerusalem.[36] The centralization of political bureaucratic and administrative functions, limited as it was to Amman and its environs, goes a long way in explaining this unique phenomenon. As Amman and the neighboring industrial zone Zarqa grew,

Jordan increasingly took on the characteristics of many other modernizing states, in which the major metropolitan area's political, economic, and demographic weight becomes so overwhelming as to suggest the emergence of a dual economy.

While the growth of Amman was partially the outcome of direct state intervention, the fate of Jerusalem was at least initially dictated by the historical events surrounding the war over Palestine. Previous to the war, Jerusalem functioned as the administrative capital of Mandate Palestine as well as the political and religious center of the Arab community. These functions were interrelated to the extent that many members of the Arab elite were prominent in both.[37] The termination of the mandate and the consequent division of Palestine by the two states, meant an end to Jerusalem's role as a Palestine-wide administrative center. A year of fighting in the city, and the loss of modern Western Jerusalem to the forces of the newly constituted State of Israel, brought in their wake a massive exodus of both Moslem and Christian Arab residents.[38]

Primarily it was the Arab elites who, bereft of position and having lost homes in neighborhoods occupied by the Israelis, were leaving the city more readily than their more disavantaged counterparts. Nevertheless, they were joined by residents originally from Nablus and Hebron who had immigrated to the city during more prosperous times. Thus the Arab population, which had reached nearly 70,000 inhabitants by the mid-1940s, dropped to little more than 44,000 in the aftermath of the war.[39] In functional terms, what was once a spiritual and administrative center was abruptly transformed into a threatened enclave of refugees facing a victorious army garrisoned in the modern city of Jerusalem. Arab Jerusalemites sustained even heavier losses than the Jews during the war. While only 5 percent of the Jewish inhabitants lost their homes in the Jewish Quarter of the Old City, over one-third of the Arabs forfeited property in some of the wealthy neighborhoods occupied by the Israelis.[40] The severe impact of the war rendered Arab Jerusalem heavily dependent on Jordanian relief and beholden to their power. This loss of population and the willingness of others, such as the Nashashibis and their supporters, to cooperate with the Jordanians, combined to quash all hope of preserving Arab Jerusalem's former role.[41]

Certainly the immediate economic recovery of East Jerusalem was beyond the scope of Jordan's meager resources. Even the State of Israel, despite its deep-seated commitment to the development of its capital, was unable during these years to promote a city growth rate comparable to other parts of the country.[42] Nevertheless there are important indications, especially in the early years of Jordanian rule, that suggest a deliberate policy on the part of the Jordanian regime to downgrade Jerusalem and enhance Amman. Indeed, given the legacy of Palestinian nationalism in the city, it must have been in the regime's interest to do so. The ensuing years witnessed repeated protests on the part of West Bank notables in Jerusalem against what they perceived to be repeated discriminatory treatment of the city.

The city councillors lost out on a number of critical issues in this regard. Perhaps the most important was their request to accord special administrative status to Jerusalem. For ten years this repeated demand fell on deaf ears. It was only in 1959, long after Amman's preeminence had been assured, that Jerusalem was declared the second capital of Jordan.[43] However, conferral of such status was by and large devoid of financial or functional significance. In a similar vein, a campaign to induce the government to retain some important ministries in Jerusalem came to naught as early as 1951, when the government began transferring the Ministry of Education to Amman.[44] At that time, the educational system in the West Bank was far larger and more developed than on the East Bank. In fact, Jordan insisted that the UNRWA central office be situated in Amman despite the fact that the overwhelming percentage of its refugee clients were located in the West Bank.[45] Perhaps the most telling expression of the regime's attempts at downgrading Jerusalem, especially in the political domain, was its refusal to grant permission for the establishment of a Palestinian university in the city.

There were other variables hindering the growth of Jerusalem. The first was the almost incessant state of tension in the region, which lasted until well after the Sinai Campaign in 1957. Fedayeen excursions into Israeli territory, Israeli reprisals, and often-violent protests in the city itself against what Jerusalemites perceived as Arab Legion inaction, all militated against the creation of an environment in which tourism could prosper. The city also indirectly suffered from low priority status in national economic policies. A heavy commitment in infrastructure development on the East Bank that characterized Jordanian development did not allow for public capital investment in tourism until the late 1950s.

Though Jerusalem failed to compete with Amman, it remained by far the most important urban locus in the West Bank and fared better than most other West Bank towns. It was the only urban center in the West Bank, with the possible exception of Ramallah, to have a poulation-growth rate matching the national average.[46] Throughout the years, the city attracted immigrants from Hebron and Nablus, reinforcing trends prevalent during mandate times; the notable difference being that these gains merely balanced emigration of veteran Jerusalemites to Amman and other foreign destinations. In addition, the city consistently exhibited higher labor-participation rates and markedly lower unemployment relative to other West Bank towns.[47] Jerusalem differed from the other towns because it functioned as a center of West-Bank-wide distribution networks and as a limited-scale banking center for the region. Its undisputed asset, however, was tourism. Easing tension on the Jordanian-Israeli border in the aftermath of the Sinai Campaign and a certain leveling of internal protest by the end of the fifties, created a climate conducive to growth of tourism. Large private and public investment, mainly in hotel construction, bore fruit in the early sixties. Remittances from tourism during these years (80 percent of which was expended in Jerusalem and the immediate vicinity) accounted for a major share of Jordan's foreign earnings.[48] The service sector was by far the most capital-intensive sector in the city, and indeed in the entire country. One reflection of this state of affairs was the higher salaries earned by workers in this sector compared to other sectors in the city.

Yet the development of tourism, however substantial, could by no means compensate for the loss in the stature and functional capacity of the city. This is indicated by the fact that Jerusalem's population, including the rapidly urbanizing villages contiguous to municipal limits, only slightly exceeded the population figures of 1947.[49] As we previously indicated, immigration only balanced emigration of veteran educated Jerusalemites and refugees who sought the administrative jobs and business opportunities in Amman and elsewhere. Jerusalem failed to emerge as a major metropolitan center integrating administrative and bureaucratic functions with a growing financial and industrial base. In fact, as far as industrial development was concerned, it was even eclipsed by the secondary city of Nablus. Thus, of the five industries in the West Bank employing over one hundred workers, not one of them was located in Jerusalem.[50] In this sense, poor industrial growth characterized both East and West Jerusalem. West Jerusalem was compensated to some extent by the fact that as the Israeli capital it continued to enjoy administrative preeminence. The transfer of the Jordanian bureaucracy was no doubt the critical factor hindering East Jerusalem's growth.

In contrast to Jerusalem, Amman's growth was spectacular. The city's population grew from 108,304 in 1952 to 277,344 in 1963, an increase of 156 percent and an increment larger than the total population increase in the West Bank during that period.[51] By 1966, 17 percent of the Jordanian population resided in Amman, including the vast majority of the 150,000 Palestinians who had emigrated from the West Bank. While the capitals of Cairo and Baghdad boasted even larger concentrations of population, it should be noted that these were to a great extent inherited situations, while the Amman center emerged only during the nineteen years that the East Bank ruled the West Bank.

Though no extensive study has been made analyzing the unusual growth of Amman, a number of general economic indices suggest the basic reasons that led to such development. Of paramount importance was the size, rate, and degree of concentration of government bureaucracy. From 1954 to

1960, public administration and defense was the fourth-fastest-growing sector in economic terms, and the second in terms of size. This activity was also concentrated in Amman. Manufacturing and mining, a sector that by 1965 ranked fourth in size out of a possible ten, was also concentrated in the Amman vicinity.[52] The same holds true for other key modernizing sectors such as electricity, and finance and banking. The geographical concentration of business opportunity coupled with a city birth rate higher than that found in the rural areas of Jordan, suggested that comparable growth rates would continue even after 1967.[53]

The available data not only chronicles Amman's development, but it also serves to highlight the relationship between Amman's development and Jerusalem's stagnation. For example, in 1946, two of the three banks operating in Palestine and Transjordan were headquartered in Jerusalem. By contrast, eight of the nine banks operating in the country as of 1965 had headquarters in Amman.[54] On the industrial scene, the situation was also reversed during this period. In a census taken as early as 1959, over one-third of the workers in the industrial sector were located in Amman and working in establishments that employed twice as many workers as the national average.[55] In sum, the fate of Arab Jerusalem clearly reflected the general trend of shifting human and material resources to the East Bank. The downgrading of the city during Jordanian rule was critical in its own right. By virtue of its history, stature, and location, it had the potential to play the role of a metropolitan center. The Hashemites made sure that this did not take place. But the incorporation of the Palestinians required more than economic and urban policies; it also involved political mechanisms of control.

Integration and Control

To the Jordanian regime, the military advantages gained during the war were a mixed blessing. On the one hand, the Hashemites gained control of Jerusalem; on the other, they were now faced with the task of absorbing a refugee population that was double the population of their own state. Reaching a modus vivendi with the Palestinians that would be something more than military control was essential if the military gains were to be translated into a politically meaningful future.

It was no easy task. Unlike other communal conflicts, the 1948 war neither entailed the annihilation of any major segment of the Palestinian community, nor the destruction of the Palestinian political forces that led them. These forces, of which the mufti and his adherents were the most prominent, continued to operate from Egypt and other neighboring Arab states, maintaining extreme anti-Hashemite attitudes. Moreover, many of the Palestinian refugees were deeply suspicious of Abdullah's motives, actions, and interactions with Israel and his affinity for the British. These suspicions could only compound the problem of coming to terms with the Palestinian majority. Consequently, Abdullah wished to consolidate the status quo with respect to Israel, while the refugees hoped that the Arab world would quickly learn the lessons of defeat and then proceed to restore Palestine to its rightful owners. Initially this proved a stumbling block to the center's political designs. Finally, the Hashemite takeover of the West Bank was strenuously challenged by the Arab world, inviting Arab government intervention in undermining Jordanian designs. Yet, despite the obstacles, the fact remains that the Jordanian regime emerged resilient and internally stable. This resilience against such formidable obstacles begs the question; namely, how was it achieved?

In comparison to the economic demographic interaction between the two banks and the eventual emergence of a center on the East Bank, political center building was a much swifter process. To begin with, many of the key central institutions were already effectively functioning before the outbreak of the war. One such institution was the Arab Legion. British patronage and loyalty to Hashemite interests provided the state with sufficient material and organizational resources to compensate for the inadequate size and the poor quality of local personnel.[56] However, a major part of the credit must be given to political acumen exhibited by the Hashemites themselves. They managed to fuse traditional and modern mechanisms of rule in the manner of neopatrimonial regimes.[57]

Broadly speaking, four mechanisms of control were involved, all designed to abort attempts at Palestinian center building. The first was symbolic integration, manifested in the conferences convened surrounding the event of annexation. This exercised the principle of equal representation in outwardly democratic and representative national institutions. The second, co-optation, also worked along traditional lines by strengthening familial ties with the regime, preserving local power bases, and dispensing material rewards to supporters. The third mechanism involved denying Palestinian participation in the control of key coercive institutions that were essential to the preservation of the regime. Finally, the principle of administrative efficiency meant providing a minimum of public services to the Palestinian community.

A sense of urgency characterized the creation of new political frameworks with which the Palestinians could identify. A number of reasons compelled the regime to move quickly and effectively in this regard. First, it was apparent that some kind of working relationship be developed with such a large constituency, in order to avoid an open conflict within Jordan. Second, there was a need to legitimize Jordanian control and eventual annexation of the West Bank in the face of serious challenges by elements of the former Palestinian center. The most serious of these attempts was the convocation of the All Palestine Government in Gaza under the aegis of the Egyptian government, which enjoyed the support of most members of the Arab League.[58]

Jordan convened two conferences in response to these dangers, and many of the leading notables in the area attended. The first was in Amman and the second in Jericho.[59] Designed to add legitimacy to the Jordanian presence, these conferences formed an integral part of the process of annexation that culminated in 1950, when the West Bank officially became part of the State of Jordan. The granting of full Jordanian citizenship to all Palestinian refugees residing within its borders indicated a bold deviation from the practice of other Arab states. By 1950, a Jordanian constitution not only ensured the existence of a bicameral legislature, but also assured equal representation for both banks in the Senate.[60] Theoretically at least, the Palestinians became full-fledged citizens secure in their right to participate in the civic and political life of Jordan.

The legislative framework, even though it did not control the resources of power, nevertheless was used as a rallying point for antiregime activities. Institutional integration in a state like Jordan, where power was monopolized by the executive, exposed the state to perpetual parliamentary opposition and scrutiny. The institution-building process was complemented by rapid moves toward co-optation. The parliamentary process was designed to contribute to the destruction of the former Palestinian center and to promote identification with the regime. Co-optation was designed to promote an instrumental relationship in which the Hashemites could be assured of the acquiescence of the West Bank elite.

Co-optation proceeded along clearly defined lines. One of the hallmarks of the Hashemite regime was the opening of the bureaucracy to Palestinians, at first in the West Bank and increasingly thereafter in the East Bank.[61] Key positions in the welfare and regional administration were conferred upon the Nashashibis and their supporters, who were the second-largest faction of the former Palestinian center in Arab Palestine and rivals of the mufti.[62] Positions were judiciously allotted to other members of major Jerusalem families.[63] This was a policy that not only co-opted individuals but was designed to protect the integrity of the social institutions from which they came. The quasi-feudal nature of the Jordanian regime characterized by parallel structures (one representative and powerless, the other executive and dominant) facilitated the process of co-optation. Thus, the Jordanian establishment could appoint Palestinians to a variety of government posts without conceding a significant share of political power.

Yet, co-optation was not only seen as a process of individual recruitment, but also as a means of reinforcing social institutions that preserved tradition and social continuity. New political and administrative frameworks were structured to reinforce local familial power bases. Among the Palestinian community of the West Bank, traditional *hamula* (extended family) elites continued to dominate the political sphere. These elites, whose composition largely survived intact from the mandate period, showed little initiative in widening political participation. Voting rights were by law granted according to the amount of taxes paid by the extended family; influence garnered in municipal and local elections brought considerable financial advantage. Through a centralized regional administration wielding wide discretionary powers, the Jordanian regime endeavored to protect the position of those families who supported it.[64] Co-optation, despite opposition and frequent disturbances, was the dominant feature of Jordanian rule in the West Bank, and in turn an important dimension of the peripheral role of the West Bank in the Palestinian community.

While the two previous mechanisms involved inclusion of Palestinians, the policy of denying access to the key coercive institutions ruling Jordan involved their exclusion. With the exception of three brief periods, Palestinians were not chosen for the post of prime minister.[65] The same holds true for a number of other key posts such as the Minister of Interior, and the senior positions in the police force, in the armed forces, and in the intelligence service.[66]

In its commitment to safeguarding the Hashemite regime, the court consistently withstood pressures and demands by the opposition to introduce universal conscription into the Arab Legion, which would effectively transform it into a national army. Instead, recruitment practices ensured that, by and large, fighting units were to be beduin while technical backup units became increasingly Palestinian.[67] Such a policy of recruitment allowed for the increasing modernization of the force without compromising the loyalty of the legion to the regime.

Subordination of the West Bank did not go unopposed. A number of political parties with proven bases in the West Bank sought to transform Jordan into a more representative state than the Hashemite regime wanted. With the exception of the Tahrir party, an ultraconservative Islamic movement, these parties were Pan-Arab oriented.[68] As Egyptian President Nasser's prestige grew, these local political parties increasingly looked to Cairo as an alternate center.[69] However, Pan-Arabism, with its radical messianism, was not an ideology that could appeal to the conservative Palestinian elite in the West Bank. It was never sufficiently attractive to most of the Palestinians to seriously compromise the basic relationship they maintained with the Jordanian center. Thus, despite disturbances that marred the first decade of Jordanian rule (over issues such as the prerogatives of the executive branch, the presence of British officers in the Jordanian army, British patronage, and universal conscription) the opposition failed to achieve their objectives.

One of the outstanding features of the Jordanian-Palestinian relationship was the absence of any attempt to develop a Palestinian center within Jordan. Those center-building mechanisms so extensively employed by the Zionists in Mandate Palestine, and to a certain extent replicated by the Palestinians in the diaspora later on, were markedly absent in the Jordanian period. Such factors as Jerusalem's role as a former capital of Mandate Palestine were never translated into center-building assets. In addition, the severe problems facing the area were rarely dealt with by local Palestinians on a collective institutional basis; neither was the diaspora ever called upon to help alleviate them. Finally, the Pan-Arab orientations of the main parties and their reliance on alternative external centers were major obstacles in the emergence of an effective territorial framework.[70] In espousing the tenets of Pan-Arabism they sought unity and pitted this unity against the idea of territorial particularism. So strong was this sentiment that when the newly constituted PLO did attempt to territorialize operations in Jordan, it was opposed by both the Jordanian establishment and Pan-Arab elements.

When the ideas of Palestinianism were first heard and the concept of the Palestinian entity began to gain ground, Jordanian center building had been underway for so long, and Hashemite control so firm, that efforts in that direction had to originate outside Jordan. By the mid-1960s the West Bank witnessed little opposition and even less Palestinianism. The West Bank continued to be dominated by centers not their own. When Israel occupied the West Bank, a center met a periphery that was poor in leadership and in organizational life, and was predominantly rural and agricultural; a territory where opposition reacted more to outside centers than to autonomous initiative. The territory was dominated by a conservative elite accustomed to accommodation even when ideological conviction dictated otherwise. In short, when Israel acquired control of the West Bank, it came in contact with a community whose fate had been determined by a center with which the community identified only partially. In 1967, the West Bank came under the control of a center that it perceived to be totally alien and illegitimate.

Notes

1. Anne Sinai and Allen Pollack, eds., *The Hashemite Kingdom of Jordan and the West Bank* (New York: American Academic Association for Peace in the Middle East, 1977), p. 27.

2. On steps towards integration in the early years see Shaul Mishal, *West Bank/East Bank: The Palestinians in Jordan, 1949-1967* (New Haven: Yale University Press, 1978), pp. 6-8.

3. Joel Migdal, et al., *Palestinian Society and Politics* (Princeton, N.J.: Princeton University Press, 1980), pp. 26-27.

4. On Bethlehem see Shabtai Brill, "The Cities of Bethlehem Region—The Main Characteristics," in A. Shmueli, D. Grossman, and R. Ze'evi, eds., *Judea and Samaria* (Jerusalem: Canaan Publishing House, 1977), pp. 318-320 (Hebrew). On Hebron see Yigal Karmon, *Eretz Yisrael* (Tel-Aviv: Yavneh Publishing, 1978), pp. 366-367 (Hebrew).

5. On the growth of the Arab community in Western Palestine see Y. Karmon, *Eretz Yisrael*, pp. 70-71.

6. Shaul Mishal, *The Conflict between the West and East Banks*, p. 123.

7. For a thorough analysis of the Transjordanian economy see A. Konikoff, *Transjordan: An Economic Survey* (Jerusalem: Economic Research Institute of the Jewish Agency for Palestine, 1946).

8. Palestine Government, *A Survey of Palestine* (Jerusalem: Government Printer, 1946).

9. Ibid., pp. 716-717.

10. Ibid., p. 137.

11. Anne Sinai and Allen Pollack, eds., *The Hashemite Kingdom of Jordan and the West Bank*, p. 27.

12. Mishal, *The Conflict between the West and East Banks*, p. 127.

13. Michael P. Mazur, *Economic Growth and Development of Jordan* (Boulder, Col.: Westview Press, 1979), pp. 8-9.

14. Mishal, *West Bank/East Bank*, p. 15.

15. Ibid., pp. 9-10.

16. International Bank for Reconstruction and Development, *The Economic Development of Jordan* (Baltimore: The Johns Hopkins University Press, 1965), pp. 66-68.

17. Mazur, *Economic Growth and Development of Jordan*, p. 12.

18. See Naseer H. Aruri, *Jordan: A Study in Political Development (1921-1965)* (The Hague: Martinus Nijhoff, 1972), table 12, p. 61. On American aid see ibid., table 14, p. 63.

19. See Y. Ben-Porath and E. Marx, *Some Sociological and Economic Aspects of Refugee Camps on the West Bank* (Santa Monica, Cal.: Rand Corporation, August 1971), Report R-835-FE, p. 5; M. Zamir, "Refugee Camps in Jordan, Judea and Samaria: A Form of Settlement," in Shmueli, Grossman, and Ze'evi, eds., *Judea and Samaria*, pp. 350-363.

20. Mishal, *The Conflict between the East and West Banks*, p. 138.

21. Ibid., table 3, p. 38.

22. IBRD, *The Economic Development of Jordan*, p. 237.

23. Eliahu Kanovsky, *Economic Development of Jordan* (Tel-Aviv: University Publishing Projects, 1976), p. 5. See also Mazur, *Economic Growth*, p. 39; and Claude R. Sutcliffe, "The East Ghor Canal Project: A Case Study of Refugee Resettlement, 1961-66," in *The Middle East Journal*, vol. 27, no. 4 (August 1973):471-482.

24. Michael Roman, "East Jerusalem: Population and Employment," in Shmueli, Grossman, and Ze'evi, eds., *Judea and Samaria*, p. 483.

25. See Mazur, *Economic Growth*, p. 98. The population share of the West Bank declined from an estimated 62 percent to 40 percent, producing only one-third of the Gross National Product.

26. Haim Ben-Shahar, Eitan Berglas, Yair Mundlak, and Ezra Sadan, *Economic Structure and Development: Prospects of the West Bank and the Gaza Strip* (Santa Monica, Cal.: The Rand Corporation, 1971), R-839-FF, p. 27; and Elyahu Kanovsky, *Economic Development of Jordan*, p. 29.

27. Mazur, *Economic Growth*, table 5-5, p. 97.

28. Kanovsky, *Economic Development of Jordan*, p. 27.

29. Ya'acov Lifshitz, *Structural Changes and Economic Growth in the Administered Territories, 1922-1972*, Research Report no. 6 (Tel-Aviv: David Horowitz Institute for the Research of Developing Countries, 1974), p. 9 (Hebrew).

30. Kanovsky, *Economic Development of Jordan*, p. 12.

31. Nabil A. Badran, "The Means of Survival: Education and the Palestine Community, 1948-1967," in *Journal of Palestine Studies*, vol. 9, no. 4, (Summer 1980):57-61.

32. Amnon Shinar, "Nablus: The Development of Building Area in an Arab City," in Shmueli, Grossman, and Ze'evi, eds., *Judea and Samaria*, p. 277.

33. See N.M. Hansen, ed., *Growth Centers in Regional Economic Development* (New York: The Free Press, 1972); and E.A. Johnson, *The Organization of Space in Developing Countries* (Cambridge, Mass.: Harvard University Press, 1970).

34. Lucian W. Pye, *Aspects of Political Development* (Boston: Little, Brown, 1966), p. 8.

35. See Elisha Efrat, *Spatial Patterns for the Implementation of Autonomy in Judea and Samaria* (Tel-Aviv: Tel-Aviv University Project on Peace, 1980), table 3, p. 9, and table 5, p. 13 (Hebrew).

36. The population of Jersualem in 1961 was estimated to be 60,000 compared to 250,000 in Amman. See Kanovsky, *The Economy of Jordan*, p. 25.

37. Daniel Rubinstein, "The Jerusalem Municipality under the Ottomans, British, and Jordanians," in Joel L. Kramer, ed., *Jerusalem: Problems and Prospects* (New York: Praeger Publishers, 1980), p. 84.

38. Emigration was equally prevalent among Palestinians born on the West Bank and among the refugees of 1948. See Ya'acov Lifshitz, *Structural Changes and Economic Growth in the Administered Territories, 1922-1972*, p. 9.

39. See Michael Roman, "East Jerusalem Population and Employment," in Shmueli, Grossman, and Ze'evi, eds., *Judea and Samaria*, p. 480.

40. Ibid., pp. 480-481.

41. Mishal, *The Conflict between the West and East Banks*, p. 143.

42. See Roberto Bachi, *The Population of Israel* (Jerusalem: The Institute of Contemporary Jewry, The Hebrew University of Jerusalem, 1974), table 18-5, p. 333.

43. Daniel Rubinstein, "The Jerusalem Municipality," in Kramer, ed., *Jerusalem: Problems and Prospects*, p. 93.

44. Ibid., p. 89.

45. Ibid., p. 90.

46. The national urban rate of growth was 25.3 percent between 1952 and 1961. Jerusalem's stood at 24.4 percent. See Aruri, *Jordan: A Study in Political Development*, pp. 66-67.

47. Michael Roman, "East Jerusalem: Population and Employment," in Shmueli, Grossman, and Ze'evi, eds., *Judea and Samaria*, p. 483.

48. See Kanovsky, *The Economy of Jordan,* p. 33.

49. Ibid., p. 67.

50. Michael Roman, "East Jerusalem: Population and Employment," in Shmueli, Grossman, and Ze'evi, eds., *Judea and Samaria*, p. 483.

51. Aruri, *Jordan: A Study in Political Development*, p. 67.

52. Roman, "East Jerusalem: Population and Emigration," p. 483.

53. On geographical concentration see Aruri, *Jordan: A Study in Political Development*, pp. 59-60. See also *MEED*, vol. 23, no. 36 (June 1979):4.

54. Roman, "East Jerusalem: Population and Emigration," p. 483.

55. Ibid.

56. Aruri, *Jordan: A Study in Political Development*, p. 27.

57. S.N. Eisenstadt, *Traditional Patrimonialism and Modern Neopatrimonialism* (Beverly Hills, Cal.: Sage Publications, 1973).

58. Mishal, *West Bank/East Bank*, pp. 41-42.

59. Mishal, *The Conflict between the West and East Banks*, pp. 108-110.

60. Anne Sinai and Allen Pollack, eds., *The Hashemite Kingdom of Jordan and the West Bank*, p. 71.

61. An analysis of the Jordanian civil service can be found in Mishal, *The Conflict between the West and East Banks*, pp. 154-156. On the absorption of Palestinians in lower echelons of Jordanian government bureaucracy see Nabil A. Badran, "The Means of Survival: Education and the Palestine Community, 1948-67," pp. 57-61.

62. Mishal, *The Conflict between the West and East Banks,* p. 99.

63. Uri Shtandel, "The Arab Population of East Jerusalem: The Origins of Major Groups and Their Leadership," in Shmueli, Grossman, and Ze'evi, eds., *Judea and Samaria*, p. 489.

64. On the ramifications of municipal laws and election processes and how they protected local clan-*hamula* structures see Sasson Levy, "Local

Government in the Administered Territories,'' in Daniel J. Elazar, ed., *Judea, Samaria and Gaza: Views on the Present and Future* (Washington, D.C.: American Enterprise Institute, 1982), pp. 106-108.

65. Clinton Bailey, ''Cabinet Formation in Jordan,'' in Sinai and Pollack, eds., *The Hashemite Kingdom of Jordan and the West Bank*, p. 103.

66. Uriel Dann, ''Regime and Opposition in Jordan since 1949,'' in Menahem Milson, ed., *Society and Political Structure in the Arab World* (New York: Van Leer Jerusalem Foundation Series, Humanities Press, 1973), p. 103.

67. P.J. Vatikiotis, *Politics and the Military in Jordan: A Study of the Arab Legion, 1921-1957* (London: Frank Cass, 1967), pp. 28-29.

68. For an extensive analysis of West Bank political parties during Jordanian rule see Amnon Cohen, *Political Parties in the West Bank under the Hashemite Regime, 1948-1967* (Jerusalem: The Magness Press, The Hebrew University, 1980) (Hebrew).

69. Mishal, *West Bank/East Bank*, pp. 48-50.

70. Mishal, *The Conflict between the West and East Banks,* pp. 453-454.

State and Periphery: The West Bank under Israeli Rule— The First Decade

In 1948, Palestine's dual society was divided into two states. The Jewish community had overwhelmed the Arab community in the struggle over Palestine. In 1967, Israel occupied the West Bank; a state met a territorial periphery. It was a rare historical occurence. Not only the swiftness of change was unique (the occupation of the West Bank took only two days) but the distances involved were strikingly small, for it is usually the nature of peripheries to be quite distant from their centers. Even though it was a union of continuous areas, it brought together two vastly different communities. Israel had been, since its establishment, one of the fastest-growing states in the world, both in demographic and economic terms. It was a polity characterized by a high degree of consensus and political cohesiveness, a strained but stable political system, and a functioning mixed economy. Israel's economy was a highly integrated one with rapidly diversifying industry and an agricultural sector demonstrating a high level of efficiency. In addition, Israel was a charismatic center for a well-organized diaspora, fulfilling the Zionist dream of a territorial communal center.

In contrast, the West Bank underwent economic stagnation and political control between 1948 and 1967. As a periphery, it was a source of continuous emigration, suffering from low incomes, high rates of unemployment, a low rate of urbanization, and almost no industrialization. While the 1967 war brought economic prosperity to Israel and strengthened ties with its diaspora, it brought mixed results to the West Bank.

The immediate implications of the interaction between the Israel center and the new periphery were:

1. Self-governing market forces created an economic relationship beneficial to both the communities concerned.
2. Proximity to the periphery and the existence of rudimentary economic structures allowed Israel to administrate the territories for a relatively small financial cost.
3. Co-optation patterns that emerged during Jordanian rule helped facilitate interaction between the Israeli military administration and the West Bank elites in day-to-day matters.

The West Bankers' ability to interact without political sentiment and the growing economic links with Israel, which resulted in a new prosperity, provided the basis for relative autonomy in internal matters. All three outcomes help explain the remarkably low cost of Israeli occupation as well as the relatively stable security situation that increasingly prevailed in the West Bank.

Compared to Jordan, which tried to be a comprehensive center aiming at political integration of the Palestinians, Israel had more limited objectives. Despite a more favorable geo-economic relationship with the West Bank than that of its predecessor, Israel did not seek to integrate the territories politically. One of the factors the Israelis had to take into consideration was that the demographic balance of the country would be upset. Israel's main concern was the creation of a strategic buffer zone on its eastern border. Though this objective was initially strategic, eventually Israel had to come to terms with its multicommunal problem. The imperatives of this situation required that Israel control the area as long as a political solution was not feasible on the interstate level; yet at the same time Israel had to seek tacit cooperation with the previous ruler and fulfill the basic needs of the local inhabitants. The result was that Israel never aspired to solve the communal problem as such. Israel was not ready to allow the whole area to revert back to sole Jordanian control; neither was it ready to allow the territories to develop their own center.

In the absence of overall peace, Israel could have achieved its major objectives only by keeping the West Bank as a periphery. Once again the development of the West Bank was deliberately directed by its controlling center. However, Israel's higher level of economic and political development was bound to influence the territories. It is against this background that we shall analyze the economic and political development of the territories under Israeli rule during the first decade of occupation.

Economic Growth in a Periphery Economy[a]

Economic analysis is open to widely varying interpretations. Jamil Hilal, of the Palestine Liberation Organization Research Center in Beirut, described the Israeli relationship with the territories as a form of economic imperialism.[1] Israel's official economist for the administered territories, Aryeh Bregman, described this interaction in more flattering terms as a mutually beneficial economic relationship.[2] Political economic analyses differ as widely as political ideas. Just as each political development necessitates a sui generis assessment, so must every economic indicator be evaluated individually. What is to one observer a positive indicator, often points to a negative trend for another.

Israel's initial relationship with the territories was neither the result of a laissez-faire policy nor the product of an imperialist design. Israeli economic

---

[a]This section is a slightly re-edited version of Shmuel Sandler and Hillel Frisch, "The Political Economy of the Administered Territories," in *Judea, Samaria and Gaza: Views on the Present and Future,* Washington, D.C. (American Enterprise Institute, 1982). Reprinted with permission.

policy in the territories was clearly influenced by both political and economic factors. The background of this government policy is best summarized by Larry L. Fabian:

> Every Israeli cabinet since 1967, while insisting that there will be no return to the June 1967 borders, has decided not to decide the political future of the West Bank and the Gaza Strip. But government policy, including economic policy, was grounded in three understandings. Israel would not formally annex the territories. Israel would not withdraw from them. And Israel would not allow them to become a net budget burden.[3]

To achieve the last objective, Israeli economic policy toward the territories involved: 1) promoting an economic common market with Israel; 2) allowing for autonomy in internal economic activity; and 3) permitting a situation of open bridges between the West Bank and Jordan.

In creating a common market between a developed economy and an underdeveloped region, self-regulating market forces were brought into play to help solve the severe unemployment problem in the West Bank that existed before and after the war. Israeli absorption of excess West Bank labor proved beneficial both to West Bank employees and Israeli employers. By adopting a policy of economic autonomy and leaving development to the entrepreneurial talents of local inhabitants, Israel relieved itself of the responsibility of playing a traditional role as a welfare state with all the obligations that role entails. Open bridges with Jordan permitted the continuation of economic relations with Jordan and the Arab world. Thus, the West Bank was allowed to export agricultural produce to Jordan that would otherwise have been diverted to the Israeli market to compete with Israeli produce. This would have forced the Israeli government to subsidize Israeli farmers hurt by such competition.

The effects of this trilateral economic framework extended beyond the fiscal domain. On the political level, it facilitated Jordanian influence and Israeli control in the West Bank. This framework also engendered unprecedented prosperity with no accompanying economic development. Both structural underdevelopment and large-scale emigration continued to characterize the West Bank under Israeli rule.

Prosperity in a Periphery Economy

When Israel took over the West Bank from Jordan, the economy of this territory came into contact with an economic reality that was in many ways revolutionary compared to its previous evolution. The Israeli economy had changed drastically since 1948. Moreover, the West Bank entered into a relationship that was essentially imposed upon it. In general, the economic development in the territories (the West Bank and the Gaza Strip) since 1967 has been determined by two major factors: the quantitative and qualitative disparities between their economies and the Israeli economy; and the political uncertainty regarding the future status of the territories.

The gap between the economies of Israel and the West Bank was of considerable magnitude. This situation can best be understood by comparing several indicators. The value of Israeli industrial-export sales in 1966 alone exceeded the Gross National Product (GNP) of both the West Bank and the Gaza Strip combined. Israel's industrial development was rapid in comparison with other countries, including countries with developed economies. Israeli industrial output increased nearly fivefold between 1950 and 1966, with an annual growth rate exceeding 9 percent. The number of workers employed in industry in 1966 was 222,000, a figure almost double the total employment in the West Bank.[4] While industry in the West Bank was concentrated mainly in the processing of agricultural produce, the major products in Israel included machinery, synthetic yarns, rubber and plastic products, chemical and petroleum products, and textiles.[5]

The gap between Israel and the West Bank was equally evident in agriculture. Israeli farm production increased almost sixfold between 1949 and 1966, as did agricultural exports. A number of factors contributed to this growth including the doubling of the number of persons employed in agriculture, a 250 percent increase in cultivated land, a fivefold increase in irrigated land, and a fourfold increase in the use of water.[6] Another important constellation of factors was the rapid increase in capital stock complemented by greater skill, rising efficiency, better organization, and technological innovation. This resulted in the tripling of productivity.[7]

In contrast to Israel's agricultural sector, the agricultural development in the West Bank was slow, even when compared to other economies at similar GNP levels. A Rand Institute study by three Israeli economists compared the distribution of products by sector in the West Bank with the arithmetic mean of Kusnets' sample. The comparison showed that "the share of agriculture was extremely low."[8] While almost half of the labor force was employed in agriculture, this sector accounted for less than one-quarter of the GNP. By contrast, in the hypothetical average country in Kusnets' sample, nearly two-thirds of the labor force was employed in agriculture, producing almost one-half of the GNP.

The disparity between the two agricultural sectors is best illustrated by the fact that the gross produce per person employed in Israeli agriculture was over four times that of the West Bank.[9] The previously mentioned factors that played such an important role in Israel's rapid agricultural growth were almost totally absent in the West Bank.

Under such conditions, the West Bank could not successfully compete with the Israeli economy. While the territories had little import-substitution industry, Israeli industry was highly developed. Protected by high tariffs, and often competitive without them, the administered territories were an ideal market for Israeli goods. Although, to the best of our knowledge, no study has been made on the direct effects of Israeli business in the territories, there is no doubt that Israeli firms enjoyed the twin advantages of commodities of scale and favored access. Aggregate statistics show that within a period of five years the West Bank had become a large export market for Israel, second only to the United States. In 1974, 12 percent of Israeli exports went to the territories, a level that has been more or less maintained since that time. As early as 1968, imports from Israel constituted 76.8 percent of the total imports of the territories, and by 1977 reached 91 percent. Exports to Israel from the territories in 1968 represented 44 percent of total exports, and in 1977 reached 61 percent.[10]

One of the main commodities the West Bank had to offer in exchange for its trade disadvantage was cheap labor. Although in the first year following the Six Day War, Palestinian laborers were not allowed to seek work in Israel, free movement of labor was permitted once the Israeli economy revived. The workers entered those sectors with the largest incremental growth and the lowest technological requirements. Construction absorbed the largest share of the incoming labor pool, as the building industry experienced its greatest boom since the early 1950s. Others worked in the growing service industry as tourism made significant gains.

Exporting labor thus became the West Bank's main economic activity. In 1974, when earnings from such employment reached their high point relative to total economic activity, they accounted for roughly 27 percent of the GNP. Brian van Arkadie estimates that, given the multiplier effect wrought by the injection of these wages into the West Bank economy, they accounted for nearly half of the incremental growth of the GNP between the years 1968 to 1973. These earnings financed Israeli imports to the West Bank.[11]

Interaction between the two economies subsequently developed along specialized lines. While the West Bank's main export was labor, Israel's exports consisted primarily of sophisticated and technological goods. This, of course, does not constitute the sum total of the relationship. There are indications that, between 1974 and 1977, the relationship between the two economies became more diversified. In this period, labor earnings from Israel accounted for less than 50 percent of total foreign receipts, with the remainder deriving from the sale of agricultural produce and industrial goods. Moreover, in recent years export revenue growth has exceeded growth in labor receipts. The export revenues of the West Bank grew by 33 percent in real terms over the years 1974-1977, compared to a 23 percent increase in labor earnings from abroad.[12]

Contact between the economies of the West Bank and Israel resulted in an accelerated economic growth in the West Bank. Growth of the GNP exceeded an average of 12 percent annually between 1968 and 1978. This figure is even more impressive if we take into account the continued emigration from the West Bank throughout this period. GNP per capita grew by 11 percent in the West Bank (see table 4-1). This rate of growth surpassed Israel's own remarkable economic growth in the boom years 1955-1964 and 1968-1973 as well as that of other fast-growing economies.[13] The growth in GNP was accompanied by a corresponding expansion of the West Bank's domestic economy. While notably lower than GNP growth rates, owing to the prominence of labor earnings from Israel, Gross Domestic Product (GDP) grew by an average of 10 percent in the West Bank.

Thus, the impact of of the Israeli economy promoted the expansion of the West Bank's domestic economy in two major spheres: Higher incomes, mainly the result of earnings in Israel, brought significant increases in levels of consumption, which in turn spurred domestic economic activity; and in the area of supply, contact with a superior technological environment resulted in innovations in virtually all sectors of the economy. Productivity gains were especially apparent in agriculture, industry, and construction. The introduction of technological innovations facilitated the expansion of the domestic economy, despite a decline in domestic manpower during the early years following the Six Day War when an increasing share of the labor force found employment in Israel. The decrease in domestic employment levels was nevertheless slight, owing to the fact that most workers employed in Israel came largely from the ranks of the unemployed. Thus, the initial absorption of workers into the Israeli economy reflected little cost in opportunity to the economy of the West Bank.

Table 4-1
Annual Rate of Growth, 1968-1978
(*percent*)

	West Bank			Israel
	GNP (Gross National Product)	*GNP* Per Capita	*GDP* (Gross Domestic Product)	*GNP*
1968-1978	12.9	11.0	10.4	5.5
1968-1973	14.5	11.8	9.9	9.9
1974-1978	7.0	5.2	5.1	1.9

Source: Adapted from *Administered Territories Statistics Quarterly*, Vol. 9:2 (Jerusalem: Israel Central Bureau of Statistics), November 1979; *Statistical Abstract of Israel 1978*, no. 29 (Jerusalem: Israel Central Bureau of Statistics); and *Central Bureau of Statistics Monthly*, no. 1 (January 1979):17.

The opportunities presented by access to the Israeli market, once the free flow of goods was allowed, contributed to the process of expansion. The Israeli market became the dominant importer of goods from the West Bank. Israel's share of the West Bank's total exports rose from 48 percent in 1968 to 70 percent in 1974.[14] Export growth was registered for industrial as well as agricultural and labor-intensive products—mainly products in which the West Bank enjoyed a comparative advantage over Israel. Exports from the West Bank increased by 8 percent annually during the years 1968 to 1977.[15] While prior to 1967 the West Bank's foreign earnings derived almost overwhelmingly from tourist services, visible exports represented an increasingly large share of foreign earnings during the period after 1968.

The double-digit growth rate that characterized the first six years of economic development in the West Bank has since declined substantially. Not only has the growth rate been halved, but labor-participation rates have dropped. Estimated emigration rates increased considerably in the years 1975 to 1978, reaching levels almost comparable to those in the Jordanian period. The labor force in the West Bank declined in absolute numbers from 139,000 in 1974, to 131,500 in 1978. Similarly, labor-participation rates as a percentage of the total working-age population declined from 39.1 percent in 1974 to 34 percent in 1978 (see table 4-2).

This analysis suggests that the 1968-1978 period should be divided in two, with 1974 as the dividing point. Several factors can explain the slow-down in growth. First, after absorbing large numbers of workers from the territories, the Israeli market reached its saturation point, particularly with the Israeli economy itself entering a no-growth period in the wake of the Yom Kippur War. While West Bank earnings continued to grow, the number of laborers working in Israel declined (see table 4-2). With Israel's current economic difficulties, the prospects for any significant reversal of this trend in the near future are unlikely. However, Israel's consistently high demand for West Bank labor accompanied by wage rigidity, as demonstrated since 1974, indicates a steady stream of future earnings for the territories. Second, a steep decline in private consumption in the face of uncertainty has weakened West Bank domestic demand. A corresponding decline in public expenditures has also contributed to slower growth. Third, unusually high savings have not been translated into business investment, although building investment throughout the second period was extremely brisk. A general unwillingness to invest in industry is characteristic of many developing countries, where there is a traditional preference for real estate. Fourth, a long-term decline in the comparative labor-wage advantage, accompanied by declining Israeli demand for goods initially subcontracted in the territories, have led to a condition of almost no growth in West Bank industry since 1974.

The most outstanding characteristic of the West Bank economy was the rise in personal affluence for a large number of West Bankers. Private con-

Table 4-2
Labor Force and Population Characteristics in the West Bank, 1970-1978

Year	Population of West Bank (in thousands)			Labor Force of West Bank		Labor Force of West Bank Employed in Israel	
	Total	Net Outflow	Natural Increase	Percentage of Total Population Over Age 14	Total Employed (in thousands)	Percentage of Total Employed	Total (in thousands)
1970	603.9	5.0	13.7	36.7	118.4	12.4	14.7
1971	617.3	2.5	15.9	36.3	119.7	21.4	25.6
1972	629.0	5.1	16.8	37.6	126.6	27.6	34.9
1973	646.2	−0.3	16.9	37.4	127.7	30.2	38.6
1974	661.6	2.7	18.1	39.1	139.0	30.5	42.4
1975	665.1	15.1	18.6	36.5	133.9	30.2	40.4
1976	670.9	14.5	20.3	35.4	131.3	28.3	37.1
1977	681.2	10.2	20.5	33.9	128.8	27.6	35.5
1978	690.4	9.4	18.6	34.0	131.5	28.0	36.8

Source: Adapted from *Administered Territories Statistics Quarterly*, vol. 9, p. 2 (Jerusalem: Israel Central Bureau of Statistics), November 1979; *Statistical Abstract of Israel 1978*, no. 29 (Jerusalem: Israel Central Bureau of Statistics).

sumption increased by 7 percent annually between 1968 and 1969.[16] In the space of five years (1974-1979) the number of families owning a gas or electric range in the territories increased from 32.7 percent to 72.8 percent; and in the space of seven years (1972-1979) the families owning television sets increased from 10 percent to 46.7 percent. Residential building increased almost twelvefold between 1968 and 1975.[17] Evidence suggests that those who enjoyed rising affluence during this period came from the weaker strata of West Bank society employed in Israel. One can safely assume then, that prosperity brought in its wake greater socioeconomic equality.[18]

Structural Underdevelopment and
Continued Peripheralization

Despite certain economic changes and rising prosperity, the West Bank continued to be characterized by structural underdevelopment. The same trilateral framework that engendered a rise of affluence also served to inhibit structural growth. In fact, some of the key modernizing sectors regressed under Israeli rule. The common market that expanded blue-collar work opportunities by providing jobs in Israel exposed the West Bank medical profession and other white-collar sectors to stiff competition from their Israeli counterparts. In a similar manner, the same relationship that was instrumental in promoting textile and furniture subcontracting also exposed critical sectors in the West Bank economy, such as tourism, to superior Israeli competition. The policy of autonomy in economic affairs was also two sided. Although the traditional commercial network remained intact, unmolested by direct Israeli competition, that same policy left local economic development to the mercy of local entrepreneurs who were scarce. Few were willing to take business risks in the face of the political uncertainty that prevailed throughout the period in the West Bank. The same can be said for the open-bridges relationship with Jordan. While this arrangement provided a much needed outlet for West Bank produce, it also facilitated the brain drain and the debilitating transfer of capital from the West Bank. Finally, these relationships both induced and reflected the administrative and economic control wielded by both Israel and Jordan in the West Bank. Both centers used economic control as a means of furthering political ends at the expense of West Bank economic development.

The persistence of structural underdevelopment in the West Bank was manifested in the decline or disappearance of critical service sectors, the poor performance of West Bank industry and tourism, and the growing imbalance between educational attainment and the supply of suitable jobs.

Industrial development, critical to a region poor in natural resources but rich in manpower, was severely limited. After twelve years of Israeli administration, the industrial sector's share of the GNP barely exceeded 5 percent.[19] In terms of growth (7 percent annually), it was the least outstanding of the sectors that make up the West Bank economy. Most of the growth was recorded in the first period, and since 1974 no growth has taken place.[20] The development of this sector has been highly dependent on Israeli market demand for subcontract material.[21] Moreover, industry was unable to diversify to meet changing consumer demands as disposable income rose. The inevitable result was that more and more disposable income was spent on Israeli products. In truth, both subcontract relationships and higher income levels did have some effect on the changing composition of local industry— the more technologically based industries, including basic metals, plastics, and quarrying, grew more rapidly than the traditional artisan industries. In addition, while the industrial labor force only increased from 12,000 in 1968 to 14,300 in 1974, total output has increased by 60 percent since 1968.[22] This development suggests that the increase in industrial output was largely the result of technological improvements. Nevertheless, in comparison to growth rates exhibited in other sectors, industrial development was indeed slight.

The lack of industrial development was attributable to both economic and political factors. For example, free and daily commuting of workers from the West Bank to Israel posed little financial or administrative burden to the Israeli entrepreneur. It did, however, reduce the Arab entrepreneur's wage-labor advantage.[23] Moreover, Arab entrepreneurs had to contend with unfair competition as a result of government subsidies and easy financing terms that were available to Israeli manufacturers. This was especially true for Israeli firms located in government-designated development areas.[24]

Political control was also exercised to the detriment of industrial development. Two requirements stringently maintained by the Jordanians retarded the growth of an already disadvantaged industrial sector. One was the requirement that all inputs in West Bank products be of non-Israeli origin, insisting, in many cases, that they be imported from Jordan. Israeli security forces, however, frequently forbade the entrance of Jordanian supplies for fear that they contained materials needed in the manufacture of explosives. Jordan's second stipulation forbade the import over the bridges of any product manufactured in industrial establishments set up in the West Bank after the Six Day War.[25] For these reasons, only two factories employing over one hundred were established in the West Bank during twelve years of Israeli administration.[26]

Tourism suffered an even worse fate. It was the pride of the West Bank economy during the Jordanian period. As Jordanians frequently point out, in 1966 more tourists visited East Jerusalem than all of Israel. Aside from the postwar loss of the wealthy Arab oil clientele, which dealt a severe blow to the Ramallah and Jericho hoteliers, the East Jerusalem and West Bank tourist industry had now to compete directly with Israel's hotel industry.

The effects of such competition on the hoteliers is evidenced by the data supplied by Israel's Central Bureau of Statistics: the number of hotels operating in the West Bank (excluding East Jerusalem) remained constant between 1969 and 1977, but the number of rooms actually declined during that period. Occupancy remained very low at 26 percent.[27] There was, as in the case of industry, virtually no hotel investment. While it is true that retail outlets serving tourists and Arab tour operators fared appreciably better under Israeli administration than did the hotels, their growth could not compensate for the poor performance of the hotel industry.

A number of reasons account for the decline of the tourist sector. The West Bank tourist sector lost its monopoly and was exposed to competition with Israel's tourist industry. Both Israeli and West Bank hotels were equally close to major places of interest. Therefore, the Arab hotel industry entered the competition without any comparative advantage. The Israeli hotel industry enjoyed preferential access to government subsidies, unburdened by political risk, and had hotels situated closer to the superior amenities offered in West Jerusalem. Thus, West Jerusalem became a center for large-scale foreign and domestic hotel investment, as indicated by the opening of the Hilton, Plaza, and other large hotels.

The disappearance of the banking sector was dictated by Israeli government fiat. Following a decision taken after the breakdown in talks between these banks and Israeli authorities, Israel demanded that these branches sever relations with their Jordanian head offices and operate as independent banking institutions.[28] The effects wrought by the absence of financial intermediary institutions, one of which was that industry lacked needed capital, were only heightened by the effects of the open-bridges policy allowing the transfer of funds to Jordan.[29] Jordan's economic boom and the growth of the Amman stock market at a time when economic activity in the West Bank peaked contributed to the disappearance of capital from the area.[30] It is ironic to observe that despite large savings by the local population, the average industrial unit in the West Bank during this period remained constant and employed the same number of paid workers.[31] A group of financial institutions able to channel these savings into industry was sorely missed.

The poor performance of these sectors, coupled with limited growth in public employment since 1975, created a growing imbalance between the educational level of those attempting to enter the labor force and the level of economic development required to absorb them.[32] Emigration, which had subsided during the height of the local boom, increased considerably from 1974 to 1978.[33]

Prosperity encouraged education, but the same framework that created that prosperity did not generate the type of development that could absorb the growing ranks of the educated. For example, the sector that modernized most, agriculture, was also the sector that considerably reduced its labor force.[34]

Two groups figured heavily among those emigrating from the West Bank. The first consisted of high-school graduates, some of whom were pursuing their studies in Arab universities. The second group was comprised of skilled workers, many of whom received their training in Israeli-administered vocational centers and Israeli factories.[35] While the first group left because of a dearth of job opportunities, the second group was attracted by more remunerative employment in the Persian Gulf states.

In sum, the West Bank, sandwiched between two centers that dictated economic realities to the territories, experienced the contradictory phenomena of affluence and extensive residential building on the one hand, and structural underdevelopment and mass emigration on the other. It was an economic relationship that did not burden Israel, and required little direct intervention. Prosperity helped buy the peace while structural underdevelopment and emigration promoted Israel's objective of holding the West Bank as a strategic buffer zone without a center. Israel's political relationship was not nearly as smooth, nor was its political policy as successful.

Political Development in a Political Periphery

Israel's occupation of the West Bank was not a planned event. After the fact, Israel's policies were not determined by a cohesive master plan. However, Israeli authorities did not act by whim. There was a clear decision regarding the reunification of Jerusalem. Thus, the largest urban configuration was detached from the West Bank immediately after the Six Day War.[36] At the same time, certain ideas concerning the relationship between Israel and the territories gained currency among Israel's ruling Labor elite.

It was taken for granted during the first decade of occupation that Israeli rule could not replicate Jordan's. As an Arab state, enjoying historical and spiritual legitimacy, however much challenged within Jordan and the Arab world, Jordan could still aspire to integrate the Palestinians in the Jordanian state. Israel, though more powerful in the instrumental sense, was constrained by political illegitimacy and religious and cultural distance. Experience during the mandate period and later Jewish-Arab interaction in the State of Israel implied a limited relationship. Another principle guiding Israeli thinking was that Israel's security interests were linked to the territories, not to their inhabitants. The Allon plan, conceived in the immediate aftermath of the war, gave eloquent expression to Israel's overriding concern—the need for strategic depth, which the West Bank provided.[37] A third mainstay of the Labor elite's thinking was the importance of the Jordanian role in the territories. Jordan was regarded as both an important partner in the control of the territories[38] and a potential partner in a possible peace solution. Indeed, the two previous ideas reinforced Israel's perception that Jordan had a role in governing the territories.

Though the military administration set up after the war had complete control of the legal apparatus developed in the mandate and Jordanian periods,[39] as well as recourse to formidable coercive power, the continued interest and influence of Jordan in the West Bank suggested to Israeli policymakers that power should, to a limited extent, be shared. This joint control implied a certain division of labor in which Israel was to be responsible for administrative and economic functions (and direct intervention when necessary) while Jordan would continue to exercise the sociopolitical influence it had wielded so effectively during the years of its rule. This entailed preserving the traditional leadership, reinforcing localism, and co-opting newcomers through traditional *hamula* (familial) channels—elements of a political control that Israel, as a non-Arab occupier, could not contrive.

Had this relationship taken root, it could have been a possible formula for the preservation of the status quo. Why subsequent political developments took place, the shape they took, and why these developments were not translated into center-building efforts will be explained in our analysis.

Liberalization in a Control Framework

Israeli policy in the early years was guided by the idea that the ultimate solution to the problem of the territories would be found within the Jordanian framework. Thus, Israeli administrative policies were directed at establishing a working relationship with Jordan along the lines we suggested previously. In keeping with its policy of preserving the status quo, Israel maintained a limited relationship with the territories. It abstained from undertaking large social and economic programs designed to solve the refugee problem in the West Bank, and from offering political insurance to potential Israeli investors. In general, the policy was to avoid extensive settlement, despite suggestion to do otherwise.[40] At the same time, Israel implemented the policy of open bridges allowing the flow of goods between the territories and Jordan.[41] This policy facilitated not only the continuation of economic relations but also the preservation of Jordanian influence in the West Bank.

Despite these overtures, a working relationship between Israel and Jordan involving a degree of joint control did not materialize. It has been suggested that Hussein (King of Jordan) overestimated annexationist tendencies among Israel's political elite; perhaps because he mistranslated public sentiment as evoking the ideas of the elite when in reality the public tended to be more extreme than the policymakers.[42] He was constrained by the rising military power of the PLO guerrilla organizations within Jordan with which he officially cooperated until his decision to rid Jordan of their presence in 1970. Hussein gave verbal support to the code of passive resistance, *sumud*, that held sway in the West Bank at the time. He activated the Jordanian bureaucracy against Israeli normalization policies by continuing to pay the salaries of striking lawyers, teachers, and judges. Jordanian interference in the Kadi crisis and Jordan's strident opposition to Jerusalem's annexation[43] (voiced at the Supreme Muslim Council located in Jerusalem), suggested an unwillingness to cooperate with the Israelis.

As the possibility of creating a tacit joint control became remote, Israel was forced to intervene more directly than it would have done if a cooperative framework had emerged. This, in turn, had significant ramifications on the West Bank.

Jordan's uncooperativeness and the lack of an overall framework intensified the importance of tactical decisions by key Israeli policymakers. Golda Meir, Israel's prime minister, and Moshe Dayan, her defense minister, were given free rein.[44] Both of them were unsympathetic to Hussein yet aware of Jordan's important role in the running of the territories and in settling the final political outcome. While Meir's plans for the West Bank were focussed on assuring the buffer zone, Dayan's designs seemed to have been more ambitious. They transcended the strategic dimension and entered into the realm of political engineering. At the basis of Dayan's thinking was the possibility that the renewed interaction between Jews and Arabs could produce the long-sought-after, but elusive, solution to the communal problem in Palestine. To Dayan, the effectiveness of Israel's military control and its economic absorptive capacity allowed for greater flexibility and risk taking in the territories. Dayan looked for an alternate Palestinian leadership that would cooperate with Israel and eventually come to terms with the existence of the Jewish state and its strategic needs.

With the passing of time, there was an inevitable infiltration of Israeli political norms into administration policies. Israel hoped that the adoption of liberal policies and the introduction of democratic procedures in the local political structure of the West Bank would encourage a more cooperative attitude amongst the Palestinians. Thus, for reasons of ideological conviction as well as political calculation, Israel proceeded to implement a number of liberal policies. Palestinian women were, for example, granted suffrage for the first time in the 1976 municipal elections; and the electoral base was further broadened through liberal interpretation of Jordanian law.[45] Of even greater significance was Israel's decision not to exercise its legal right to appoint two municipal-council members, one of whom would serve as mayor.[46] This political restraint ultimately resulted in the assumption of the mayoralties by PLO supporters in the 1976 elections. In addition, the Israeli military administration granted to Bir-Zeit College the right to seek university acreditation in the Arab states, which was the first step in the emergence of a university system in the West Bank.[47]

These and other policies, by democratizing political and educational opportunity, served to undermine Jordan's influence in the West Bank, which had historically been based on the co-optation of traditional elites. It became apparent that the policies of Israel and Jordan were not conducive to a tacit joint-control system. This inability to cooperate brought about significant political changes in the West Bank.

Institution Building in the West Bank

Although a definitive study of political modernization in the West Bank has not been made, there are nevertheless salient indications that such a process has taken place under Israeli rule. Some of these changes were the direct result of Israeli policy which deviated sharply from Jordanian practice; others emerged as a result of greater economic prosperity. Israeli policy was directly responsible for the emergence of strengthening of territory-wide institutions, a phenomenon that had been inhibited under the Jordanian regime. In this area, three developments need some elaboration: the growing importance of local councils as autonomous political units, the emergence of an independent Palestinian press, and the creation of a network of institutions of higher learning. In addition, growing economic prosperity facilitated the expansion of high-school education in both the rural and urban sectors.

The Municipalities: Israel, as a nonlegitimate control center, could not operate along traditional lines of co-optation so extensively employed by Jordan. There were no family ties connecting local elites with the Israeli center, and no positions in Israeli political and bureaucratic institutions that could be offered to local notables in exchange for cooperation. Lacking these mechanisms, Israel departed from the standard mode of governing in which notables acted as intermediaries between the central authority and their constituencies. Instead, benefits and services were accorded by the Israeli authorities on the basis of nonpolitical administrative rules.[48] Such a departure from Jordanian practice involved not only a change in the manner of distribution of these benefits, but also a change in the actors. Instead of working almost solely with local notables, Israel dealt with municipalities as collective entities and functioning organs, enhancing their power as political institutions. The mere transfer of power from traditional familial authority to local political institutions, although still dominated by traditional elements, was an important step toward political modernization.

The role of the municipalities as political institutions was further enhanced by events surrounding the elections of 1972. An unprecedentedly large turnout following an intensive campaign and Israel's decision not to interfere in either the election results or in the nomination of mayors strengthened the representative role of these organs.[49] With the addition of female suffrage in 1976 and the lowering of financial barriers in the right to vote, Israel further broadened political participation and thereby indirectly increased the prestige of the municipalities. Political modernization was also reflected in the changing composition of local council members. The trend toward the election of younger, more-educated and professionally trained candidates, many of whom enjoyed positions of power independent of the extended-family structure, was already apparent in 1972 and became the general norm in subsequent elections.[50]

The Press: Israel allowed the reemergence of a local Palestinian press, which had been quashed by the Jordanian authorities in 1965 and 1966. Two of the three reestablished newspapers generally supported the PLO and were allowed to continue publication despite their denunciations of the occupation and Israeli administration policies. The granting of publication permission to the newspaper *Al-Quds* represented no serious deviation from Jordanian practice since its editorial board was largely composed of pro-Hashemite conservatives, but the same cannot be said for the subsequent decisions allowing the publication of *Al-Sha'ab* and *Al-Fajr*.[51] Both publications were rabidly and consistently anti-Jordanian. *Al-Fajr*'s editorial board included leading personalities identified with the PLO; and two of its most prominent and influential members were Karim Khalaf, the mayor of Ramallah, and Hilmi Hanun, the mayor of Tulkarm, elected in the 1972 elections. The newspaper, owned by the wealthy emigrant Paul Ajlouny, could also count on financial support from the PLO.[52]

Though the total copies sold of all three newspapers rarely exceeded 8,000 (with *Al-Quds* at 4,500; *Al-Fajr* at 2,000; and *Al-Sha'ab* at 1,500),[53] they are reputedly read by at least double that number of people, as copies are passed from one individual to another. All three of the newspapers are published in East Jerusalem, thus perpetuating a remnant of the Palestinian character of the city that formally became the unified capital of Israel. Ironically, as Jerusalem-based newspapers, they have enjoyed one more advantage: the protection of Israeli law which is much more lenient than the Jordanian press laws operating in the West Bank.

The press acts as a politically modernizing institution. The idea of a Palestinian entity pervades all three newspapers. Even *Al-Quds*, regarded as the establishment paper, whose board has been wary of overstepping Israeli censorship laws, has nevertheless been adamant in calling for Israeli withdrawal and for the establishment of a Palestinian political framework different from both past and present. The newspaper regularly features articles against expropriation and settlement written by prominent members of the professional and political elite, many of whom held senior positions in the Jordanian government.[54] An interesting feature that appears regularly in *Al-Quds*, as well as in the other two newspapers, is notices by readers welcoming relatives, usually graduates of professional schools to the homeland and wishing them productive and rewarding careers in the service of the Palestinian people. Such inserts are another illustration of the newspapers' role in promoting Palestinianism.

Having shown skepticism in the past toward developments that West Bankers interpreted as promised signs of salvation, *Al-Quds* has generally taken a more sober view of the Palestinian problem, calling for deep structural reform within the West Bank and in the Arab world as a whole. It has, throughout the years, firmly supported Palestinian institution building. It has consistently defended the West Bank's largest economic enterprise, the East Jerusalem Electric Company against the termination of its concession by Israel on the grounds of inefficiency.[55] The paper has encouraged schemes by various West Bank investors, few of which have materialized, and urged the creation of a higher-education system as a first step in stemming the critical manpower drain that it regards as one of the critical problems facing the area.[56]

By contrast, *Al-Fajr* has consistently upheld the PLO, has regularly run afoul of Israeli censorship laws, and its closure has always been in the offing.[57] The newspaper has strived to promote the development of an ideological Palestinian literature and culture, a genre characteristic of other radical national movements. The newspaper features both lengthy editorials and an extensive literary section, unrivaled by the other newspapers. One distinct characteristic of *Al-Fajr* has been its close relationship with municipalities and municipal leaders who are most stridently anti-Jordanian and least cooperative with the Israeli authorities.

The press played a major role by introducing issues of national identity into the municipal election campaign of 1976. All three newspapers have given coverage to the increasing organizational activity in the West Bank;[58] and all of them have featured translated articles from the Israeli press, often accompanied by editorial comment. They disseminate information about the state and at the same time shape views about Israel's policies. Although generally preferring political articles critical of Israeli policies to those featuring aspects of Israeli technology and culture, the West Bank press has nevertheless served to disseminate knowledge of a more highly democratic and industrialized society.

The breadth, relative sophistication, consistency, and the location of these newspapers help explain the efficacy of the West Bank press for political modernization and mobilization. For a number of years they were the only institutions whose impact was felt throughout the West Bank; their monopoly, moreover, was never challenged by a local regional press.

The Universities and Secondary Education: In 1967, there were no university-level institutions in the West Bank. Instead, a total of eight institutions were involved in postsecondary education, mainly in teacher training. Two of these institutions offered vocational training on a junior-college level. Enrollment in each of the eight schools never exceeded a few hundred.[59]

By granting Bir-Zeit College the right to seek accreditation in Arab states as a university in 1973, Israeli military authorities were breaking with a cardinal aspect of Jordanian policy. Given the fact that there were two other colleges of Bir-Zeit's size eager to make the transition to accredited university, it was inevitable that the decision would not be the only one of its kind. The decision to allow Bir-Zeit to develop as a university must have been difficult for Israel to make, as the PLO envisioned one of the objectives of the Palestinian movement to be the rise of cultural institutions in the territories.[60] Within five years of the Bir-Zeit decision a territory-wide university system did emerge. The reinstatement of Bir-Zeit University, located in a village bearing that name near the twin cities of Ramallah and Al-Bireh, was followed by the establishment of Bethlehem University in 1974 and the transformation of Al-Najah College into a university in 1975.[61] By that year, then, three of the six districts constituting the West Bank and three of the four of its most populated areas boasted a local university. Two institutions of higher learning, the Islamic College of Hebron and Bethlehem University (Freres), founded under Israeli rule, are awaiting accreditation from the Association of Arab Universities.[62] Once these are secured, a full-fledged regional network of institutions of higher learning with locations in or near all major population centers will be in place.

All of these institutions have witnessed remarkable growth in student enrollment and faculty positions and the three universities are successfully tackling the problems of diversification into fields of study critical to modernization.[63] Bir-Zeit University has introduced additional science courses, is presently in the process of setting up an engineering school, and has recently launched its first master's program in education. Al-Najah, located in Nablus, the largest city in the West Bank, has overtaken Bir-Zeit in student enrollment and has opened departments in the natural sciences and architecture, in addition to the traditional liberal arts and education curricula. It is also in the process of opening up a school of engineering. Freres, which was established as a liberal arts college in 1973, has been offering degrees in managerial fields such as business administration and hotel management since 1979. Enrollment in Bir-Zeit, Al-Najah, and Freres universities and in the Islamic College exceeded six thousand students in 1980, over five thousand of whom are attending courses in the three universities. The system, as it stands today, is proportionately as large as that found in the average Arab country.[64]

The growth of a local university system has also spawned considerable organizational activity, most notably a Committee of Higher Learning headed by Hakmat al-Masri, chairman of the Board of Governors of Al-Najah

University. The committee is located in Jerusalem.[65] In addition to assuming fund-raising and coordinating roles, the committee has also attempted to draw up a policy for higher education. The trend toward high-level technical education and the decision to promote the expansion in enrollment beyond the availability of jobs for future graduates, even at the risk of increasing emigration in the short run, are two policy decisions implemented by the committee. In addition, each of the three universities are overseen by Boards of Governors, whose membership is composed of major professional and organizational figures in the area.[66]

With continued prosperity, there has also been a considerable expansion of high-school education, appreciably greater than on the primary or preparatory levels. For example, in 1969-1970, 16,025 students attended secondary schools; in 1976-1977 the figure increased to 25,247.[67] The impact of this educational expansion on political and social modernization has been considerable. West Bank high schools have long been noted for their intense political and ideological involvement, often encouraged by the teaching faculty and taught in the classrooms themselves. As early as 1968 and 1969, high-school youth as individuals and often high schools as collective bodies were in the forefront of opposition to Israeli normalization policies.[68] Participation in political demonstrations continued in subsequent years. In general, the high-school and university sectors have been the only segment of the West Bank population participating in activities against Israeli administration.

Certain characterisitics of the high-school educational structure in the West Bank contribute to the politicization and restlessness of the student body. First, approximately two-thirds of the students concentrate in the humanities and social sciences. Thus, the overwhelming majority of the student body concentrates on studies that are intimately related to national identification. Second, there is an almost total absence of high-school vocational education (less than 4 percent of the student body are enrolled in vocational or commercial studies).[69] Employment opportunities do exist for the vocationally trained but are in short supply for the humanities, social science, and science students. Because of the lack of economic opportunities available to those who score low or fail the matriculation examinations and the insufficient number of university places in the territories for those wishing to pursue their education, the student is left with an unhappy choice between emigration and pursuring a vocation below his expectations.[70]

To gauge the importance of high-school education, one should note that the high-school education system in the West Bank is as large proportionately as many Western countries, matriculating more students per capita than Israel.[71] The high-school student body constitutes approximately 3.7 percent (in Israel, 3.6 percent) of the population. This student body increased by 83 percent between the years 1967 and 1977, compared to an overall population increase of 15 percent for that period.[72]

The Role of Jordan in the West Bank

Neither political changes witnessed in the West Bank under Israeli control nor the political separation between the two banks of the Jordan River resulted in the total loss of Jordanian influence in the West Bank. Quite to the contrary, Jordan continued to assume a diminished but important role as both a legal-institutional center and as a geographic gateway to the Arab world. In the words of Menahem Milson, a former advisor to the Israeli military government, "There was the immutable fact that all the land routes connecting the West Bank with the rest of the Arab World ran through Jordan, a situation that placed a very powerful sanction in the hands of the Jordanian government with regard to West Bankers."[73] Demography also linked the two banks: "Many West Bankers had relatives in Jordan (often relatives highly placed in the Jordanian establishment)." These realities alone assured Jordanian influence despite changing political fortunes in the West Bank.

With the inception of Israeli administration, residents of the West Bank became neither Palestinian nor Israeli. Jordan continued to provide the only legal identity West Bankers possessed. Jordanian passports allowed members of a highly peripheral, and therefore mobile, community the ability to travel, work, and study abroad. The importance of this document is indicated by an Israeli census taken soon after the war showing that one out of every three households had at least one child living outside the West Bank—60 percent of whom resided outside Jordan.[74]

Another source of influence emanated from Jordan's continued role as the official registrar of all profit and nonprofit organizations in the West Bank. Jordan frequently suppressed moves by various professional organizations toward organizational autonomy in the West Bank; insisting instead that they remain affiliated with the parent bodies on the East Bank, thereby maintaining their Jordanian identity in their official titles.[75] Control over passports and registration of local organizations enabled Jordan to continue to wield influence on both the individual and institutional levels. Jordan also continued to pay salaries to 40 percent of the civil servants and teachers in the West Bank, disbursing, for example, $18,000,000 in 1978. This figure represents approximately $3,800 for each employee—a sum exceeding well over half of the average annual earnings of Israelis.[76]

While the Israeli military authorities were responsible for the maintenance of the growing education system, the curriculum employed (except for minor revisions involving the excision of anti-Jewish literature from textbooks) was Jordanian. Jordan also continued to allocate education grants to municipalities as well as to individual institutions. Jordanian control over the transfer process of the *sumud* (steadfastness) funds financed by wealthy Arab states was yet another source of influence. The impact of these funds was heightened by the fact that the education system was, throughout these years, desperate for funds. The West Bank had to cope with both an annual 5 percent enrollment increase and strict budget ceilings set by the Israeli administration, which was determined to keep down the costs of its occupation.[77]

Jordan's role in local municipal affairs was best reflected in the recurrent pilgrimages made by West Bank municipal officials to Amman.[78] The most important item on the agenda was financial. Jordan either directly provided or supervised the allocation of monies that in some years exceeded, and at other times equalled, Israeli contributions to the municipalities.[79] The actual amounts involved are hard to assess as many payments are made in Amman and remain unrecorded.[80] The role of these funds in promoting Jordanian influence was even more considerable than the education grants.

Like the educational institutions, the municipalities were also faced with growing financial difficulties. On the one hand, local revenue accounted for a small percentage of total revenues (poor tax collection is a feature endemic to the Middle East). On the other hand, growing personal prosperity among the citizenry resulted in demands for more and better municipal services.

Other items frequently discussed by municipal councillors in their meetings with Jordanian officials concerned trade and business matters. The importance of these issues was of course a reflection of Jordan's larger role both as a gateway to markets in the Arab world and its own important role as the second-largest national market for West Bank produce. Jordan had virtually total control over the nature, mode, and operation of such commercial intercourse. In a manner similar to the way Jordan dispensed funds to municipalities, these decisions were made on the executive administrative level, unconstrained by legal or parliamentary oversight.

Though the outstanding features characterizing Israeli rule were the deviation from Jordanian practice and the subsequent modernization of the territories, Jordan continued to wield considerable influence in the West Bank. The immutable realities connecting the two banks, and the multiple channels of influence that continued to exist despite political separation, allowed for the continuation of Jordanian control in various areas of political and social life in the region.

Political Development without Center Building

The contact between a developed Israel and the underdeveloped West Bank that occurred following the 1967 war generated changes in both the economic and the political domains. In the first domain, we saw how prosperity coincided with more-limited structural development. In the political arena, there was increasing political participation, formal as well as informal, and institutions assumed roles independent of traditional political structures. Despite this evolution, the development of a national indigenous leadership never took place. Its absence can partially be explained by the lack of political independence, but this fact alone fails to explain why attempts to create a territorial authority decreased over time.

Given the existence of other features of political development, the opposite should have been true. Despite social and political modernization, the inalterable rise of Palestinian consciousness throughout the period, and demographic concentration in distinct territorial units, there were few attempts at center building. By center building we mean the creation of a territorial authority that would represent the West Bank on the international and inter-Arab scenes, as well as direct and coordinate territory-wide political and economic activities.

An inverse relationship between political modernization and support for a territorial Palestinian entity characterized the West Bank under Israeli rule. Indeed, the only serious attempts at establishing a local territory-wide leadership that would negotiate the political future of the territories with Israel and the other concerned parties, took place in the early years of Israeli rule. The creation of National Fronts in most West Bank towns can be regarded as the most important of such attempts.[81]

The National Front organizations were composed both of local notables and of young professionals and students formerly associated with the Jordanian opposition. By 1968, these groups identified to some extent with the guerrilla organizations but were not totally subservient to their wishes. Publicly they professed loyalty to the Hashemite regime, demanding reforms that were the staple of opposition demands during Jordanian rule; in reality they were seeking a framework that would give political expression to yearnings for greater independence. Their subsequent demise after two years of political activity (from late 1967 to 1969) is indicative of the difficulties of acting unilaterally against so formidable an array of opponents. According to David Farchi, a former chief advisor to the Military Government, a delegation of local notables failed to receive Nasser's blessings for their efforts. His lack of assent meant a lack of political legitimacy in the eyes of the Arab world.[82] It had been hoped that he would persuade the Jordanians to regard their efforts in a more positive light. Jordan's response was no less negative. Hussein, who then hoped for a quick return to the status quo, was unwilling to consider concessions of the magnitude presented by the leaders of the movement.[83] Even more strenuous opposition came from PLO quarters. The PLO and its member organizations, who at that time were attempting to create a guerrilla base in the territories, were understandably opposed to political initiatives that could have ultimately undermined their perceived role and aggrandized the stature of territorial Palestinians.[84] Israel responded by banning territory-wide political activities, including attempts at recreating political parties.[85]

Opposed from all sides, the National Front movement had little choice but to disband. Its failure was followed by political resignation both to the prospects of continued Israeli administration and political abnegation. The subsequent strengthening of instrumental relationships between the new rulers and ruled was the natural corollary of such a political mood.[86]

The National Front attempt was not the only effort at center building; it was, however, the only territory-wide effort enjoying the support of major segments of the population. The two other serious initiatives were dominated by the personalities that led them. Muhammad 'Ali al-Jabri, the veteran mayor of Hebron and a powerful notable in Jordanian times, intermittently attempted to cull support for the notion of negotiating with the Israelis.[87] Hamdi Kna'an, the mayor of Nablus, appealed to less traditional elements of West Bank society. Nablus, as the most nationalist of West Bank towns, counted among its inhabitants a relatively high proportion of politicized intellectuals and technocrats, many of whom took part in activities of the National Front including demonstrations, protests, and strikes against the occupation.[88] Both of these attempts proved ineffective. Al-Jabri was tainted by his close working relationship with the Israelis. Kna'an was rebuffed by the Israeli administration and was undermined by radical elements who were gaining ground in the West Bank. These elements warned against the dangers of such efforts, especially as Dayan had begun voicing his support for the emergence of a local leadership.

By the mid-seventies, the hope that West Bankers would be able to negotiate their own political future had evaporated. Indeed, the doctrine of *sumud*, with its cardinal tenets being political abnegation, held sway. Political representation of the interests of local Palestinians was henceforth to be in the hands of forces other than themselves.

The doctrine of *sumud* was created well before the attempts we have described. It was the doctrine of holding out against the occupier, who was presumed to be bent on reducing the Arab presence on the West Bank. In fact, *sumud* became the password for resistance activities soon after the war. It had emerged as a competing principle to those calling for territory-wide leadership, even though the National Front movement sought to reconcile both approaches and became involved in attempts at center building and opposition activities. Initially the doctrine of *sumud* called for the freezing of all institutional public life, including opposition to elections conducted under the auspices of the military administration. It also included the prohibition of formal and informal ties beyond the minimum necessary to sustain the activities of existing organizations. In its later modified form, it has principally sought to block any attempt at local representation. However, a growing awareness of the importance of promoting local Palestinian institutions and the awareness that the opportunities of doing so existed within the more lenient environment created by the Israelis, resulted in the discarding of those prohibitions against institutional development.[89]

In retrospect, if moves toward liberalization on the part of Israel were designed to create an environment conducive to the development of an alternative leadership, then Israel's efforts were counterproductive. Center-building efforts were frozen while liberalization measures facilitated the growth of politically modernizing and mobilizing institutions such as the universities and the press. In the short run, this state of affairs was highly amenable to Israel. Relations between the mayors in day-to-day matters improved considerably in comparison to the situation prevailing in the first two years of Israeli rule. Despite the content of the West Bank press, Israel viwed the institutional buildup as a positive sign of normalization. It seemed to the Israelis that the smoothness that characterized the economic relationship between Israel and the territories was being carried over into the political domain. The Israelis regarded with favor what seemed to them a preoccupation with civic and organizational development and local abstention from dealing with national political issues.

Israeli optimism might have been misplaced; the parallel between the prevailing political and economic situations was far from perfect. Unlike the economic framework in which both external instrumental centers (Israel and Jordan) monopolized control, in the political domain a vacuum was created that neither center filled. Neither Jordan nor Israel could meet the rise of Palestinian consciousness gaining ground in the West Bank or gauge the importance of institutional activities engendering it. Jordan had already failed to be the comprehensive center it had sought to be during its own rule; still less was it able to command charismatic identification indirectly, especially after the 1970 civil war in Jordan. Both centers were unwilling to make the necessary concessions to any potential leadership that could direct political consciousness in the West Bank along more amenable lines than the PLO alternative. By the 1970s, the West Bank was a politically modernizing periphery—a territorial community characterized by a high degree of political awareness and the absence of a representative territory-wide leadership. This situation paved the way for the subordination of the West Bank to an external charismatic center—a development that was contrary to both Israeli and Jordanian interests.

Notes

1. Jamil Hilal, *The West Bank: Its Social and Economic Structure, 1948-1973* (Beirut: Palestine Liberation Organization and Research Center, 1975).

2. Aryeh Bregman, *The Economy of the Administered Territories, 1974 and 1975* (Jerusalem: Bank of Israel Research Department, 1976), pp. 7-9.

3. Larry L. Fabian, "Prologue: The Political Setting," in Brian van Arkadie, *Benefits and Burdens: A Report on the West Bank and Gaza Strip Economics since 1967* (New York: Carnegie Endowment for International Peace, 1977), p. 12.

4. State of Israel, Prime Minister's Office, Economic Planning Authority, *Israel Economic Development: Past Progress and Plan for the Future* (Jerusalem: Israel Program for Scientific Translations, 1968), p. 394. For the data on employment in the territories see Haim Ben-Shahar, Eitan Berglas, Yair Mumdeax, and Ezra Sadan, *Economic Structure and Development: Prospects*, p. 21. For GNP data, see ibid., pp. 26-27.

5. State of Israel, *Israel Economic Development*, p. 403.

6. Ibid., pp. 313-315.

7. Ibid., p. 339.

8. Ben-Shahar, et al., *Economic Structure and Development: Prospects*, p. 33. Kuznets analyzed the distribution of means and shares of product and labor in countries at various levels of per capita income, with the view of assessing the structural features of economies at different levels of development. The sample mentioned comprises countries with an average per capita income of $200. See S. Kuznets, "Quantitative Aspects of the Economic Growth of Nations II, Industrial Distribution of National Product and Labor Force," *Economic Development and Cultural Change*, vol. 5 (July 1957), Supplement.

9. Ibid., pp. 28-30.

10. Figures computed from State of Israel Central Bureau of Statistics, *Statistical Abstract of Israel, 1978*, no. 29 (Jerusalem: State of Israel, 1978), table 8-1, p. 212.

11. Van Arkadie, *Benefits and Burdens*, pp. 163-164.

12. Figures computed from *Statistical Abstract of Israel*, table 27-6, p. 769.

13. State of Israel, *Israel Economic Development*, p. 10.

14. Bregman, *The Economy of the Administered Territories*, p. 46.

15. Uri Litwin, *The Economy of the Administered Territories, 1976-1977* (Jerusalem: Bank of Israel Research Department, 1980), pp. 8-9 (Hebrew).

16. State of Israel, Minister of Defense, Coordinator of Government Operations in Judea and Samaria, Gaza District, Sinai, Golan Heights, *A Thirteen Year Survey (1967-1980)*, Mimeographed report, 1981, append. 4B, Comprehensive Data on Judea and Samiara, p. 42.

17. See Gideon M. Karsel, "Consumption Patterns in the Administered Territories after Ten Years of Israeli Rule," in Raphael Israeli, ed., *Ten Years of Israeli Rule in Judea and Samaria*, (Jerusalem: The Magness Press.

The Hebrew University, 1980) pp. 87-89; and State of Israel, *A Thirteen Year Survey*, append. 14, Household Equipment, p. 58.

18. For an analysis of the redistribution of wealth in the West Bank under Israeli rule see Mark Heller, "Politics and Social Change in the West Bank," in Joel S. Migdal, et al., *Palestinian Society and Politics*, pp. 193-195.

19. Computed from data in Ben-Shahar, et al., *Economic Structure and Development*, table 11, p. 27; and in *A Thirteen Year Survey*, append. 2, p. 40, and append. 7, p. 50.

20. Computed from append. 7, in *Thirteen Years of Israeli Rule*, p. 50.

21. On the impact of subcontracting see van Arkadie, *Benefits and Burdens*, pp. 84-85.

22. Computed from *Statistical Abstract of Israel, 1978*, table 27-22, p. 788.

23. An indication of diminishing comparative labor-wage advantages for West Bank workers employed in Israel is reflected by the fact that earnings of West Bank laborers employed in the West Bank were 60 percent of after-tax earnings of West Bank workers employed in Israel in 1968-1969, and were 90 percent of those wages in 1976-1977. Computed from data in Uri Litwin, *The Economy of the Administered Territories, 1976-1977*, table 13, p. 30; and Mark Heller, "Political and Social Change," in Joel S. Migdal, et al., *Palestinian Society and Politics*, table 11, p. 192.

24. For an extensive analysis of the impact of government subsidies on Israeli industry and the market distortions that ensue see Nahum Finger, *The Impact of Government Subsidies on Industrial Management* (New York: Praeger Publishers, 1971).

25. Arieh Shalev, *The Autonomy: Problems and Possible Solutions* (Tel-Aviv: Center for Strategic Studies, Tel-Aviv University, 1979), p. 130.

26. Hisham M. Awartani: *A Survey of Industries in the West Bank and Gaza Strip* (Bir-Zeit: Birzeit University Publications, September 1979), p. 12.

27. *Statistical Abstract of Israel, 1978*, table 27-35, p. 801.

28. See Israel National Section of the International Commission of Jurists, *The Rule of Law in the Areas Administered by Israel* (Tel-Aviv: Israel National Section of the International Commission of Jurists, 1981), pp. 64-65.

29. The need for local banks in the development of the local economy was the subject of an editorial in *Al-Quds*, August 11, 1979, entitled "Bank Filastin—A Step in the Right Direction." On the importance of foreign bank accounts and portfolios see *The New York Times*, October 13, 1981.

30. See section on Jordan in Michael Field, ed., *The Middle East Annual Review, 1978* (London: The Middle East Review Co., 1977); and *MEED*, (September 25, 1980) vol. 25, no. 39, p. 24.

31. Ya'acov Lifshitz, "Economic Growth in the Occupied Territories, 1968-1975," in Israeli, ed., *Ten Years of Israeli Rule*, p. 81.

32. See Dan Izenberg, Government Press Office correspondent, "Civilian Aspects of the Military Government in Judea and Samaria" (Jerusalem: Government Press Office, August 1981); and State of Israel, *A Thirteen Year Survey*, append. 23, p. 67.

33. See *The Jerusalem Post*, September 24, 1973; and *Israel Economist* (October 1978):25. See also *MEED* no. 4 (October 12, 1979):12.

34. The number of workers employed in West Bank agriculture decreased from 42,500 in 1970, to 33,450 in 1977. *Statistical Abstract of Israel*, table 27-22, p. 788.

35. Litwin, *The Economy of the Administered Territories, 1976-1977*, pp. 14-15.

36. Jerusalem was officially unified as Israel's capital on June 28, 1967.

37. For details on the Allon plan see Yigal Allon, "Israel: The Case for Defensible Borders," in *Foreign Affairs*, vol. 55, no. 1 (October 1976):38-53.

38. Ibid., 44.

39. For an analysis of the legal structure of the West Bank see Moshe Drori, *Local Government, Democracy, and Elections in Judea and Samaria: Legal Aspects* (Jerusalem: Jerusalem Institute for Federal Studies, and Bar-Ilan University, Institute of Local Government, 1980), pp. 23-42 (Hebrew).

40. A group of prominent economists and sociologists from Israeli universities proposed that the government embark upon large scale-rehabilitation of refugees both in the West Bank and Gaza. They called for an annual commitment by the State of 50 million dollars a year over eight to ten years. The proposal was privately rejected by the Eshkol government in September 1967. A similar proposal was rejected by Golda Meir in 1969, though some minor projects were undertaken. See Michael Bruno's article, "The Economy of the Territories—Prosperity Without Development," *Ma'ariv*, May 18, 1972. Concerning insurance, see Mordechai Nisan, *Israel and the Territories, A Study in Control 1967-1977* (Ramat-Gan, Israel: Turtledove Publishing, 1978), p. 93.

41. On the evolution of the open bridges in theory and practice see Vivian Bull, *The West Bank: Is it Viable?* (Lexington, Mass.: Lexington Books, D.C. Heath and Co., 1975), pp. 50-51 and 73.

42. Zvi Elpeleg, *King Hussein's Federation Plan: Genesis and Reaction* (Tel-Aviv: Tel-Aviv University, December 1977), p. 6 (Hebrew).

43. On the Kadi crisis see Ann Mosely Lesch, *Israel's Occupation of the West Bank: The First Two Years* (Santa Monica, Cal.: The Rand Corporation, August 1970): Report RM-6295-ARPA: 17-19, 45.

44. Golda Meir's "Kitchen Cabinet" was an excellent example of the way the executive has traditionally dominated Israeli politics. For a general

discussion as to how that effected Israeli policy in the West Bank, see Nisan, *Israel and the Territories*, pp. 21-56.

45. See Drori, *Local Government*, pp. 87-88.

46. Sasson Levy, "Local Government in the Administered Territories," p. 113.

47. On the reasons for the Israeli decision see text of a letter sent by Ambassador Yehuda Blum, permanent representative of Israel to the United Nations, February 28, 1979 (A/34/101 - 5/13/76).

48. The point was made by Menahem Milson, later head of civilian administration in the territories, in "How to Make Peace with the Palestinians," *Commentary*, vol. 71, no. 5 (May 1981):31.

49. Shaul Mishal, "Judea and Samaria: An Anatomy of a Municipal Elections," *HaMizrach HeHadash*, vol. 24, no. 1-2(93-94)(1974):63-67. (Hebrew).

50. On the 1972 elections see ibid. On the composition of candidates in the 1976 elections see Yehuda Litani in *Ha'aretz*, April 11, 1976.

51. See Yosef Tzuriel, "A Press under the Magnifying Glass," *Ma'ariv*, weekend supplement, April 13, 1981, p. 18.

52. Ibid.

53. Various estimates have been presented for the circulations of the three East Jerusalem papers. See Clinton Bailey, "Changing Attitudes toward Jordan in the West Bank," p. 165. See also Nissim Rejwan, "The Palestinian Press under Israeli Administration," in *Midstream*, vol. 14, no. 9 (November 1973):16.

54. Some of the regular contributors to *Al-Quds* include Anwar Nuseibeh, former minister of defense of Jordan and present chairman of the East Jerusalem Electric Company; Elias Freij, mayor of Bethlehem, and chairman of the Association of West Bank Chambers of Commerce; and T. Kan'an, former judge in the Jordanian Court of Appeals.

55. The company has, in its struggle to maintain the concession, applied to the Israeli Supreme Court. See State of Israel, Ministry of Foreign Affairs, Department of Information, "Excerpts from the Statement Submitted to the Supreme Court on Behalf of the Attorney General of Israel," January 11, 1981, 119/1.11.061.

56. See, for example, Anwar Nuseibeh's article, "On the Meaning of Autonomy," *Al-Quds*, April 4, 1979.

57. Tzuriel, "The Press under the Magnifying Glass," *Ma'ariv*, p. 18.

58. See, for example, the wide press coverage given to the "Jam'iyyet 'al-Multakah al-Fikri al-Arabi," in the West Bank. *Al-Quds*, April 15, 1979; *Al-Sha'ab*, July 15, 1979.

59. See Khalil Mahshi and Ramzi Rihan, "Education: Elementary and Secondary," in Nakhleh, ed., *A Palestinian Agenda for the West Bank and Gaza*, (Washington, D.C.: American Enterprise Institute, 1980), pp. 46-47.

60. See "Aims of the Political Programme of the Palestinian Revolution Adopted by the 11th Palestine National Congress, Cairo, January 12, 1973," article 8, in *Journal of Palestine Studies*, vol. 2, no. 3 (Spring, 1973), p. 170.

61. Musa Budeiri, "The Universities of the West Bank," in *Middle East International*, no. 110 (October 1979):9.

62. Ibid.

63. Mahshi and Rihan, "Education: Elementary and Secondary," in Nakhleh, ed., *A Palestinian Agenda*, pp. 47-50. On the limits of this diversification see ibid., pp. 50-51; and Muhammad Hallaj's "Mission of Palestinian High Education," in ibid., pp. 71-72.

64. See Hallaj, "Mission of Palestinian High Education," in Nakhleh, ed., *A Palestinian Agenda*, pp. 59-60.

65. See Norman C. Hunt, "Report on a Visit to the West Bank Council for Higher Education," July 1979 (unpublished).

66. Ya'akov Chavakuk, "Bir-Zeit," *Ha'aretz*, weekend supplement, December 19, 1980, p. 18.

67. Mahshi and Rihan, "Education: Elementary and Secondary," in Nakhleh, ed., *A Palestinian Agenda*, pp. 36-37.

68. Ann Mosely Lesch, *Israel's Occupation of the West Bank*, pp. 55-56, and 90-94.

69. Israel Central Bureau of Statistics, *Administered Territories Statistics Quarterly*, vol. 9, no. 7 (1979), table 2, p. 62. In 1977 there were over 8,000 high-school graduates in the West Bank, approximately 6,000 of whom either did not take the matriculation exam or scored below the minimum threshhold of 70 percent which permits entrance to university. Approximately 5,000 sought work in occupational categories appropriate to their educational attainment (administrative, technical and clerical). On the entire West Bank there were only 13,000 positions extant in these categories—which produces a job seeker/position ratio of 1:2.6.

70. Computed from data in Hallaj, "Mission of Palestinian High Education," in Nakhleh, *A Palestinian Agenda*, pp. 69-70; and Mahshi and Rihan, "Education: Elementary and Secondary," in ibid., p. 48, table 8, note g.

71. See *Statistical Abstract of Israel*, no. 29 (Jerusalem: Central Bureau of Statistics, 1978), table 22-32, p. 679; and *Administered Territories Statistics Quarterly*, vol. 9, no. 1, table 6, p. 74.

72. Figures computed from data in Mahshi and Rihan, "Education: Elementary and Secondary," in Nakhleh, ed., *The Palestinian Agenda*, table 2, p. 33, and table 4, p. 37.

73. Menahem Milson, "How to Make Peace with the Palestinians," p. 32. Reprinted from *Commentary*, by permission; all rights reserved.

74. Israel Defense Forces, "Households with Sons or Daughters Outside the Territories in 1967," *Demographic Characteristics of the Popula-*

*tion in the Administered Areas Publication No. 3 of the Census of Popula-
tion 1967* (Jerusalem: Central Bureau of Statistics, 1968), pp. 30-32, and
62-64.

75. On the Jordanian involvement of this type, concerning for example
the establishment of the Council of Chambers of Commerce in 1968, see
Shaul Mishal, "The Palestinian West Bank Political Elite—A Behavioral
Portrait," in Asher Arian, ed., *Israel—A Developing Society* (Assen, The
Netherlands: Van Gorcum, 1980), pp. 136-137. On Jordanian intervention
in other attempts at organizational autonomy (medical and legal) see
Shimon Shamir, et al., eds., *The Professional Elite in Samaria* (Tel-Aviv:
Shiloach Center, Tel-Aviv University, 1975), p. 82 (Hebrew).

76. Arieh Shalev, *The Autonomy: Problems and Possible Solutions*, p. 54.

77. On specific educational problems see Fatiyya Said Nasru, *West Bank
Education in Government Schools, 1966-1977* (Beir-Zeit: Bir-Zeit University,
1977). On the economic aspect, see Gideon M. Karsel, "Consumption Patterns
in the Administered Territories after Ten Years of Israeli Rule," in R. Israeli,
ed., *Ten Years of Israeli Rule in Judea and Samaria*, p. 101.

78. See Clinton Bailey, "Changing Attitudes toward Jordan in the West
Bank," *Middle East Journal*, vol. 32, no. 2 (Spring 1978):968; and Asher
Susser, "Jordanian Influence in the West Bank," *The Jerusalem Quarterly*,
no. 8 (Summer 1978):60-61.

79. See Shalev, *Autonomy: Problems and Possible Solutions*, p. 53.

80. Levy, "Local Government in the Administered Territories," p. 112.
Levy provides no source for his assertion. The author's background of
former military governor of Hebron lends it credibility.

81. David Farchi, "Society and Politics in Judea and Samaria," in
Raphael Israeli, ed., *Ten Years of Israeli Rule in Judea and Samaria*, pp.
162-164.

82. Farchi, "Political Stances in the West Bank," in R. Israeli, ed., *Ten
Years of Israeli Rule*, p. 149.

83. Elpeleg, *Hussein's Federation Plan*, p. 6.

84. Abraham Sela, "The PLO, the West Bank, and Gaza Strip," *The
Jerusalem Quarterly*, no. 8 (Summer 1978):69.

85. Nisan, *Israel and the Territories*, p. 79.

86. Dan Horowitz and Shaul Mishal, "The Political Elite in the West
Bank—A Research Report," Dept. of Sociology/Dept. of Political Science,
The Hebrew University of Jerusalem, 1972):52-53 (Stencil in Hebrew).

87. See *Shu'un Filastiniya*, no. 12 (August 1972):250; *Al-Quds*,
September 28, 1972; and *Al-Fajr*, September 29, 1973 (Arabic).

88. See Mishal, "The Palestinian West Bank Political Elite," in A.
Arian, ed., *Israel: A Developing Society*, pp. 138-139; and Clinton Bailey,
"Changing Attitudes toward Jordan in the West Bank," *Middle East Jour-
nal*:160.

89. On the change from negative to positive *sumad*, see Farchi, "Political Attitudes in Judea and Samaria 1972-1973," *Ma'arachot*, no. 231 (July 1973):9-10.

5

The Palestine Liberation Organization and the West Bank: Center and Periphery in the Palestinian Communal Structure

In the preceding chapters we have analyzed the position of the Palestinians in the territories following two phases of conquest. Though they retained a separate identity, more marked under Israeli rule than Jordanian, they nevertheles failed to develop an indigenous representative organ that could command their allegiance. Such an organ emerged outside the territories. The reality of a separate public and the absence of a territorial body representing their aspirations prompted the emergence of a new Palestinian communal structure. This structure was composed of an external charismatic organ and a territorial public both involved in an ongoing political relationship.

The creation of a new communal structure in which the territories also played a role was a new phenomenon. Until this period, the rise of the Palestinian national movement was primarily a diaspora event. The circumstances in the West Bank since 1948 made the development of a territorial-based movement difficult. In contrast, the environment in the neighboring Arab states was conducive to the creation of such a movement because Palestinian aspirations corresponded with those of the host Arab countries. Unlike the situation in Jordan where the Palestinians comprised a majority of the population, in other states they did not constitute the same demographic threat. In calling for the liquidation of the State of Israel, they were echoing one of the maxims of contemporary Pan-Arabism. It was only after the consolidation of the Palestine Liberation Organization (PLO) and its subsequent rise to international prominence that the territories began playing a role in the national Palestinian movement. The emergence of a distinct Palestinian community comprised of two nonsovereign sectors (one in the diaspora and the other in the territories), each playing a highly differentiated role, will be the main topic of this chapter.

The Emergence of a Palestinian Diaspora Center

The PLO has emerged in recent years as a focus of Palestinian identification. This development may be considered the greatest PLO achievement in the absence of visible military and economic gains. In doing so it filled a vacuum that had existed since 1948. While Jordan and Israel have succeeded in becoming functional centers, neither could satisfy the national aspirations of the Palestinians. It was this void that assisted the PLO in their drive to become a center of identification for the Palestinians. Two questions must be posed about this phenomenon. First, what were the elements that qualified the PLO to serve as a center? Second, why was center building an exclusively diaspora event?

The creation of the PLO was sanctioned by all of the Arab states in the 1964 Cairo Summit. It was realized four months later when delegates to the Palestinian conference, meeting in East Jerusalem, set up the PLO and ratified its national covenant. The thirty-three-article covenant, a quasi-constitutional document, was "embraced by all the organizations affiliated with the PLO."[1] This document defined the Palestinian community, asserted the imperative of destroying Israel and replacing it with a "secular democratic state," and detailed the means by which this goal was to be achieved.[2]

The importance of the Palestinian National Covenant (al-Mithak al-Watani al-Filastini) from our perspective is that its essence and character laid a basis for a spiritual center. One observer of the PLO described the significance of this document in these terms: "the fundamental properties of the ideology of the PLO are encompassed in the national covenant."[3] This role of the covenant as receptacle for PLO ideology is manifest in the major change that was instituted in 1968. In the 1964 version of the covenant, the title used for *national* was *kawmiyya*, the Pan-Arab concept of nationalism; but in the 1968 version the term used was *wataniyya*, which implies territorial patriotism to a specific geographic unit. This shift in emphasis to Palestinian particularism was essential in order to draw the attention of the Palestinian masses from a broader, but more messianic, goal to a term with which they could identify and base their actions. At the same time, in order to draw support from the Arab states, the Palestinians had to draw upon major ideological norms within the Arab world. Article 1, for instance, tried to integrate both territorial nationalism and Pan-Arabism. It stated: "Palestine is the homeland of the Palestinian Arab people and an integral part of the great Arab homeland, and the people of Palestine is [sic] a part of the Arab Nation."[4] The spiritual element of the movement appeared also in Articles 2 and 3, which tried to integrate land and people. This conception of the homeland as a mythical whole is in accordance with the general spirit of the covenant which excluded any compromises regarding the land or the enemy.

The covenant was also an operational document which outlined specific goals and strategies, and how these goals were to be accomplished. The goal was the liberation of the whole of Palestine, and armed struggle was the strategy (Article 9).[5] This strategy was to be accomplished through means such as Fedayeen guerrilla action (Article 10), mobilization of the resources of the whole Arab nation (Article 15), and suspension of internal differences

(Article 8).[6] Finally, the injection of concepts such as revolution, vanguard, and "imperialism as the ally of Zionism,"[7] provided a contemporary ideological quality to the Palestinian national movement.

Another aspect of center building was the organization and structure of the PLO. The ideological shift from *kawmiyya* to a more Palestinian focus was also reflected on the organizational level. In 1969, the original leadership of the PLO was replaced by Fatah—the largest Palestinian guerrilla force, under the leadership of Yassir Arafat. There was an urgent need to integrate the various, newly formed Palestinian terror organizations under one umbrella organization. This was a difficult task as most of these organizations were supported by different Arab states. This effort achieved partial success when, in 1974, the executive committee of the PLO was increased from nine to fourteen members and seats were given to the major organizations according to the following distribution: Fatah had 2 seats; the Popular Front for the Liberation of Palestine (PFLP) had 1; Democratic Front for the Liberation of Palestine (PDFLP) had 1; Popular Front for the Liberation of Palestine, General Command (PFLP-GC) had 1; the Syrian Ba'athist al-Saika had 1; the Arab Liberation Army had 1; the Iraqi-sponsored Arab Liberation Front (ALF) had 1; Independents had 2; and exiles from the West Bank had 4.[8]

The structure of the PLO reflected political realities. At first there seemed to have been a genuine attempt to build a central body that would encompass all the major forces in the Palestinian movement. As a nonsovereign body depending to a large extent on voluntary cooperation, the only way to unite forces was by giving the various organizations representation. Although this structure did not prevent the organizations from acting independently, at least from the outside it appeared as a united whole and thus could attract support from various elements of the Palestinian community within Israel and in the diaspora. Through the inclusion of organizations that were direct offshoots of political parties in the West Bank during the Jordanian period and that represented different Arab states, the PLO tried to incorporate both Palestinian continuity and Arab ideological norms. Besides the Syrian Al-Saika and the Iraqi ALF, another organization that represented Arab states was Ahmed Jibril's PFLP-GC, which was directly supported by Libya's Colonel Gadaffi.[9] To be sure, the inclusion of differing groups in one umbrella organization did not prevent direct warfare between the various organizations, as for example when Al-Saika and the Palestine Liberation Army fought on the Syrian side during the latter's crackdown on the Palestinians in 1976. Nevertheless, the umbrella organization of the PLO eased the way for general Arab support for the organization. Likewise, the allocation of four seats for West Bank exiles in the executive committee was an attempt to provide the population of the territories with a feeling of inclusion in the PLO's decisionmaking process.

The institutional structure of the PLO was another facet in the emergence of a diaspora center. Despite the fact that the PLO objected to the establishment of a government in exile, in effect it was designed to be one. Formally it had a parliamentary body—the Palestinian National Council (PNC); an executive body—the Executive Committee, with eight departments; an intermediate body between the two organs—the Central Council; an army—the Palestine Liberation Army (PLA); it included supporting bodies such as the research center, planning center, and information council; and a financial body—the Palestine National Fund.[10]

In practice, the executive bodies (the military ones in particular) reflected the Arab states' influence. The PLA contingents, for instance, were under the control of host Arab states. The Palestine Armed Struggle Command (PASC), which was designed to be a military coordinating body, was actually a military police force keeping law and order within the refugee camps and maintaining peace between rival Palestinian factions.[11] The Palestine National Fund distributed aid payments made by Arab governments among the various organizations. However from the point of view of a center, the formal side was more important than the operational side. The formation of institutions with which a maximum number of sectors in the Palestinian community could identify contributed to the charismatic nature of the PLO.

One of the most important factors that contributed to the emergence of the PLO as a potential center for the Palestinians was its ascendance in the international arena. The major breakthrough for the PLO came at the Rabat Conference of 1974, when it was recognized by all of the Arab states as the sole representative of the Palestinian people. This recognition combined with growing Arab oil power resulted in political gains in many international forums: the conferring of observer status to the organization at the United Nations General Assembly, and its inclusion in all international conferences convened under the auspices of the General Assembly. Subsequent gains include admittance to the nonaligned group in August 1975, acceptance as a member of the "Group of 77" developing nations, and full membership in the Arab League and in the Economic Commission for West Asia (ECOSOC). By mid-1978, the PLO had representatives in more than fifty countries.[12] One example of the impact of these developments on the West Bank was reflected in an *Al-Fajr* editorial following the Rabat conference and Yassir Arafat's address at the United Nations entitled: "The Palestinian, lost and dispossessed before June 1967, is now sitting on top of the world, dictating events and holding sway over history."[13]

Although the PLO received its earliest international recognition from communist countries such as China and the Soviet Union, its prestige in the West Bank increased when it succeeded in developing relations with the West. The fact that the PLO, with the help of oil and petro-dollars, succeeded in transforming what were considered the patrons of Zionism into a more favorable position vis-à-vis the Palestinian problem strengthened the status of the PLO among the inhabitants of the territories. International recognition of Palestinian rights as legitimate, which was perceived as being the accomplishment of the PLO, gave the PLO a special status in the territories.

Having examined the elements that qualified the PLO to act as a potential center, the question that arises is why was center building limited to the diaspora? Why were the territories not assigned a larger role in the Palestinian movement, now that they were a distinct Palestinian region occupied by a foreign power?

Indeed, the PLO tried to establish a territorial base in the early years of Israeli rule. Influenced by the Algerian and Vietnamese experiences, the PLO sought to promote popular armed struggle in the territories against Israel. This strategy called for close cooperation between the local inhabitants and guerrilla fighters; the former's role was to serve as "human forest," to hold general strikes and demonstrations, while the latter's role was to wear out the enemy.[14]

The doctrine did not pass the practical test. The failure of the guerrilla organizations in attaining their general aims and their subsequent expulsion from the territories by Israel forced the PLO into reassessing their overall strategy. One of the main lessons drawn from their failure concerned not only Israeli military effectiveness but the ineffectiveness of the local inhabitants as participants in the national liberation struggle. The status of the local inhabitants as a revolutionary force in the eyes of the guerrilla organization was, therefore, inevitably reduced.

Following their failure in the territories, the Palestinian organizations attempted to operate from the other side of the Jordanian border. Their expulsion from Jordan, which took place in 1970 and 1971, and the subsequent decision by Jordan to forbid PLO activity in its domain, left the PLO with little choice but to establish an operational center abroad.[15] The establishment of the center in Lebanon, which was neither Palestinian territory nor heavily populated by Palestinian refugees, contributed to the exclusive nature of the PLO. Their previous experience indicated that the revolution could not rely on the Palestinians living either under Israeli or Jordanian rule because that population was exposed to reprisals and material benefits. They concluded that political authority must be confined to the diaspora where the revolutionary consciousness was strong and uncorrupted.

Not only political and military events dictated that the center emerge as an exclusive diaspora event. Massive financial aid and political support from a number of Arab states freed the PLO from dependence on local resources, obviating the need to root mass-based political organization in the territories. The emergence of an exclusive diaspora center is also attributable to the elitist nature of the PLO. The PLO perceived itself as a vanguard not only of the Palestinian revolution but also of a social revolution that would ultimately sweep the Arab world. Finally, it should be pointed out that the Palestinian national movement had been a diaspora phenomenon since 1948. The short period following the 1967 war when they tried to build a territorial-based movement was the exception rather than the rule. In concentrating efforts on building the movement in the diaspora, the PLO was continuing, not breaking, Palestinian practice.

Concentrating on building the movement in the diaspora did not mean, however, disengagement from the territories. The role of *sumud* assigned by the PLO to the inhabitants in the territories called for passive resistance and noncooperation with the Israeli authorities even in matters of daily life. As we have indicated in the previous chapter, this policy implied that the local population was not allowed to build its own framework for political action. PLO efforts were focused on preventing the West Bank Palestinians from deciding their own political fate. In the words of one observer, "the Palestinian organizations waged a bitter and relentless struggle against any attempt at independent political organization in the territories."[16] Political activity was allocated exclusively to the diaspora.

In sum, since its inception in 1964, the PLO has developed characteristics that have prepared it to act as a diaspora center. Its semiconstitutional document (the National Covenant), its organization and structure, and its status both in the Arab world and on the global scene (since 1974) prepared it for this role. It is another important characteristic of the PLO that its center-building efforts were carried out exclusively in the diaspora. It is against this background that the role of the territories should be examined.

The Diaspora Center and the Role of the Territories

Ideology, organization, and international support facilitated the development of a center with which Palestinians in the territories and abroad could identify. The main problem remaining for the PLO was the lack of a territory that could be the base for the Palestinian national movement. Although the material support provided by Arab states and the Soviet Union relieved the PLO of the need to seek support from the largest concentrations of Palestinians, the lack of a defined territorial base posed a threat to the PLO's credibility as a national liberation movement. The PLO's credibility could be defended by the nature of its struggle, which was aimed at organizing resistance against the conquering power. Nevertheless, there was no substitute for support from the inhabitants of the territories. The need for such support became even greater following the PLO's expulsion from Jordan in 1971, King Hussein's attempt to mobilize support within the territories through his federation plan of March 15, 1972, and the subsequent victory of moderate forces in the 1972 municipal elections. Moreover, the longer the Israeli presence in the territories lasted, the greater was the possibility that the local population would cooperate with the authorities and abandon the policy of *sumud* that the Arab states and the PLO had demanded. Indeed, the growth in economic prosperity and the PLO's military ineffectuality led to resignation on the part of the local inhabitants and cooperation with Israeli authorities in matters of daily life.

The PLO's attempt to politically penetrate the territories was a move fraught with dangers. First, by increasing political activity within the territories, the PLO ran the risk of acting as a catalyst for the emergence of a local leadership that could eventually turn into a local center. The combination of territoriality and populace was an advantage which the West Bank and the Gaza Strip possessed and the PLO lacked. Raising political consciousness could have led to the undermining of the PLO as the representative of the Palestinian people or even to mutual recognition with Israel.

Another problem, although less threatening, was in the ideological sphere. Concentration on political activity in the West Bank and the Gaza Strip could have been interpreted as a reordering of priorities in which the Palestinian revolution lost ground: in terms of territory by diminishing claims with regard to the rest of Palestine; in terms of strategy by shifting from military activity to political activity. Such interpretations did indeed emerge from the more extreme wing of the PLO. Finally, there was a danger that the local leadership, whose interests were focussed on matters relating to daily life, would have a moderating effect on the PLO and the Palestinian revolution.

In retrospect, it seems that the first set of considerations, favoring political activation of the territories, prevailed. Developments on the international scene and within the territories apparently helped the PLO in their decision to politically activate the territories. Their failure to establish a foothold in the territories and to activate them militarily following the 1967 war also influenced their new strategy. Before analyzing this new strategy, we will examine the Palestinian National Council resolutions in order to substantiate our argument and reveal the role that the diaspora allotted to the territories.

The first signs of change in PLO policy toward the territories were expressed in the tenth session of the Palestinian National Council held in Cairo in 1972, only one month after Hussein came out with his federation plan. The resolutions produced at this session called for organizing trade unions and providing assistance to organizations and institutions in the territories.[17]

At the eleventh session held the following year, the need for political mobilization was reiterated. Article 5 of the 1973 resolutions was divided into two parts; in the first part, the concept of mobilization was spelled out; in the second, the call to arm the masses was repeated. From the context, it was clear that the word *mobilization* meant the promotion of political activities in the territories. The order in which the two aims appeared, first mobilization and then the call for armed struggle, indicated the new importance of political action for the Palestinian movement.[18]

Recognition of the imperative to politically penetrate the territories was qualified by forceful statements limiting the control of the reins of leadership to the PLO. Article 15, for example, stressed that the PLO constituted the "legitimate political leadership of the Palestinian people and its sole spokesman for all fateful matters."[19] Clearly, for the territories, participation in the realization of the goals of the national movement did not mean the right to decide them. Finally, the eleventh session's resolutions ended on a practical note with a decision to establish a framework organizing all political forces in the territories—an organization that came to be known as the Palestinian National Front.[20]

An even more radical innovation was introduced in the resolution produced at the twelfth PNC (June 1974). Whereas the previous resolution explicitly rejected the idea of a "Palestinian state on part of the Palestinian national soil," this resolution introduced the idea of stages and called for the establishment of an "independent combatant national authority for the people over every part of Palestinian territory that is liberated."[21] This entity was conceived to be a first stage in the strategy of liberating all Palestinian territory. Although this new strategy was motivated by a variety of reasons, especially new developments emerging after the Yom Kippur War, it had bearing on the relationship between the PLO and the territories. The recognition of the territories as the first stage in the liberation process highlighted the importance of the West Bank and the Gaza Strip as a territorial base in the Palestinian enterprise. For several years the PLO had concentrated on building the diaspora organ. Once again the territories became the focus of Palestinian strategy, as they had been in a different context following the Six Day War. As the two previous PNC resolutions indicated, the territories were now to become a territorial base not only for guerrilla activities, as in 1968 and 1969, but also the focus of political activity. At the same time, the PLO guarded its role as the highest authority dictating the Palestinian struggle.

While the resolutions of the tenth, eleventh, and twelfth PNC sessions facilitated the integration of the territories into the PLO strategy, the two subsequent resolutions produced a clearer structure for the relationships. The thirteenth PNC resolution (March 1977), which was issued following the victory of PLO supporters in the 1976 West Bank municipal elections, states in Article 2: "The PNC affirms the stand of the PLO and its determination to continue armed struggle, and its concomitant form of political and mass struggle to achieve our inalienable rights.''[22] In other words, the struggle of the population in the territories is recognized as a central component of the PLO strategy. In the following article, however, it was made clear that the PLO would guide and direct the struggle and strengthen the steadfastness of the territories against defeat and occupation. Finally, in order to reemphasize the PLO role in the Palestinian national structure, Article 5 stressed again the "necessity of national unity, both political and military, among the contingents of the Palestinian revolution within the framework of the PLO."[23]

Having established the desired relationship between the territories and the PLO, the fourteenth PNC session (January 1979), which convened in the wake of the Camp David Accords, emphasized the diaspora center's role in the Palestinian movement. Consequently, the resolution stressed the PLO's role as the sole legitimate representative of the Palestinians on the Arab and the international scenes. Aware of intentions by the Camp David participants to find an alternative to the PLO with whom they could negotiate the autonomy plan, the PNC added that the Palestinians would "resist all attempts to harm, override or circumvent the PLO, or to create alternatives or partners to it . . . " and "adhere to the resolution of the Arab summits of Algiers and Rabat and its UN resolutions . . . which affirm our inalienable national rights . . . "[24] In essence, autonomy could not be regarded as an alternative to the stage strategy and neither the West Bank leadership nor Jordan could be regarded as representatives of the Palestinians.

A close examination of the PNC resolutions thus reveals a growing awareness by the PLO of the need to penetrate, activate, and encourage political organizational activity in the territories. At the same time they clearly delineated the roles of the diaspora and the territories. These resolutions indicated that while the political activity of the territories was upgraded in Palestinian strategy, the PLO would retain its leadership role and maintain the sole right to represent the Palestinian cause.

The Emergence of a Center-Periphery Relationship

Having described the organizational network of the PLO in the diaspora and having demonstrated the importance for the PLO of political penetration of the territories, we will analyze the emergence of a center-periphery relationship in the Palestinian communal structure. The question that we confront is: how did the PLO politically activate the territories in a Palestinian framework despite Israel's control and Jordan's influence?

Political penetration would have been unlikely without the emergence of the PLO as an international actor and without institutional changes that took place in the West Bank under Israeli rule. It was the charisma the PLO acquired during this period that enabled it to demand and receive the obedience of the territories. It was the growth of key modernizing institutions in the territories that enabled the execution of PLO objectives. Finally, it was a change in tactics that transformed these developments into tangible political assets.

Unlike their previous attempt to penetrate the territories following the 1967 war, the PLO chose to concentrate its efforts on the political rather than military infrastructure. Israel's effective military control of the territories and its determination to prevent the emergence of a guerrilla movement in the territories prohibited a military strategy. Because of its political structure and sensitivity to public opinion, Israel was more lenient with regard to political organizational activity. During this campaign, the PLO concentrated primarily on the charismatic sphere, which they were not in a position to do previously. Having established a political framework in the diaspora, the goal was to promote political and spiritual identification with the external organ. It was a linkage that Israel could not control; neither could it aspire to provide the inhabitants with an alternative. The PLO's previous attempt had been carried out through illegal means, a military network. This time they chose to operate through instrumentalities that Israel could not eradicate by force without changing its overall strategy toward the territories.

As mentioned previously, the eleventh session of the PNC decided to politically activate the territories through the establishment of a Palestine National Front. It was anticipated that this framework would include all the national forces operating in the territories. In August 1973, the National Front published its platform and stated its loyalty to the PLO. Despite its verbal commitment to the PLO leadership, the nucleus of the Palestine National Front was the Palestine Communist Party. This situation presented a potential threat to the diaspora leadership. Despite the close relations between the PLO and Moscow, the PLO could not afford to have political activity coordinated by an organ loyal to another force. Therefore, the PLO started concentrating on territory-wide organizations that were gaining prominence during that time and were more likely to be subordinated to PLO management.[25]

In pursuing its strategy, the PLO set about channeling political developments that had already been put into motion by the local inhabitants. This was more effective than trying to initiate activity from abroad. The institutions which began to flourish under Israeli control expressed an explicit Palestinian orientation. As modernizing institutions, their tendency was to identify with a national movement rather than a conservative monarchy. They exhibited several other attributes that complemented PLO aspirations. The mere fact that institutions, unlike personalities, could not be exiled or easily pressured, provided the PLO with a degree of permanence that it desperately needed—especially in light of its changing fortunes as a diaspora center. These institutions were also valuable to the PLO because they had the potential of influencing the public on a scale far greater than any group of notables could ever do.

Strong ties did develop between the emerging modernizing institutions and the PLO. As noted in the previous chapter, there were strong affinities between the editorial board of *Al-Fajr* and the diaspora center. *Al-Sha'ab,* which adopted a cautious approach at its inception, with time changed its editorial policies and became a clear supporter of the PLO line.[26] Even *Al-Quds*, the most moderate of the three newspapers, in time recognized the role of the PLO as a legitimate representative of the Palestinians.

Another target of PLO political penetration was the institutions of higher learning. The role that the universities started playing in the Palestinian enterprise could be discerned in the new attitude of the PLO toward a university system. The PLO now began to actively campaign for Arab recognition of academic institutions in the West Bank. On March 13, 1977, the PNC issued a resolution recommending the establishment of a university in the occupied territories.[27]

The cooperative relationship between the institutions of higher learning and the PLO produced two different kinds of activity. The first was the formalization of the links between these institutions and the PLO. Bir-Zeit University's board of managers, for instance, is directed in absentia by its president, Hanna Nasser. Nasser was deported from the West Bank in 1974 for subversive activity, because he was held responsible for the violent disturbances that characterized the university's activities. Once expelled, he became a member of the PLO's executive, the PNC, and of the PLO-Jordan Joint Commission. Later he was appointed a member of the PLO Actions Committee, which at that time was responsible for higher education in the territories. The Board of Trustees of Bir-Zeit University, composed of fourteen members, has included prominent PLO supporters such as Hayder Abdul Shafi, director of the Red Crescent Society of the Gaza Strip; Karim Khalaf, the mayor of Ramallah until his expulsion from office in 1982; and Jawad Abdal-Salah, the exiled mayor of Al-Bireh.[28] There has also been a trend toward the inclusion of more PLO supporters on the boards of trustees of the other West Bank colleges.

The second type of activity was the expression of support for the PLO. "Palestine Week," an annual event held at Bir-Zeit that has taken on the characteristics of a national pilgrimage, is one vehicle for this expression. Beginning in 1976 as an exhibition of Palestinian arts and crafts and a book fair, it has since become explicitly political, replete with PLO flags, literature, politicized drama, and other activities supportive of the diaspora center.[29]

It was the events surrounding the 1976 municipal elections that gave shape to the realization of the diaspora-center-territorial-periphery relationship. This was manifested in the election campaign, the election results, and especially in the behavior of the mayors in the postelection period.

The PLO never actively supported the election process. It could hardly support municipal elections initiated by the Israelis which were designed to conform with existing Jordanian law but also to illustrate the libertarian style of Israeli rule. There was always the danger, moreover, that public support for candidates would entangle the PLO in local political rivalries and undermine the declared consensus of support for the PLO among all political circles in the West Bank. On the surface, then, the PLO continued to oppose the elections. In reality it adopted a posture of strict neutrality that could only be interpreted as silent support.

In retrospect, the PLO's change of heart was a position well taken. In 1972 there was a real possibility that an alternative leadership in the West Bank could emerge. By 1976 that seemed a much dimmer prospect in light of the rising stature of the diaspora center, the development of modernizing institutions that supported the PLO, and the growing influence of young professionals in the political elite of the West Bank.

Despite the lack of vocal PLO support, the election campaign reflected the successful community-wide mobilization of the West Bank inhabitants and their identification with the diaspora center. Though the elections were officially municipal, they were conducted as if they were territory-wide, with municipal issues overshadowed by expressions of nationalist Palestinian sentiment. The national blocs—those local coalitions of PLO supporters who were swept into office in all the big West Bank towns—campaigned relentlessly with PLO themes. The Tulkarm National Bloc, headed by veteran PLO supporter Mayor Hilmi Hanun, based its campaign on the theme of preserving the Arab character of the West Bank (*uruba*). Al-Bireh's National Bloc captioned its newspaper advertisement in *Al-Fajr* with the slogan "the fatherland first, the fatherland second, the fatherland forever."[30] *Al-Fajr* editorials and feature articles called upon voters to regard the campaign as one concerned with more than municipal affairs.

In one such editorial, two weeks before the elections took place, the newspaper reminded the readers that candidates should not be elected merely for their abilities to get streets paved or cleaned, but for their opposition to Israeli attempts to create an alternative leadership.[31] Other articles defended political involvement, and attacked those extremists who continued to advocate negative *sumud*, which called for the freezing of all public organizational life.[32] Even *Al-Quds* refrained from limiting the elections to municipal issues. In an article entitled "The Voter's Responsibility," T. Kan'an, former president of the Court of Appeals during the Jordanian period, encouraged the electorate to vote in accordance with the interests of the homeland and the people rather than local issues.[33]

The success of the PLO's mobilization efforts was demonstrated by the election results. A comparative analysis of the 1972 and 1976 West Bank election results reflects the impact of the PLO's influence. The 1972 elections, although reflecting certain important changes from the 1963 elections under Jordanian rule, ended for the most part along traditional lines. The most notable developments were increased voter participation (from 50 percent in 1963 to over 85 percent in 1972), the higher turnover of mayoralties (fourteen of twenty-one mayors were newly elected), and the candidacies of a number of younger professionals largely from towns closest to the former border.[34] With the exception of PLO supporters Karim Khalaf of Ramallah, Jawad Abd al-Salah of Al-Bireh, and Hilmi Hanun of Tulkarm, all those elected represented traditional elements.[35] Of particular significance as well was the fact that a large percentage of the electorate chose to participate despite the outright rejection of the elections by the PLO, which in Nablus and elsewhere took the form of violence designed to obstruct the voting process.

In sharp contrast, the 1976 election results were a decisive PLO victory. National bloc lists composed of PLO supporters, many of whom had been involved in radical politics during Jordanian rule, took over the majority of the city councils in the larger towns of the West Bank. The only pro-Jordanian mayor of a larger West Bank municipality to be elected was Elias Freij of Bethlehem. Otherwise, Jordanian supporters and traditional leaders who maintained good relations with the authorities were swept out of office. Instead, several declared supporters of the PLO assumed office as mayors: Bassam Shak'a in Nablus; Fahd al-Kawasmeh in Hebron; Sulayman al-Tawil in Al-Bireh; and Bishara Da'ud in Beit Jalla. Karim Khalaf of Ramallah and Hilmi Hanun of Tulkarm were reelected.[36] Thus, the 1976 elections were greatly affected by the crystallization of a unified, PLO-oriented front that was West Bank-wide. Five of the six biggest towns in the West Bank were among the ten towns that witnessed a national bloc victory. Furthermore, for the first time, the two regional capitals in the area, Nablus and Hebron, came under the domination of national blocs.[37] The newly elected mayors of these two towns replaced two of the leading traditional figures in the West Bank: Ma'zuz al-Masri of Nablus and Shaykh Ali al-Jabri of Hebron.

Israel's reaction to these results was negative. One Israeli observer described the elections as "a demonstration of unified support by the area's leaders and population for the PLO—and the radical nationalism the terrorist organization represents."[38] The consensus of opinion among Israeli observers was that the elections signified a fundamental change in the political elite structure of the West Bank in that for the first time a majority of those elected were under 50 years old, and a sizeable minority were technocrats.[39] Many bemoaned the fact that Israel had failed to create a more amenable leadership in the territories.[40]

Just as the election campaign mobilized most of the West Bank behind the PLO, the election results seated a majority of PLO-oriented mayors. The behavior of these mayors following the elections strengthened the PLO's hold in the area. Initially it seemed that nothing had changed. The newcomers took office, devoting themselves almost exclusively to municipal affairs in a manner little different from the previous office holders.[41]

It was not long before the newly elected mayors parted from traditional ways. First, relations between the Israeli military authorities and many of the mayors soured. The close relations between Ali al-Jabri (former mayor of Hebron) and the Israeli military authorities were not continued by his successor Fahd al-Kawasmeh. There was a similar situation in Nablus. Second, many of the more prominent mayors of the major towns in the West Bank "held frequent consultations about general political issues affecting the entire West Bank as well as purely municipal matters."[42] During their consultation they sought the opinion of prominent PLO supporters. Third, the mayors showed both commitment and the ability to act in concert, frequently placing ideological commitments before municipal or regional loyalties (the reverse of which was a distinguishing characteristic of their predecessors). They unanimously condemned proposals for home rule put forward by former Defense Minister Shimon Peres,[43] despite Israeli pressures in the form of delayed budget approvals and cancellation of soft-term loans. At the same time they sought alleviation of pressing financial problems through participation in PLO-sponsored appeals held in the Persian Gulf states and PLO-initiated twin-city agreements.[44] Concerted action was again evinced during U.S. Secretary of State Cyrus Vance's visit to Israel in August 1977. A meeting scheduled at Moshe Dayan's home between Secretary Vance and West Bank mayors was boycotted by the latter.[45] It was their reasoning behind the decision to boycott the Vance meeting, rather than the cancellation itself, that indicated the emergence of a subordinate leadership to a charismatic center. As Bassam Shak'a explained to a visiting U.S. academic delegation, "we did not receive a mandate from the people to negotiate the creation of a Palestinian state; the elections were held for the municipal councils only. We are not here as substitutes for the PLO and we do not represent the whole of the Palestinian people."[46] This position, incessantly repeated over the following years, not only reflected its wide currency in the West Bank among all political forces but it also paralleled PLO arguments against previous attempts at independent West Bank initiatives.

The Camp David Accords of 1978, which called upon Israel, Jordan, and the West Bank Palestinian leaders to negotiate the future of the territories, was the first significant test of the territory-diaspora relationship. Despite the extensive courting of West Bank leaders by Egypt and the United States, the nearly unanimous response was that the mandate to represent the Palestinian people resided solely with the PLO.[47] Aware of the threat implicit in the autonomy plan, the PLO rejected it. Despite the promise of Palestinian self-rule and the concomitant reduction of Israeli control contained in the plan, the PLO must have felt threatened by the possibility that a territorial center would emerge, usurping its function and ultimately its raison d'être.

It was at this point that an interesting development took place in the West Bank. A National Guidance Committee was established in 1978 under the leadership of Karim Khalaf. The committee was comprised of twenty-three members including the mayors of the six largest towns, two Gaza residents, and representatives of various professional organizations. The committee was principally involved in coordinating protest activities against settlement, occupation policies, and alleged brutality. According to Israeli military sources, it was especially active in promoting organized political activity at the West Bank universities (Bir-Zeit, Bethlehem, and Al-Najah in Nablus).[48]

Rafik Halabi, who covered the territories for Israel Television, has provided the most accurate analysis of the committee:

> The area was divided into three subdistricts, with committee seats apportioned on a geographical basis. The north was represented by Bassam Shaka of Nablus, Wahid Hamdallah, the mayor of Anabta, and Hilmi Hanoun, the mayor of Tul Karem. From the central region came Karim Halaf of Ramallah, Ibrahim Tawil of el-Bireh, Bishara Da'ud of Beit Jalla, and Samiha Halil, representing the women's organizations. The delegates from the southern district were Fahed Kawasmeh and Mohammed Milhem, of Hebron and Halhul respectively. Also affiliated with the committee were representatives of labor unions, student organizations, and three newspapers—*a-Shab*, *al-Fajr*, and *a-Tali'ah*. Two representatives from the Gaza Strip, the lawyer Zuheir Rayes and Dr. Haydar Abdul Sahfi, the president of the Red Crescent, were also named. Though there were pro-Hussein people among the committee's membership, they seemed to be only a token group.
>
> The new organization's steering committee likewise reflected the spectrum of political factions in the territories. It consisted of Karim Halaf as a representative of the Democratic Front, Bassam Shaka speaking for the Ba'ath party and also as a supporter of Ahmad Abdul-Rahim's Front for Arab Struggle, Dr. Haydar Abdul Shafi as a supportor of George Habash's Popular Front for the Liberation of Palestine, and Fahed Kawasmeh as a supporter of Arafat's el-Fatah and not above preserving a dialogue with King Hussein. The committee established branches in all the large cities of the West Bank, placing local activists in charge.[49]

The committee's ability to coordinate political activities in the West Bank was first tested in the winter of 1979, during U.S. President Carter's visit to Israel. A wave of demonstrations swept the West Bank, with Bir-Zeit University as the focal point of well-coordinated protest activities. These demonstrations led to the closing of Bir-Zeit in May 1979.[50] Two junior colleges and the Bethlehem high school were also closed down.[51] (It should be noted that it was at Bir-Zeit that the mayors collectively denounced the Camp David talks, precluding any possibility of their participation in the autonomy negotiations.) According to at least one source, the National Guidance Committee could be credited with making 1979 the most unrestful year in Israeli rule since the normalization of the security situation in the territories in 1968 and 1969.[52] But the significance of the committee went beyond its ability to organize resistance to the Camp David talks and the autonomy plan. It represented a territory-wide leadership, that activated territory-wide institutions and coordinated policies for the diaspora center.

The relationship between the West Bank leadership and the PLO is further revealed in several incidents. In a protest meeting against the Israeli government's decision (March 1980) to resettle Jews in Hebron, delegates from local councils in the Hebron area suggested an en-masse resignation. In the middle of the meeting, a message from the PLO arrived forbidding resignation before the organization discussed the matter. Mayor Kawasmeh accepted that decision.[53] Even more revealing was a statement made by the ex-mayor of Halhul a year after his and Kawasmeh's expulsion in May 1981 following a terrorist attack against Jewish settlers in Hebron. In an interview with the American Enterprise Institute, Mayor Mohammed Milhem stated:

> Mayor Kawasmeh and I attended the last meeting of the Palestinian National Council (PNC) in Damascus. We did not speak; we listened, we learned, and we saw certain things. Yasser Arafat spoke to 400 or 500 Palestinian delegates. He spoke my thoughts, with no differences. He spoke as if he were an elected official of the occupied territories. He spoke of what the Israelis should get and of what the Palestinians should get.[54]

The mayor of Halhul was speaking in a manner appropriate for a periphery spokesman. Territorial leadership for the PLO could not progress beyond the point of a territorial periphery.

The above quotation also reflected another element in the PLO's policy. Even when exiled, the territorial leadership did not assume a position of leadership in the national movement. Milhem described it explicitly when he said, "We did not speak; we listened, we learned, and we saw certain things." One of the factors that contributed to this phenomenon is implicit in the continuation of that discussion:

> Mr. (Herbert) Kelman: As you found at the PNC, are there strong differences between the Palestinian diaspora and the Palestinians on the West Bank and Gaza?

Mayor Milhem: They are getting closer. In diaspora people do not understand the Israeli mentality in the same way as those who are living in the occupied territories. We have to deal with the Israelis day and night, and we
come to understand what is the best way to tackle the problems of relations
between the Arabs and the Israelis. We have succeeded in the last decade in
reflecting this experience to Palestinians outside. Our chairman's attitude
did not come from a vacuum. It came from people like us.[55]

If this was the case, why did the territorial leaders not speak at the council? Why did not one of the mayors become a national leader when he joined
the PLO outside? The fact that Milhem represented the territorial leadership may have been a reason for their decline once in the diaspora. The role
allocated to the West Bank was that of a periphery and no more.

In sum, an integrated Palestinian communal structure emerged from the
Palestinian national movement based on a distinct division of functions between center and periphery. The center formulated strategy, acted as sole
representative of the movement, and monopolized the military domain. The
periphery reacted to the directives of the diaspora center by mobilizing inhabitants against partial solutions to the Palestinian problem, and above all
by deepening the affinity between West Bank inhabitants and the PLO
center. The emergence of the diaspora-center-territorial-periphery relationship can be traced to the growth of certain key modernizing institutions (the
press, the universities, and municipalities); it was consecrated in the 1976
elections and was cultivated through the growth of a coordinating institution and funding organization. The relationship's test was the Camp David
Accords.

By the end of the 1970s, the PLO could see the decade as a period of major accomplishments. Although at the outset of the decade it faced one of the
most difficult periods in its history (Black September of 1970 in Jordan), at
the end of the decade the PLO had gained worldwide recognition and a com-
prehenive organizational network that radiated authority over the largest
Palestinian territorial base—the West Bank. Despite this significant development, the center-periphery relationship remained vulnerable. To understand
why this was so, one must examine this relationship in the broader context of
all the parties involved in the politics of the West Bank.

Conclusion: Competing Centers and the
Peripheralization of the West Bank

The evolution of a diaspora-center-territorial-periphery relationship is not
uncommon in contemporary history. Many of the national movements that
emerged during the period of decolonization were comparably structured.
In a number of instances, national liberation struggles were conducted by a

leadership in exile which in time developed into a charismatic, organizational center. These movements, in most cases, confronted declining colonial powers that had come to accept the negligible value of their continued possession of the colonies. Thus, confrontation was essentially between a colonial administration and an aspiring, indigenous center often located in the diaspora. A comparable relationship developed between external guerrilla movements and their supporters in the territories in the struggle against minority-settler regimes.

The conflict between the Palestinian national movement and the Jewish state differed radically from these phenomena. Neither the colonial nor the settler-regime models accurately characterized Israel. A more accurate image would be that of a sovereign territorial center commanding the allegiance of the majority of its citizenry; and a communal-spiritual center for a large, well-organized diaspora. Moreover, the Palestinian national movement encountered the opposition of not one but two centers, both of which felt threatened by the aspirations of the Palestinian center. In the colonial model, the metropolitan center had the option of either abandoning all interest in the colonies or retrenching its position under a different framework. That sort of detachment was impractical for these two centers for they regarded the Palestinian movement as a direct threat to their national security. It is in this context that we should note that the expansion of the Palestinian movement encountered two centers, each one dominating key functional areas that the PLO could not penetrate.

A comparison of the setting the Zionists had encountered with the environment the Palestinian movement faced illustrates the problematic nature of the Palestinian movement. When Zionism first took on the characteristics of an organized movement, dedicated to the creation of a Jewish political entity, it faced a declining imperial power. The Ottoman Empire was succeeded by limited colonial rule in the form of the British mandate. Both the framework of mandate government and the fact that it was specifically the British who ruled the area allowed the Zionists to expand their enterprise. Despite the obstacles the British administration frequently placed in the path of the Jewish national movement, a tradition of limited colonial rule that included dedication to legal governance ensured the Zionists ample freedom to build institutions, purchase land, and set up key functional agencies. In sum, the Jewish settlers crafted those instrumentalities necessary for the territorialization of the Jewish center while under mandate rule.

The Palestinian situation was different. Their early attempts to penetrate the two largest territorial concentrations of Palestinians—the West Bank and Jordan—were crushed by the Israelis in 1968-1969 and 1970-1971 respectively. Under such circumstances they transferred their efforts to the only place where a weak mechanism existed and from where they could act relatively freely—Lebanon. In Lebanon, the PLO was vulnerable; in the West Bank its existence was threatened.

The PLO, being aware of the inherent weakness of a diaspora-based movement confronting two opposing states with considerable influence, tried to overcome this weakness through the consolidation of a diaspora-center-territorial-periphery relationship. In their drive to establish such a structure, they concentrated their efforts in an area in which they enjoyed a relative advantage. In essence, they filled a vacuum that neither center could realistically fill. They took advantage of both the inability of Israel and Jordan to establish themselves as a charismatic center of the Palestinian community and their inability to cooperate against their common enemy. At the same time, despite the impressive achievements of the PLO in establishing itself as a charismatic ideological center, the PLO was apparently aware that further expansion would have entailed the transformation of the three-center structure.

The relationship between the three centers that controlled the West Bank was competitive. The fact that neither the Palestinians nor the Israelis were prepared to grant the other the right to national self-determination in the contested areas was at the root of the competition. Jordan, which also laid claims to the territory, was a contender against the two other centers. In effect, because of the distinct individual constraints of each party, the competitive aspiration became complementary. Thus the PLO, lacking a sovereign territorial base, could not fulfill certain functions (legal and institutional) providing an economic bridge to the Arab world, which Jordan was able to do. Similarly, the PLO could not supply the territories with the necessary instrumental services that Israel provided. Jordan was aware of the fact that it could not at this juncture become a spiritual center for a community subordinated to a diaspora center. Obviously, Israel could never aspire to become a spiritual center for the Palestinians. Also, because of demographic and political concerns, Israel was not able to radically transform the legal and institutional relationship between the local Arab inhabitants and Jordan.

This complementary division of labor between the three centers was particularly significant from the perspective of the territories themselves. Local political forces by and large justified compliance with this reality as a transitory phenomenon, which enabled them to function on a day-to-day basis.[56] It was this structure that contributed to their ability to function as a separate community without abandoning their hope of forming a national entity. Each center, in its specialized domain, provided the minimum services required for the preservation of the territories as a separate political community. The Palestinians in the territories preferred compliance with these centers to an extended open confrontation with any or all of them. Such confrontation might have exposed them to dangers that they were unwilling to face. Total noncompliance and active resistance to Israel could have led to the destruction of their political and civic life. This fear was reflected in the idea of *sumud*; the strategic goal of this code being to hold out under difficult circumstances. Confrontation with Jordan could have left them in a worse position. Severance of ties with Jordan followed by Jordanian retaliation could have left them isolated from the Arab world and all it entailed in terms of material and organizational support, exposing them to a more-constraining Israeli presence. Rejecting the PLO as their legitimate spokesman might have undermined the Palestinian issue in the world view. An open rift in the Palestinian community could have reduced the Palestinian issue in the Arab-Israeli conflict and limited it to other aspects of the conflict, such as Jerusalem and territorial withdrawal on other fronts.

But the West Bank Palestinian community had to pay a price for the de facto structure. The division of labor between the three centers created a complete control that effectively peripheralized the territories. By granting the PLO the exclusive right to represent them on the international scene and by rejecting any territory-wide representative for talks with Israel or any other interested parties (such as the United States following the Camp David Accords), they basically relinquished the right to determine their own political future. At the same time, the legal-institutional role played by Jordan in the territories reduced their capability of building the institutional infrastructure that was so crucial in political modernization and nation building. Jordan's control over the West Bank school curricula, for example, inhibited the development and dissemination of a Palestinian identity. By the same token, Israel's dominance in shaping economic activity, despite its beneficial effects, left some of the problems basic to economic development unresolved. The lack of an autonomous economic authority that could create financial institutions (which in turn could finance investment in infrastructure and industrial activity or impose a tariff policy) illustrates the hidden costs of peripheralization.

The West Bank thus became a peripheralized community; that is, a community where all power is in the hands of external centers. These centers may be states, such as Israel and Jordan, or diaspora organizations such as the PLO. The difference between a peripheral community and a regular periphery is that a periphery refers to a situation where one segment of a community is dependent on one center to whom it delegates all functions of authority. A peripheralized community, in contrast, describes a situation where authority is taken by one or more external centers and the community complies with those authorities, willingly or not. The source of authority of the various centers may be legitimized, partially legitimized, or not legitimized at all in the eyes of the subordinate community. Under such circumstances, the fact that the peripheralized community is territorial while another segment of the community is in the diaspora does not prevent its being subordinated to the diaspora center. The fact that other functions of authority are external may contribute to the willingness of the territorialized segment of the community to abandon the leadership role to the diaspora.

Three decades after the partition and the collapse of the Arab community in Palestine, a new framework of relationships emerged in the West Bank. During that period, the West Bank went through three waves of subordination—the Jordanian, the Israeli and that of the PLO. Each wave reduced the control of the other parties, but most of all each added to the subordination of the West Bank. Even the PLO's political penetration, designed to relieve the West Bank from foreign influence, in fact added to the territory's subordination. Instead of reversing the trend that began in 1948, when the West Bank lost out to external forces, the PLO's relationship with the West Bank reinforced the peripheralization process. The implications of the peripheralization of the West Bank became more evident when a transformed Israeli polity launched a new drive to penetrate the West Bank through massive settlement, through attack on the PLO political establishment in the West Bank, and finally through a direct assault on the PLO in Lebanon.

Notes

1. A. Yaniv, *PLO—A Profile* (Haifa: Israel Universities Study Group for Middle Eastern Affairs, 1974), p. 12. For a comprehensive study of the covenant see Y. Harkabi, *The Palestinian Covenant and Its Meaning* (London: Vallentine, Mitchell, 1979). For a brief account of the origins and development of the PLO, see Rashid Hamid, "What Is the PLO?", *Journal of Palestine Studies*, vol. 4, no. 4 (Summer 1975):90-109.

2. See articles 19 through 22 of the covenent in Yaniv, *PLO—A Profile*, pp. 51-52.

3. Ibid., p. 12.

4. Ibid., p. 48.

5. Ibid., p. 49.

6. Ibid., pp. 49-50.

7. See especially articles 14, 15, and 22, ibid., pp. 50-51.

8. Ibid., p. 9. For the composition of the Central Council see Rashid Hamid, "What Is the PLO?", p. 103. In the same article see the composition of the National Council.

9. Yaniv, *PLO—A Profile*, pp. 7-11.

10. Rashid Hamid, "What Is the PLO?", pp. 101-107.

11. On the PLA see Sara Bar-Haim, "The Palestine Liberation Army: Stooge or Actor," in Gabriel Ben-Dor, ed., *The Palestinians and the Middle East Conflict* (Ramat-Gan, Israel: Turtledove Publishing, 1978), pp. 173-194.

12. On PLO external relations see Foreign and Commonwealth Office, London, "Palestine Liberation Organization," *Background Brief* (November 1979), pp. 3-4.

13. Quoted in Clinton Baily, "Changing Attitudes toward Jordan in the West Bank," *Middle East Journal*, vol. 32, no. 8 (1978):162.

14. For the impact of guerrilla models on the PLO, see Yehoshafat Harkabi, *On the Guerrilla* (Tel-Aviv: Ma'arachot, 1971), pp. 303-352 (Hebrew). See also Abraham Sela, "The PLO, the West Bank, and Gaza Strip," p. 67.

15. On the transformation of the guerrilla base from the West Bank to Jordan see Yitzchak Baily, "The Palestinians and Jordan between the Six Day War and the Yom Kippur War," in Eytan Gilboa and Mordechai Naor, eds., *The Arab-Israeli Conflict* (Tel-Aviv: Israel Defense Ministry, 1981), pp. 173-195 (Hebrew).

16. Sela, "The PLO, the West Bank, and Gaza Strip," p. 69.

17. Ibid., p. 70.

18. See append. D in Y. Harkabi, *The Palestinian Covenant and Its Meaning*, p. 139.

19. Ibid., p. 141.

20. Ibid.

21. Ibid., p. 147.

22. Ibid., p. 152.

23. Ibid., p. 154.

24. *Journal of Palestine Studies*, vol. 8, no. 2 (Winter 1979):166.

25. On the relationship between the PLO and the Palestine National Front see Sela, "The PLO, the West Bank and Gaza Strip," pp. 70-71.

26. See Yosef Tzuriel, *Ma'ariv*, March 13, 1981, weekend section, p. 19.

27. Sela, "The PLO, the West Bank and Gaza Strip," p. 76.

28. "How the Abuse of Academic Freedom Led to the Temporary Closure of Bir-Zeit University," (Jerusalem: Israel Information Center, 11c/423/22.11.81/3/3.08/12); and Ya'akov Chavakuk, in *Ha'aretz*, weekend supplement, December 19, 1980, p. 18.

29. "Institutions of Higher Learning in Judea and Samaria," *Information Briefing* (Jerusalem: Israel Information Center, 361/30.8.81/3.08.12), p. 11.

30. *Al-Fajr*, April 3, 1976.

31. *Al-Fajr*, April 1, 1976.

32. Adil Samarah, "Behind the News," *Al-Fajr*, April 1, 1976.

33. T. Kan'an, "The Voter's Responsibility," *Al-Quds*, April 10, 1976.

34. Shaul Mishal, "Judea and Samaria: An Anatomy of the Municipal Elections."

35. *Ha'aretz*, April 12, 1976.

36. Yehuda Litani, "Leadership in the West Bank and Gaza," *The Jerusalem Quarterly*, no. 14 (Winter 1980):103-104.

37. This data is based on an analysis conducted by the researchers of candidate lists as they appeared in various sources, including final election results in *Al-Quds* on April 15, 1976.

38. Yosef Goell, "A Different Breed," *The Jerusalem Post*, magazine section, May 16, 1976.

39. Of the 577 candidates, 408 were under the age of 50, of which 40 percent were university educated. See Yehuda Litani, *Ha'aretz*, April 11, 1976. On the prominence of technocrats among the newly elected see Kasm Ziad, "White Revolution in the West Bank," *Al-HaMishmar*, April 16, 1976.

40. See Zvi Elpeleg, "Without Illusions," *Yediot Aharonot*, May 16, 1976.

41. Shaul Mishal, "Jordanian and Israeli Policy on the West Bank," in Anne Sinai and Allen Pollack, eds., *The Hashemite Kingdom of Jordan and the West Bank*, p. 219.

42. Litani, "Leadership in the West Bank and Gaza," p. 105.

43. Ibid.

44. *Ha'aretz*, April 27, 1977, and June 17, 1977.

45. *Ha'aretz*, September 19, 1977.

46. Sinai and Pollack, *The Hashemite Kingdom of Jordan and the West Bank*, p. 251.

47. See for example, "The Mood of the West Bank: Interviews with Three West Bank Mayors," *Journal of Palestine Studies*, vol. 9, no. 2 (Autumn 1979):114-116. See also "Statement by the West Bank Municipalities and Nationalist and Professional Institutions on the Egypt-Israel Peace," *Journal of Palestine Studies*, vol. 8, no. 2 (Winter 1979):163.

48. This information was drawn from two articles on the subject written by Shmuel Segev, "The Night the Telephones Went Dead," in *Ma'ariv*, June 6, 1980; and Ya'akov Chavakuk, "The National Steering Committee, *Ha'aretz*, May 16, 1980.

49. Rafik Halabi, *The West Bank Story* (Konigstein, Germany: Athenaum Verlag Gmbh, 1981), p. 122. Reprinted with permission.

50. See "How the Abuse of Academic Freedom Led to the Temporary Closure of Bir-Zeit University," Israel Information Center.

51. *Davar*, June 8, 1979.

52. Arieh Shalev from the Center for Strategic Studies in a symposium on "Is there a solution to the Palestinian problem?" held at the Van Leer Jerusalem Foundation, February 16, 1981.

53. Halabi, *The West Bank Story*, pp. 155-156.

54. *A Conversation with the Exiled West Bank Mayors, A Palestinian Point of View* (Washington, D.C.: American Enterprise Institute for Research, 1981), p. 4. Reprinted with permission.

55. Ibid., p. 10.

56. For an early study pointing to this phenomenon see Dan Horowitz and Shaul Mishal, "The Political Elite in the West Bank—A Research Report," pp. 46-56.

Part III
Israel and the West Bank

The Transformation of the Israeli Polity and Its Impact on the West Bank

In 1967, Israel was ruled by a veteran Labor elite which believed Jordan to be the key to political settlement and discouraged extensive settlement in the territories. A decade later the Israeli polity was governed by a coalition of nationalist and religious elements which considered the Jordanian option a dead issue and which was dedicated to extensive Jewish settlement in Judea, Samaria, and the Gaza Strip. By the end of the 1970s, the West Bank and Gaza were no longer regarded by the Israeli government as collateral to be exchanged for peace but as an integral part of the land of Israel, to be settled and developed by the Jewish people as part of their historical mission. Thus, transformations in the Palestinian communal structure were paralleled by changes in the Israeli polity. The ramifications of Israel's political transformation for the territories were no less significant than the consolidation of the new Palestinian communal structure.

The 1967 war had a profound impact not only on the Palestinians in the territories and on the Palestinian communal structure but also on Israeli society. In the weeks preceding the Six Day War, the State of Israel and its Jewish community faced an acute threat to their existence; the sudden turnabout that occurred in the war when that threat was removed and Israel found itself controlling the holy city of Jerusalem and other ancient Jewish land was bound to have a major impact on the political and social life of the state.

The outpouring of emotion which followed on the heels of the conquest of Jerusalem inspired the Labor party to act quickly and decisively. The city was formally annexed less than three weeks after its conquest. Beyond their strategic importance, Judea and Samaria were also significant emotionally to various segments of Israeli society. Unlike the case of Jerusalem, where Jewish aspirations were satisfied, the Israeli government did not fulfill the goals of these factions. With time these thwarted aspirations were translated into organizational and political realities which came to play a central role in changing the Israeli political setting. Israel's ruling Labor elite, which had dominated the Israeli political system since the Yishuv period, had a clearly defined policy toward the territories, which could be traced back to pre-State days. Despite its pluralist composition there was a common denominator on which the various segments of the Labor camp concurred: that Israel must remain a state with a predominantly Jewish majority. They agreed that annexation of the territories would eventually threaten the Jewish character of the State of Israel. As far as the Labor camp was concerned, the territories served two purposes—a bargaining card to be exchanged for peace with the Arab states, and a strategic buffer zone that would provide greater security.

To the coalition that came in 1977, Judea and Samaria were no longer the means of attaining objectives; they were an end in themselves. The dominant elements in the new coalition (Herut and the National Religious Party) perceived Judea and Samaria as integral parts of the historic Land of Israel. This attitude on the part of the new Likud government created an environment in which a new settlement movement, Gush Emunim, could thrive. This outlook dictated a new pattern of extensive settlement and a new regional orientation. Labor's selective, strategic settlement policy gave way to intensive settlement in the heartland of Judea and Samaria; and the partition approach highlighting Jordan's role gave way to a combination of annexation and self-rule.

The Transformation of the Israeli Polity[a]

The results of Israel's victory in 1948 transcended concerns of geography and security and influenced the political and social domains of the Jewish polity. Mapai, the dominant Yishu-era party since 1935, and its leader David Ben-Gurion emerged from the victory with greater strength and support than ever. Mapai's renewed mandate was reflected in the first elections held in 1949. Mapai, which later became a major element of the Labor coalition, ruled Israel until its sudden decline in May 1977. Mapai's consecutive rule for nearly three decades should not be taken for granted, especially given the democratic nature of the Israeli political system, the pluralism of Israeli society, and the large immigration that changed the face of the Jewish state. At the time of the establishment of the state, the Jewish population numbered around 650,000; it was more than 3 million by the mid-1970s. Between 1948 and 1975, more than 1.5 million immigrants arrived from Jewish communities all over the world.[1] Despite the heterogeneity of these immigrants, the political map did not change drastically in the first two-and-a-half decades of statehood, from 1949 to 1973. In all the elections held during this period, Mapai-Labor emerged as the only party capable of putting together a majority coalition. It is ironic that one of Mapai's greatest accomplishments—the conquest of the West Bank and other territories—would come to be one of the factors contributing to its fall.

---

[a]This section is a slightly re-edited version of Shmuel Sandler, "The Transformation of Israeli Policy," *Midstream* 27, no. 2 (February 1981):13-18. Reprinted with permission.

Ben-Gurion's Political Strategy

Mapai's dominance of the Israeli political system was to a large extent the result of the political strategy of Ben-Gurion, the first prime minister of Israel. His strategy applied political pragmatism to both foreign and domestic politics. In both environments he sought forces with whom he shared political interests, thus establishing relationships that increased his own political power. In foreign affairs, he found King Abdullah to be a reliable and tacit ally who, although he had his own aspirations for the West Bank of the Jordan River, opposed the Palestinians and their radical leadership, the Husseini family. Similarly, Ben-Gurion sought potential domestic allies who, although belonging to other camps enabled him to rule Israel without achieving an absolute majority.[2] The most important consequence of this strategy from our perspective was the decline of the antipartition forces both on the foreign scene and on the domestic scene.

Although the roots of Ben-Gurion's strategy go back to the Yishuv period, his behavior during the 1948 war further illustrates his strategy of divide and rule. In both foreign and domestic affairs, he took advantage of conflicts among his opposition. Thus, comprehensive attempts were made to exploit the conflicting interests of Egypt and Jordan in order to enable the Israel Defense Forces (IDF) to strike freely against Egypt while negotiations were going on with Jordan concerning the West Bank. Moshe Dayan, who held talks with Jordanian representatives, recalled one of Ben-Gurion's instructions: "to continue the talks, even if they did not seem to be productive, for as long as the fighting with the Egyptians continued in the Negev . . . so as to preserve the truce in the Jordanian sector."[3] Early on, the Israelis tried to persuade Abdullah to stay out of the fighting. His cooperation would be repaid with territories in the West Bank.[4] Though these negotiations failed, he did avoid a major confrontation with the Jordanian Legion. When Jordanian forces took over the Hebron mountain area from the Egyptians on October 25, 1948, Israel did not try to take the area despite the fact that the conquering forces were relatively small.[5] At the same time, a major attack in the north was postponed until a decisive victory had been achieved in the south. Following an Egyptian defeat, the central Galilee and a part of Lebanon were conquered. Only afterward was Ben-Gurion ready to turn to the eastern front. Abdullah was forced to relinquish certain positions in diplomatic negotiations, and Israel took over Eilat with no confrontation.[6]

While the fighting was still going on, a similar strategy was followed on the domestic scene. There were two forces in Israel that represented a potential threat to Ben-Gurion's dominant role in the political system—the Revisionists on the Right, and Mapam on the Left. The fact that these groups controlled their own politically loyal military forces (the Irgun and the

Palmah respectively), prior to and during the establishment of the Israeli army, implied a potential threat not merely to the stability and performance of the new state institutions but also to Mapai's rule. In a decisive move in the midst of the war, Ben-Gurion destroyed the military power of the right-wing Irgun underground organization with the help of Mapam's Palmah. After finishing with the right wing, he turned to the left wing, dismantled the Palmah and brought it under the control of the IDF. Although the Palmah assisted him in destroying the Irgun, and despite the fact that these forces never demonstrated any disloyalty to the central government, ultimately Ben-Gurion could find no room for such an organization in his political framework. In the midst of Israel's struggle for existence, Ben-Gurion was also able to destroy opposing political centers.[7] However, this device was not limited to the war period; later on, in fact, it became one of Ben-Gurion's elementary tools in insuring his dominance in the domestic political system as well as in the country's national security interests.

Despite the temptation to complete the liberation of the rest of the Land of Israel after defeating the invading armies in the south and the north, Ben-Gurion stopped himself. His realistic instincts overcame his idealism. In retrospect, this inaction established a tacit alliance between Israel and Jordan. Facing the realities of a hostile Arab world dedicated to the destruction of the new Jewish state, Ben-Gurion sought and found a principal whose interests could be reconciled with the security interests of the only non-Arab country in the region. Thus, by letting Abdullah occupy the West Bank of the Jordan River, Ben-Gurion helped the expansion of a country and the reinforcement of a regime that in the future would also have an inherent interest in maintaining the status quo. By creating this common interest, moreover, he helped to secure his eastern border and to concentrate the defense efforts of the newly established state against imperialist drives originating from the south and north.

This pragmatic policy also complemented two other principles Ben-Gurion strongly believed in. One was that Israel should try to avoid a confrontation with the great powers, particularly the Western powers.[8] The second was that the Jewish state should avoid governing substantial numbers of Arab inhabitants.[9] The common interest with Jordan advanced both goals. The pro-Western orientation of the Hashemite Kingdom that now ruled over areas heavily populated with Arabs coincided with this tacit partnership. When Ben-Gurion was once asked by an Israeli author why he did not liberate the whole country, he answered: "There was a danger of getting involved with a hostile Arab majority, which would have brought about either another Dir-Yassin and massive expulsions of Arabs, or the presence of a million Arabs in the State of Israel. There was also a threat of a confrontation with the United Nations and the great powers."[10]

In the period between 1948 and 1967 this framework of relationships was basically maintained, despite foreign and domestic pressures. Terrorist actions from Jordan were countered by an Israeli policy of controlled retaliation.[11] Israel's military reactions were designed to reduce internal pressures, yet they were sufficiently limited so as not to threaten the Jordanian regime. Moreover, despite the terrorist attacks from Israel's eastern neighbor, Ben-Gurion confined the Sinai Campaign in 1956 to the Egyptian front. Israel and Jordan cooperated with respect to the Jordan-Yarmuk River system and against the internationalization of Jerusalem.[12] Most important was Israel's declaration with regard to the preservation of the status quo on the West Bank.[13] Israel warned that control of the Jordan "bulge" by a state or a united command other than Amman would be an automatic casus belli. Finally, by permitting British troops to fly over Israeli territory in 1958 and to land in Jordan, Israel actively assisted in preserving the independence of Jordan and its pro-Western regime and in countering Nasser's attempt to rule over a united Arab world.[14]

As in Middle Eastern affairs, Ben-Gurion was determined to divide his domestic opposition, and thus establish his party as a pivotal force that would henceforth be the center of any future government. Although he paid lip service to the desires of a unified Socialist camp, no serious attempt was made during his reign to advance such an alignment. To be sure, he would have liked to achieve a majority for his party, through an alignment with the Left, but not under existing political coalitions. He desired to accomplish this through a change in the electoral system which would replace the existing proportional system with one based on regional electoral precincts.[15] Only through such a reorganization was he ready to ally himself with the leftist parties. In 1954, he appealed to Meir Yaari and Yitzhak Tabenkin, the leaders of the two sections on the Left, to support such a change, but the reform never materialized.[16] Thus, in the early years of Israel's independence Ben-Gurion preferred coalitions with parties from the religious and the Civil (nonsocialist) camps instead of the Mapam bloc, which were supposedly closer to his party's ideology. Mapam, which emerged in the 1949 elections as the second-largest party in Israel and therefore a threat to Mapai's rule, also presented an alternative foreign policy to that of Ben-Gurion. Resisting Ben-Gurion's partition policies in the pre-State period, Mapam now objected to Israel's growing Western orientation and supported a closer relationship with the communist world. Only after Mapam divided into two smaller parties was Ben-Gurion ready to accept the two splinters as coalition partners in his new government formed in 1955[17] (see table 6-1).

In retrospect, therefore, Ben-Gurion's strategy could be described as one in which he would choose his partners from the moderate Left and Right, thus positioning himself in the middle of the political spectrum. The ideological differences between the opposing parties made an alternative coalition inconceivable. Moreover, in order to prevent drastic shifts in the

Table 6-1

The Various Cabinets Headed by Ben-Gurion and the Participating Parties

Number of Cabinet and date installed	Mapai	Religious Camp			Civil (Right) Camp		Socialist Camp	
		National Religious Party	Agudat Israel	Progressives (Independent Liberals)	General Zionists (Liberals)	Ahdut ha-Avodah	Mapam
1st Cabinet March 10, 1949	+	+	+	+	−	−	−
2nd Cabinet November 1, 1950	+	+	+	+	−	−	−
3rd Cabinet[a] October 7, 1951	+	+	+	−	−	−	−
4th Cabinet December 23, 1952	+	+	−	+	+	−	−
5th Cabinet[b] January 6, 1954	+	+	−	+	+	−	−
6th Cabinet[b] June 28, 1955	+	+	−	+	−	−	−
7th-8th Cabinet[c] November 3, 1955	+	+	−	+	−	+	+
9th Cabinet[d] December 17, 1959	+	+	−	+	−	+	+
10th Cabinet[e] November 2, 1961	+	+	−	−	−	+	+

Source: Adapted from *Encyclopedia Judaica*, Vol. 9, pp. 664-675.

Notes

+ signifies Coalition party

− Opposition party

[a]Agudat Israel left the Cabinet on November 3, 1952.

[b]Neither Cabinet headed by Ben-Gurion.

[c]The NRP left the government on July 1, 1958.

[d]The small workers faction of Agudat Israel joined the government.

[e]The Progressives and the General Zionists formed the Liberal party prior to the 1961 elections. The new party did not join the government.

electorate, he castigated the extreme factions in Israel's political system. Thus, while accusing Menachem Begin of right-wing radicalism, he also attacked the Left, asserting that they were Moscow's slaves.[18] Ben-Gurion proclaimed a priori that he would never enter into a government with either the Communists or Herut (Begin's party), thus creating for the latter movement an image of ominous irresponsibility. Indeed, the net outcome was that Mapai emerged in all the elections as the plurality party, without any viable alternative which could put together a working coalition. Even more important was the fact that although this party controlled only a plurality, it behaved, particularly in foreign and defense policies, as if it had a majority. A contributing factor was the cooperation of the National Religious Party (NRP).

One aspect of the relationship between Mapai and the NRP was a trade-off between religion and foreign and economic policies.[19] In practice, this deal implied that while the NRP conceded to the secular party the decisions in foreign policy, defense, and economics, Mapai in exchange guaranteed NRP dominance over religious institutions and a commitment to preserve the status quo in relations between religion and state. In this setting, the NRP established itself within the governing elite, controlled government ministries (interior, religion, and welfare) and power centers (the rabbinate and religious councils), established financial institutions, and took control of a large portion of the education system. Obviously, the greater portion of political and economic power went to Mapai, which dominated the Histadrut (the federation of trade unions), central economic institutions, the civil service, and other centers of power. But most important, under such a framework Ben-Gurion had almost a free hand in conducting Israel's defense and foreign policies. With the help of the Progressive party, which had no independent line on foreign policy, Ben-Gurion enjoyed a built-in majority that enabled him to form a government without the need to compromise with dissenting figures. This special relationship, despite occasional ups and downs on religious issues, persisted after Ben-Gurion's retirement until it started to decline in the early 1970s.

Thus, an equilibrium emerged during the first fifteen years of Israel's independence. It was based on a relatively stable government, dominated by a pragmatic leadership that conducted its country's foreign and defense policies with no serious challenges to its doctrines from outside. The ruling party, Mapai, was dominated by one person who maneuvered freely among the various centers of power and dictated his country's national-security policies, suppressing through democratic means any opposition both within and beyond his majority. In terms of the region, the equilibrium was based on a tacit understanding between the Jewish state and the only Arab state participating in the partition of Eretz Yisrael-Palestine, which was ruled by an elite interested in the preservation of the status quo. Both sides had to relieve internal pressures from time to time by limited action and retaliations, but the central structure of interests was maintained. This framework started to collapse in the mid-1960s.

The Strategy of Ben-Gurion's Heirs

The seeds of change were no doubt planted in the coalition formed after the elections of 1961, when Ahdut ha-Avodah was chosen over the Liberal party (a new party created in a merger between the Progressive party and the General Zionists—two parties from the Civil camp) as a partner in the new government.This action laid the foundations for the establishment of alignments within the Labor and Civil camps—alliances Ben-Gurion had avoided throughout his political life. At that time, after the reemergence of the Lavon affair, Ben-Gurion was already weakened in the party as well as in the country. The chief negotiator of the new coalition was Levi Eshkol; another indication of Ben-Gurion's decline in the party. The anticipated struggle for succession between the old guard of the party and the younger Ben-Gurion protégés was probably the motivating force behind this move. Taking into account a possible split with the Dayan-Peres group, the veteran element was looking for a substitute defense-oriented leadership to counterbalance the lack of security expertise in its image.[20] They found what they sought in the leadership of Ahdut ha-Avodah.

The political result of these and ensuing maneuvers was the emergence of two large camps: the Left included Mapai and the other Social-Democratic parties that composed the Alignment; the Right included the Liberals (formerly the General Zionists) and Herut, together forming Gahal. Had the Liberals joined the 1961 coalition, they would not have formed the bloc with Herut (see table 6-2).

Though Levi Eshkol won the 1965 elections, the political map had been transformed. The multipolar system preserved by Ben-Gurion was replaced by two contending alliances on the Left and the Right. Although the coalition system was not terminated, the Israeli voter was in fact offered, for the first time, an alternative to the rule of Mapai. It took another three elections to end the rule of the Socialist parties, but by 1965 Menachem Begin was heading a broad-based party (not limited to the Revisionist component) that could eventually offer an alternative government. It is true that Ben-Gurion spoke about the creation of two large political camps through a change in the electoral system, but what he envisioned was a system that would give him an absolute majority. It was this aspiration that, as long as Mapai was in power, had motivated Begin to oppose such a transformation. Ben-Gurion's heirs, on the other hand, preferred to achieve an absolute majority through political alliances and mergers without abolishing the proportional system. Accordingly, the alliance of 1965 was followed by further mergers and an alignment that in 1969 encompassed every Zionist party on the Left. Still, the Labor Alignment, despite these political alliances, did not achieve the absolute majority that was the main motive for the process of unification.[21]

A parallel change took place in the international environment. As on the domestic scene, this transformation cannot be attributed to a deliberate strategic deviation, but rather to a sequence of events that had an impact on the structure of relationships and perceptions. The turning point in the external realm can be traced back to 1966. Throughout that year Fatah terrorist actions, some of them planned and controlled by the new leftist junta in Damascus, were launched from Jordan and Lebanon against Israel. The

Table 6-2
The Various Cabinets in the Post-Ben-Gurion Era
and the Participating Parties

Number of Cabinet and Date Installed	Religious Camp		Civil Camp		Labor Camp	
	National Religious Party	Agudat Israel	Gahal-Likud[a] (Herut and Liberals)	Independent Liberals	Labor-[b] Alignment (Mapai and Ahdut ha-Avoda)	Mapam
11th-12th Cabinet June 26, 1963 December 22, 1964	+	−	−	−	+	+
13th-14th Cabinet[c] January 12, 1965 (Eshkol died in February 1968 and was replaced by Golda Meir)	+	−	− +	+	+	+
15th-16th Cabinet[d,e] December 15, 1969	+	−	−	+	+	+
17th-18th Cabinet[f] March 10, 1974 Meir was replaced by Rabin in May 1974	+	−	−	+	+	+
19th Cabinet[g] June 19, 1977	+	+	+	−	−	−
20th Cabinet[h] August 5, 1981	+	+	+	− disappeared	−	−

Source: Adapted from *Encyclopedia Judaica*, Vol. 9, pp. 664-675; and *Israel at the Polls*, The Knesset Elections of 1977.

Notes
+ signifies Coalition party
− Opposition party
[a]The Likud contested under this name since 1973 campaign.
[b]Ahdut ha-Avoda is here included in the Alignment which came into being on November 15, 1964 between Mapai and Ahdut ha-Avoda.
[c]Gahal joined the government on the eve of the Six Day War.
[d]Mapam joined the Alignment while Ahdut ha-Avoda became an integral part of Labor.
[e]Gahal was a member of the coalition for a short period.
[f]The NRP was out of the coalition for a short while.
[g]The Democratic Movement for Change eventually joined the government but slowly disintegrated.
[h]TAMI, a new party split from the NRP, was also included in the new coalition.

Eshkol government, hesitating to retaliate against Syria because of the close ties of the new regime with Moscow, focussed its reprisal against Jordan at Samua. This move was intended to force Israel's eastern neighbor to cease the forays from its territory, as well as to warn Syria without actually attacking it. As in previous reprisals, there were domestic considerations and political repercussions.[22] Unlike the raids during Ben-Gurion's time, the Samua raid was executed in broad daylight by an armored force. The internal reactions to this raid within Jordan were very dramatic; the Hashemite regime almost toppled.[23] One of the conclusions apparently drawn by Hussein was that his alliance with the West and his shared interest with Israel provided him with no immunity from retaliation.

Whether Jordan's participation in the 1967 war was determined by the Samua raid has yet to be substantiated. In any event, Hussein's agreement on the eve of the war to the establishment of common military headquarters with Egypt and his inability to stay out of the Six Day War, despite promises and pleas from the Israeli leadership to abstain, brought about the conquest of Eastern Jerusalem and the West Bank and hence the termination of the partition that was established in 1948.

The separation of the West Bank from Jordan weakened the common interest that had existed for almost two decades between the two governments. At the same time, the traumatic experience of the period preceding June 5, 1967, transformed the security perceptions of the Israeli policymakers and diminished the credibility of the Jordanian monarch as a reliable guardian of Israel's eastern border. Hussein's participation in the war and his agreement to let other Arab forces be stationed in Jordan convinced many Israelis that the West Bank was strategically too important to be left in hostile hands.

The strengthening of Palestinian identity and the emergence of the PLO as a result of the breakdown of partition has been analyzed in previous chapters. One point, however, should be made at this juncture: Before 1967, Palestinian Arabs were divided not only between Israel and the Arab states, but they were also dispersed among several Arab countries. Following the 1967 war, Arabs who had previously been living in three separate countries—Israel, Jordan, and Egypt—were now living within one political entity. The ingathering of the Arabs from the Gaza Strip, the West Bank, and Israel was bound to create new realities. Thus, contacts between Israeli Arabs and the Arabs living in the territories promoted the Palestinization of the Israeli Arabs.[24] Israelis, who had hoped that these two Arab communities would eventually form a bridge between the Jewish state and the Arab world, overlooked Israel's role as the bridge connecting the Arabs of the West Bank, Gaza, and Israel.

Even more profound was the impact of the new situation on the Israeli domestic system. The acquisition of the new territories aroused new emotions within Israeli society toward Judea and Samaria. Ideas and aspirations that had previously been limited to the Revisionists (and even there had already started to phase out) were now revived not only by Begin's supporters but also by a wide cross-section of traditional political elements.[25] The war brought about the creation of the National Unity Government in which Begin was a senior member, a fact that undoubtedly assisted in the political legitimization of Herut's leader. The breaking up of the National

Unity Government by Begin in 1970, which at that time seemed a political blunder, turned out to be a blessing. This demonstrated that it was not his participation that blocked the road to peace, as many argued, but Arab unwillingness to accept Israel's existence. In the long run, Labor's inability to convince the Arab states to exchange territories for a genuine peace was destined to erode their political status both within the electorate and vis-à-vis competing elites.

A significant transformation also took place in the relations between Labor and the NRP. On the ideological level, the attitudes of the NRP, as a religious Zionist movement, could not but be affected by the liberation of ancient Jewish territories where the kingdoms of Judea and Israel had prospered and that contained religious monuments of the ancient past. Nevertheless, these feelings were somehow suppressed as long as the old leadership dominated the party. There were early interactions between the NRP and Herut even before the death of M.H. Shapira, the NRP leader whose style of leadership was close to that of Ben-Gurion. Shapira played a major role in setting up the National Unity Government.[26] The real change came after Shapira's death in 1970 when the Youth Circles, a new contender for the leadership of the party, started to accumulate power. In its struggle against the veteran leadership, this group tried to take advantage of the new nationalistic attitudes among the party's members and supporters, and questioned the traditional partnership with Labor.

The deterioration in the relations between the two parties should not be blamed on the NRP alone. As a matter of fact, a larger portion of the blame could be placed on Labor which, under internal pressures (partly as a result of its new mergers with parties to its left and partly through the emergence of its young leaders), started to retreat from its support of the religious status quo. Labor's betrayal aided the younger leadership within the NRP who argued that their party's political exchange with Labor was neither balanced nor politically intelligent. They asserted that their party supplied Labor with the necessary power to govern and in exchange received shaky support for religious priorities accompanied by a public image of a party interested only in power without any ideology or independent line in foreign policy. The territories issue was the perfect cause under which they could combine political and ideological independence.[27] The historical partnership between the two parties thus started to collapse. However, a major contribution to that process was the acquisition of the West Bank by Israel. In addition to right-wing opposition, Labor now had an opposition party within its coalition.

The Decline of Labor and the Emergence of a
New Majority

These major transformations were not translated into clear political realities in the period immediately following the Six Day War. During these years, the ruling party enjoyed the fruits of the 1967 victory and the charisma of Golda Meir. However, the stage was set for a transition; what was needed was a major crisis to launch it. The Yom Kippur War served that function.

In the elections that followed the 1973 war, the power of the Alignment (Labor and Mapam) declined from 56 to 51 seats in the Knesset; and the parliamentary strength of the Likud, which now incorporated almost all the parties of the center and the Right, increased from 32 to 39 seats.[28] Despite the fact that Labor still enjoyed a plurality, its flexibility in domestic and foreign affairs was severely curtailed. It was ironic that the process of unification, designed to reduce the dependency of the ruling party on its coalition partners, brought about the opposite result. The party was now torn between the right and left wings, a fact that ultimately paralyzed its foreign and economic policies. Another irony was the failure of traditional Mapai to sustain its rule through the process of unification. After Golda Meir's resignation in April 1974, Mapai no longer controlled the three senior positions in the government. The new prime minister, foreign minister, and defense minister did not belong to the traditional Mapai establishment. Thus, Mapai's rule was ended even before the 1977 elections.

At the same time, relations between the ruling party and its religious partner continued to deteriorate. The protest vote following the October War also affected the potency of the NRP, thus strengthening the case of the Youth Circles in regard to the wisdom of association with Labor. Even more significant was the treatment of the party by its traditional ally, which was perceived by the NRP as an attempt to bring them to their knees. Although the religious party ultimately joined the government, its positions on foreign policy were more those of an opposition party. The traditional framework of autonomy in foreign policy in exchange for religious conces-sions, under which the ruling party had operated for a quarter of a century, finally collapsed. With a strong parliamentary opposition on the outside and opposition within the government, accompanied by a struggle between Prime Minister Rabin and Defense Minister Peres, decisive leadership in foreign policy was inconceivable.

A similar trend also developed in the relationship between Israel and Jordan. After the Six Day War, the Israeli government left the door open for a political deal with Jordan regarding the West Bank. The open-bridges policy that maintained the links between that area and its former sovereign was intended to preserve some common interest between the two countries. Moreover, both countries demonstrated a certain degree of cooperation on two occasions. When Hussein cracked down on the Palestinian Arabs and expelled their leaders in September 1970, Israel deterred Syrian intervention on their behalf. Likewise, during the 1973 war, Jordan limited its interven-tion on the Arab side. Nevertheless, these actions were not followed by a comprehensive territorial settlement. The West Bank problem, a major link between the two countries, was not resolved. The 1973 war was followed by limited agreements between Israel and the two other confrontation states without a comprehensive deal between the two interlocked neighbors.

When the Labor party suffered its unexpected defeat in the May 1977 elections, there were sound reasons for it. A deteriorating economy, a ruling party paralyzed by internal struggles and disclosures of corruption, and mounting external pressures were all good reasons for a vote of nonconfidence. Yet despite these manifestations, not many responsible people would say they had foreseen the upcoming political upset. For decades, basically the same elite had ruled the central institutions of the country, and nothing seemed able to remove them. During its history, the party survived the economic hardships of the 1950s, the absorption of more than a million immigrants, internal struggles accompanied by accusations of corruption and security failures in the early 1960s, the recession of the mid-1960s, and finally the misjudgments and early failures during the Yom Kippur War. In the light of such a capacity for survival, it was only natural that the informed observer should fail to anticipate a drastic upset. For years the Israeli voter trusted the party which stood for defense experience and social justice, and rejected the militants and the capitalists of the Right (as successfully portrayed by the Left). What happened to the images that had persisted for years?

Undoubtedly, the Israeli voter shifted loyalties because of salient issues such as inflation, corruption, and failures in foreign policy. However, the collective decision was abetted and translated into political reality only because the electorate had for several elections been offered a steadily improving alternative. While the ruling party was hindered by its allies and losing flexibility, the opposition was accumulating power and legitimacy. The combination of this process and the appearance of a new party in the center—the Democratic Movement for Change (DMC)—was sufficient to send the Socialist camp into the opposition for the first time in Israel's history.

The election upset of May 1977 was more dramatic than the conventional transformation of power that is experienced in Western democracies. The event was of major importance for Israeli politics. It signaled the end of an era in which one elite dominated the political scene and shaped Israel's economic, social, and national-security policies. From an international perspective, the change of guard heralded a significant change in the approaches and relationships that had dominated the political scene in Palestine-Eretz Yisrael for more than four decades. Mapai-Labor, the party of partition, in power since 1935, was now replaced by a coalition that was opposed to the repartition of the Land of Israel. The main partners in this new coalition were Herut—the major force in Likud and heir of the Revisionist movement—and the NRP which for all practical purposes was a nonpartition party. Although the DMC eventually joined the government, with time it became clear that the Likud government was essentially a religious-nationalist coalition rather than a center-Right one. The disintegration of the DMC, and the marginal role of the liberal section in Likud enabled the nationalist and the religious elements in government to have their way.

The 1981 elections provided a clear indication that the Israeli polity was transformed and that the 1977 elections were not a fluke. The coalition that emerged from the 1981 elections presented a new majority composed of three main elements: hawks, religious voters, and Oriental Jews. This new majority was not only reflected in the parties composing the new government—Likud, NRP, Agudat Israel, and T'nuat Masoret Israel (TAMI, a newly established list representing primarily Oriental Jews)—but also in the main elements of the Likud constituency.[29] These three elements overlap to a large extent, as Oriental Jews tend to be more hawkish and religious Jews are more committed to the ideal of Eretz Yisrael. These three elements also provide supportive margins that add to the strength of the coalition, as Agudat Israel voters are not hawks and there are hawks which are neither religious nor do they come from an oriental background. In short, the traditional coalition that ruled Israel (composed of moderate religious and center parties dominated by the Labor camp) was replaced by a new coalition composed of more radical religious and hawkish forces dominated by the heirs of the Revisionist movement. Within this new coalition, the antipartition forces have nearly attained total freedom in implementing their policies on the West Bank and the Gaza Strip.

The Emergence of a Religious Zionist Vanguard

Since 1967 Israel's political society has undergone a transformation of its ruling elite from Labor to the right wing and has also witnessed the emergence of a new group which perceives itself, and has largely won acceptance, as the new vanguard of the Zionist revolution. In the Yishuv and the pre-1967 periods, and to a certain extent even during the early years following the 1967 war, Labor took the lead in redeeming the land (*Geulat Ha'aretz*). After 1967, the national religious youth emerged as the main force behind settlement (*Hityashvut* or *Hitnachlut*)[30] and concentrated their efforts in the newly acquired areas of Judea and Samaria.

Because of the different orientations of the two camps and because these developments coincided with Labor's decline in power, these efforts had a powerful impact on the relationship between Israel and the West Bank. In order to understand the full significance of this development, embodied primarily in the emergence of Gush Emunim, one must look at the process that led to the reversal of roles.

The main question that arises is: how did a segment of the Israeli society succeed in moving from the sidelines of the Zionist enterprise into a principal position? This question is all the more compelling in light of the fact that between the religious and secular camps in Israeli society, the religious camp has always constituted a minority. Moreover, how do we explain the fact that the dominant-socialist political culture gave way to a religious interpretation and initiative?

Religion and State in Israel

Although several of the early Zionist ideologues were Orthodox rabbis, Orthodox Jewry in general was ambivalent toward the idea of Jewish self-determination. Though it could not remain indifferent to the idea of the return to Zion (*Shivat Tzion*) many of the leading Orthodox authorities could not accept the idea that this norm would be fulfilled through human enterprise. Believing that the long-awaited return would be a manifestation of divine intervention meant that Theodor Herzl, a secular Jew, was totally unacceptable as the leader of this movement. It was over this dilemma that Orthodox Jewry split between Zionists, non-Zionists, and even anti-Zionists.[31]

The religious Zionist movement, despite its inherent difficulties in cooperating with nonobservant Jews, became an integral part of the World Zionist Organization and with time even became a loyal partner of the anti-clerical Socialist camp. Cooperation with the nonreligious Zionist movement was based on two rationales that evolved in religious Zionist thought. The first was developed by Rabbi Isaac Jacob Reines, one of the founders of the Mizrachi, and came to be known as the pragmatic approach. According to Rabbi Reines, cooperation between religious and secular Zionists should overlook differences in ideology in order to accomplish what was in his estimation Zionism's primary goal: to establish secure refuge for Jews in light of the threat to the existence of the Jewish people in the modern world. The second approach was that of Rabbi Abraham Isaac Kook, first chief rabbi of Palestine, who not only supported cooperation with secular Zionism but also found grounds for its sanctification. According to Rabbi Kook, the nonreligious Zionist was really motivated by an inner divine desire of which he may not be aware. It was therefore the duty of the religious Jew to cooperate with the secularist anticipating that ultimately the latter will recognize his holy inner motivation.[32]

On the practical level, cooperation between religious and secular Zionism resulted in a relationship that began in the Yishuv period and continued into independence. The alliance came to be known as the historical partnership. Within the framework of this partnership, whose formal mentors were Mapai and Mizrachi-Ha-Poel ha-Mizrachi (the two main organs of religious Zionism), the two movements became genuine partners in the Jewish state-building process. Both movements developed parallel Labor organizations (Histadrut ha-Kelalit and Histadrut Ha-Poel ha-Mizrachi), youth organizations, kibbutzim, and moshavim, which cooperated in many areas. Cooperation was also supported by an ideological evolution. Ha-Poel ha-Mizrachi, the offshoot of Mizrachi, adopted labor as a sanctified idea in the realization of the Zionist revolution. Thus, the Mizrachi movement integrated both Zionism and religion on the political level and Torah and labor (Torah va-Avodah) on the social level as basic norms of its ideological fabric.[33]

However well grounded this cooperation may have been, the basic schism between the religious and secular elements of Iraeli society could never be completely alleviated. Indeed, the relationship between religion and state was the most explosive issue during the early years of Israel's independence, causing several governmental crises. Despite the ongoing debate, cooperation between Mapai and the NRP continued.

Several Israeli political scientists have applied the theory of consociational politics in order to explain this phenomenon. They argue that the relationship between Mapai and the NRP was influenced more by their conflicting attitudes on questions of religion and state than by their ideological proximity in other matters. Both parties, realizing that the only alternative to cooperation was a conflict that would divide irreparably the Jewish community along religious and secular lines, decided to find a modus vivendi.[34] The coalition that emerged resembled other systems of deeply divided societies where accommodation is based on compromise and power-sharing arrangements. Within this framework, the NRP secured for itself the right to direct its own school system within the state education system, veto power on religious legislation concerning personal-status law, and maintenance of the status quo in matters of public religious life. Of these areas of accommodation, educational autonomy is the most significant from our perspective. Its significance went beyond the fact that the NRP could now ensure the survival of the religious sector in the Zionist enterprise; Gush Emunim would later recruit many of its supporters from the ranks of the national religious education system. While the Labor movement was relinquishing its own educational network (Zerem ha-Ovdim—the Labor Trend) for the sake of integration, the national religious movement was developing an autonomous ideological education system.[35]

In retrospect, both the ideological and the practical elements of the cooperation between Labor and the religious Zionist movements had far-reaching implications for the development of contemporary religious Zionist ideology in general and for Gush Emunim in particular. The modern religious Zionist, in sharp contrast to the non-Zionist Orthodox Jew, continued to see the secular Jew as a potential convert to his ideology. It was no coincidence that the ideological center for the dissemination of nationalist religious norms was Yeshivat Merkaz ha-Rav. The Yeshiva was headed by Rabbi Tzvi Yehuda Kook, the son of the late Rabbi Kook who had described modern Zionism as representing the beginning of redemption. Secular Jews who contributed to the fulfillment of Zionism and settlement of the land were, according to this view, preferable to religious Jews who stayed away or objected to the Zionist enterprise.[36] Moreover, the traditional cooperation between Labor and the NRP in nation-building enterprises, such as land purchases and establishing settlements, influenced the behavior of Gush Emunim. In other words, some of Gush Emunim's norms were rooted in normative Socialist Zionism with whom the religious Zionist movement cooperated for many years.

On a different level, the consociational arrangement made its own impact on the emergence of a new religious Zionist approach. One of the necessary conditions for a consociational bargain is a compromise in which each party receives its minimal demands but at the same time relinquishes other demands for the sake of mutual accommodation. Arend Lijphart described the dilemma in these words:

> Consociational Democracy entails the cooperation by segmental leaders in spite of the deep cleavages separating the segments. This requires that the leaders feel at least some commitment to the maintenance of the unity of the country as well as a commitment to democratic practices. They also have a basic willingness to engage in cooperative efforts with the leaders of other segments in a spirit of moderation and compromise. At the same time, they must retain the support and loyalty of their own followers. The elites must therefore continually perform a difficult balancing act.[37]

In the Israeli situation, these concessions resulted in peculiar compromises which may have seemed to the nonelite in each segment as motivated by the elites' desire to stay in power. For instance, Labor's bargain with the religious camp forbade Sabbath bus transportation in many cities but cabs, which are also subsidized by the government, were permitted to function.

The younger generation of the NRP, which was brought up in an idealistic environment, rejected the pragmatism of their established leaders.[38] While accepting the results of these compromises, they despised the processes by which they were accomplished. Thus, the autonomous education system, which was the outcome of consociationalism, was the breeding ground for fundamentalism and rejection of compromise and moderation. Ironically, the ideology of Rabbi Kook and the system that promoted mutual cooperation and the adoption of certain Labor norms by the national religious movement proved to be the elements that alienated the younger generation from that partnership. They were looking for an ideological leadership more in keeping with their own fundamentalist orientation.

Another explanation for the transformation of the national religious movement, forwarded by several students of religion and politics in Israel, was that the movement suffered from an inherent dilemma. The Mizrachi ideology was based on an attempt to reconcile the norms of secular Zionism, which was relatively progressive, with Orthodox Judaism, which was conservative and resistant to modernization. The synthesis of these approaches resulted in a hybrid ideology which prevented its followers from attaining the lead in either the national or the religious arena. Mizrachi followers felt rejected by both worlds: the secular public viewed them as an antidemocratic element committed to imposing archaic religious laws on a modern state, while the non-Zionist Orthodoxy regarded them as dissenters. The central state institutions like the foreign service and the military were headed by secular leaders; the more advanced rabbinical colleges were headed by leading non-Zionist Talmudic scholars.

One manifestation of the NRP compromise was the network of *Yeshivot Hesder*, rabbinical colleges that combined military service and Talmudic studies. The Hesder program divided the four post-high-school years between abbreviated (one-and-a-half year) military service and Talmudic studies. As a result, Hesder students never felt as fully involved in the army as those who served three years, and never felt as accomplished as those who were exempt from military service and studied Talmud full time for those years. Uriel Simon described their dilemma in the following words: "These youngsters had decided that they were less Orthodox than Agudat Yisrael and less nationalist than secular movements. They felt they were falling between two stools."[39] Consequently they were looking for an issue or an area in which the synthesis between religion and nationalism could best express itself.

The acquisition of Judea and Samaria, the heartland of the ancient Jewish kingdoms, provided this generation with a cause that could relieve them of their frustrations and alienation and give them an opportunity to express their special brand of Zionism. Unlike other religious concerns, the territories issue was not the exclusive purview of observant Jews; it concerned the whole people of Israel and cut across the traditional division of camps. In this area there was no room for compromises. It was an issue that concerned security and foreign policy, two areas the traditional NRP leadership shied away from. Even more important, settling and struggling for the Land of Israel justified their unique religious upbringing. Now NRP youth were in a position to criticize nonreligious Zionists for betraying traditional ideals of Zionism such as settlement and security. At the same time they could feel superior to the non-Zionist Orthodox who, despite their religious commitment, were not fulfilling the obligation of settling the Land of Israel. Thus, the young religious nationalists could now become the vanguard of modern Zionism, not in spite of their religious outlook but because of it.

One of the contributing factors of Gush Emunim's ascendance in Zionist circles was that its members communicated their belief that they were the keepers of accepted Zionist norms. Another factor contributing to Gush Emunim's success, despite its limited recruiting base, was the fact that its growth coincided with the decline of normative Zionist socialism.

The Decline of Normative Zionist Socialism

One of the highlights of the 1981 Israeli election campaign was Menachem Begin's challenge to Labor's leader Shimon Peres to refer to socialism as a basis for his party's platform. Indeed, the disappearance of socialist norms from Labor's campaigns in recent elections is a definitive illustration of the transformation Israeli society underwent in the post-1967 period. In the estimation of many sociopolitical analysts, this transition is rooted in the establishment of the state and in the waves of immigrants that the new state had to absorb. Under those circumstances, Dan Horowitz argued, the Socialist elite could not afford to develop a gradual political socialization process as had been the case in the Yishuv period. Instead, during the early years of statehood, the masses of new immigrants were absorbed directly through a political apparatus that efficiently preserved Labor's dominancy but failed to instill Labor values.[40]

Two Israeli political scientists have written recently on the transformation of Israeli normative values or, in their terminology, on the development of Israel's civil religion. Charles S. Liebman defines civil religion as "the system of beliefs and practices which serves to legitimate the social order, integrate the population around a system of shared values and mobilize the energies of the citizenry in the fulfillment of social tasks."[41] On the basis of this definition, Liebman and Eliezer Don-Yehiya demonstrate how Israel's civil religion changed from a Zionist-Socialist central value system to statism (*mamlachtiyut*) during the early years of statehood, and was succeeded by a new civil religion, "which gave greater emphasis to Jewish history, tradition and peoplehood."[42] Amnon Rubinstein, a member of Knesset, also observed a decline in Socialist values in Israel, accompanied by new attitudes toward tradition and religious symbols which even encompassed the kibbutzim, the hard core of Labor ideology.[43]

What are the main reasons for the decline of the Zionist-Socialist norms in Israeli society? Rubinstein tied this decline to the failure of the Labor movement to implement its vision of a new social order and create an egalitarian model to be emulated by the nations of the world. The realities at home and the hostility of the Soviet Union, the New Left, and other progressive forces tended to modify the promises of the Left; and "The attempt to fill the idea of a chosen people and the role of the Jewish people with a Socialist content failed."[44] Ze'ev Shternhal blamed the decline on the abandonment of segmentalism, and ideological uniquness for the sake of statism or generalism. While the Left watered down its ideology for the sake of building an integrated nation, the Right did not change its purist norms. Thus, when confrontation between the two ideological camps was revived after the Six Day War, Labor lost out.[45]

Labor succeeded in implementing many of its broader goals: state building, nation building, and the institution of a welfare state that was acceptable and just to the average citizen. At the same time it had limited success in accomplishing two important goals of normative Zionism—the ingathering of the exiles (*Kibbutz Galuyot*) and providing full security to the Jewish people.[46] Following the establishment of the state, it became clear that these two goals would not be fully accomplished in the near future. This reality became even more apparent following the Six Day War when Israel's astonishing victory did not stimulate a massive *aliya* (immigration) or peace with the Arabs. The failure of the territories-for-peace policy, which was identified with Labor, and the decline in *aliya* following the 1973 war encouraged a search for a new direction for Zionism.

Israel, as both a new society and an ideological democracy, to use Daniel J. Elazar's teminology, could not afford to live in an ideological vacuum for any period of time. "While the founders of the new societies obviously brought with them a cultural heritage derived from their societies of origin, their motive in migrating was almost invariably a revolutionary one," Elazar writes in *Israel: From Ideological to Territorial Democracy*.[47] As the U.S. experience indicates, new societies create a sense of national purpose "developed out of a combination of the frontier experiences they passed through and the ideological grounding (essentially religious in origin) they brought with them. The mystique they created has served as the basis for a national consensus and as a major stimulus for national action ever since."[48] Israel, as a new society and an ideological democracy which had suffered the erosion of Labor's value was ready for new ideological content. However after fifty years of leading the Zionist movement, Labor had so deeply affected the national character that the new approach would have to use similar symbols in order to gain popular support.

Labor's ideological decline was not accompanied by an upsurge of Revisionist ideology, which would seem the obvious alternative to Labor. The exclusion of the Revisionists from the central organs of the Yishuv, together with Herut's apparently permanent opposition role following independence served to hinder the spread of their ideology in Israeli society. Lacking a developed network of organization and institutions, such as Labor's kibbutzim or NRP's *yeshivot*, Herut was left with no mechanisms for political socialization or ideological renovation. Similarly, Ben-Gurion's adoption of statism as a system of orientation and values implied the adoption of certain Revisionist values, making it more difficult for them to present a comprehensive alternative ideology. "The operative principles of statism," Liebman and Don-Yehiya argue, "were certainly closer to the platforms of the pre-State Revisionists and civil parties than to platforms of pre-State Zionist-Socialists."[49] The political reality of sections of the Land of Israel being under Jordanian rule, accepted by the majority of the population until 1967, rendered another part of Revisionist ideology irrelevant.

Betar, the youth movement of Herut, never developed as a mass movement that could in any way compete with the Labor or the religious youth movements. Their share in the realization of Zionist tasks, such as settlement, was minimal and essentially they never developed an ethos of pioneering. Revisionist ideology, in contrast to the political movement, could not fill the vacuum that Labor's decline had created.

The only movement that could legitimize the application of traditional Zionist values to the new territories was the new national religious ideology. Having cooperated with Labor for most of the previous period, the national religious movement was already involved in such ideals as settlement and pioneering. It had an institutional network that was breeding ideology, and an idealistic youth movement, B'nei Akiva, that had participated with Labor's youth movement in nation-building enterprises such as combining military service and pioneering. But unlike their secular partners, the national religious Zionists were not affected by the general decline of Labor values. It was no coincidence that Gush Emunim started to come to the fore following the Yom Kippur War, when Israeli society was going through a deep crisis of self-identity and doubt regarding the future of Zionism. It was at this point that many of the graduates of B'nei Akiva and Merkaz ha-Rav felt that it was their duty to pull Israeli society out of its despair and return to the fundamental ideas of Zionism. They felt that they could accomplish this task because they possessed one element that the secular camp lacked: the religious conviction that the Almighty was accompanying His people and that the return to Zion was an integral part of the redemption process.[50] Thus, while conceiving of themselves as the heirs of genuine Zionism they also saw themselves as a better and more idealistic element of the Zionist movement.

It was this self-perceived role that also dictated their approach to the territories captured in the 1967 war. While the Labor youth movements were bound by their parent party's policy of strategic settlement and the eventual return of most of the newly acquired territories to their previous owners in exchange for peace, the Gush Emunim attitude was that Judea and Samaria constitute an integral part of the Land of Israel and therefore a Jewish government was not allowed to return them to the control of non-Jews.[51]

In accordance with this belief they pressured the government to start settling in the heartland of Judea and Samaria, volunteering to be the first settlers. By doing so they provided, in their perception, not merely a new vigor but also a new challenge to modern Zionism. Rather than conceptualizing settlements as security outposts they presented the nation with a new vision—the settlement of the whole Land of Israel. Instead of stating with complacence that Zionism had essentially accomplished its main goal through the establishment of the State of Israel and that the only aim left was Arab recognition of the state, Gush Emunim challenged the people to take upon themselves a new task—the task of Zionism in the 1970s.[52]

The settlement of the West Bank, the Gaza Strip, and other parts of historic Eretz Israel was perceived by Gush Emunim, and by many of its outside supporters, not as a revolution of Zionist ideas but rather as a continuation of normative Zionism. This attitude was best summarized by one of their spokesmen in the following words:

> The critics of Gush Emunim praise moderation and realism and condemn the "stiff-necked" and unrealistic approach of the settlement movement. Part of the criticism derives, as Agriculture Minister Ariel Sharon has pointed out, from feelings of jealousy by those segments of the population whose past is a glorious tale of patriotic, pioneering successes which have not, however, been continued by the present generation. Gush Emunim is doing, with courage and sacrifice, what they did and should now be doing, but are not. Another basis of the criticism is pure weakness, a feeling of exhaustion, a loss of will, and its justification as the 'calm of strength' which is forebearance from reaction. This is really the 'calm of exhaustion'—not a divine self-control but a human failing.[53]

Similarly, they did not see themselves as the heirs to Revisionist ideology which had always fought against partition. Gush followers saw themselves and wanted to be thought of as continuing the approach of pioneering rather than declaratory Zionism. An article published in memory of Yigal Allon, one of the ideologists of Gush Emunim, attacked Begin's agreement to withdraw from the "Rafah Salient": "Yigal and his freinds could not, under any circumstances negotiate over Jewish settlements. . . . They were holy to them as they were holy to us. . . . Begin's government reintroduced an approach that was not bound to the soil."[54] Indeed, despite the clear dividing line between a socialist-secular and a national religious movement, Gush Emunim saw itself as continuing the Zionist revolution rather than presenting a new radical interpretation of Zionism.[55] The decline of Zionist socialism in Israeli society contributed to the legitimacy of such a claim.

External Factors

Thus far we have analyzed factors indigenous to Israeli society which contributed to the emergence of what we have termed the religious Zionist vanguard. But there were also external developments which influenced the tenets of Gush Emunim and contributed to its legitimation within Israeli society. These developments took place in the West Bank and the international arena.

As we have seen, the Six Day War brought in its wake the strengthening of Palestinian identity in the West Bank, the Gaza Strip, and abroad. This new Palestinian nationalism was especially evident following the Yom Kippur War as the PLO became prominent in the international scene and its influence on the West Bank was taking root. Although the ideological roots of Gush Emunim were linked directly to the acquisition of ancient Jewish land, the strengthening of a competitive identity with national claims to the land of Israel stimulated the articulation and elaboration of a Zionist response. The fact that this new identity was growing stronger at a time when the Gush and others sensed that Israeli self-confidence and idealism was going through a crisis, made the need for the revitalization and consolidation of modern Zionism more acute. To many Israelis who might not have agreed with Gush claims over the West Bank under normal circumstances, it seemed important to advance a more positive Israeli claim in light of the Palestinian ideological claims which were finding sympathizers in Israeli leftist circles.

Why did Palestinian nationalism seem more threatening than the pre-1967 Arab hostility and determination to destroy the state? In certain circumstances an ideological threat is more dangerous than a physical one. "Part of the reason why Israel survived against the onslaught of Arab hatred for over thirty years is because the Jews wanted to live more than the Arabs were able to prevent them from living," argued Mordechai Nisan, a Gush supporter.[56] In the same article he writes, "Gush Emunim represents the force of ideology as opposed to the method of pragmatism. . . . Israel's pragmatism—no matter how civilized and pleasant it appears—will never be able to compete with the Arab world's ideological strength."

A second development was the growing isolation of Israel on the world scene. One of the basic ideas of classic Zionism was the transition of the Jewish people from its abnormal situation—as a people without a land dispersed among the nations of the world—to a normal nation. It was believed that the creation of a Jewish state would provide the basis for such a transformation, as the Jews would possess, like all the other nations, a territorial state. Normalization of the Jewish people would resolve once and for all the phenomenon of anti-Semitism which was a direct result, so ran the Zionist doctrine, of the abnormal situation of the Jews. Once the Jewish state came into being, the relationship between the Jews and the Gentiles would be based on equality in accordance with the nation-state paradigm. Indeed, during the first two decades of Israeli independence, the slogan of "a nation like all the nations" was the accepted norm in Israeli political-cultural life. It was only following the Six Day War and particularly after the Yom Kippur War that a new catchword started to gain currency in Israel: "a people that dwells alone.''[57] The implicit meaning of this new definition of Israel's relationship with the world is that the Jewish people were destined to be isolated from other nations. This destiny is so strong that even under conditions of sovereignty the Jewish people would be treated differently than other people.[58]

Amnon Rubinstein traces the roots of this new designation to Israel's traumatic experience in the weeks preceding the Six Day War when the Jewish state suddenly found itself facing a hostile Arab coalition declaring explicitly its intentions of destroying Israel.[59] The unwillingness of the international community to come to Israel's aid, despite previous promises regarding free navigation, only strengthened Israeli distrust of other nations and their international guarantees. Following the Six Day War, the mounting condemnation of Israel, by the same international community, for refusing to withdraw from territories occupied through self-defense strengthened feelings of unfairness toward the Jews, and the popular song in Israel became "The Whole World Is against Us." The condemnation of Zionism as racism, following the Yom Kippur War, and the pressures that were put on Israel by the United States, without considering the fact that early Arab victories resulted from Israel's delay in mobilizing its forces and refusal to mount preemptive strikes, served to further strengthen Israeli feelings of betrayal. These feelings not only contributed to the emergence of Gush Emunim but also served to legitimize Gush views in the eyes of Israel's nonreligious society. The anti-Zionism that gained acceptance on the world scene was to many nonreligious Jews only a cover for anti-Semitism. In such a climate, the Gush Emunim policy of settlements in the West Bank seemed the right response to the world's hypocrisy and betrayal.

A slightly different approach to the factor that shaped the evolution of Gush Emunim and its acceptance in Israeli society is that of Janet O'Dea.[60] In contrast to Rubinstein, O'Dea links the emergence of Gush Emunim directly to the atmosphere of "doubt, discontent and fears which arose in Israel following the Yom Kippur War, reversing the triumphant confidence of the post-'67 period," which she describes as an anomie. "The wide tolerance and even encouragement which the movement has received from the Israeli population," writes O'Dea, is explained by the fact that "Gush Emunim represents a recrystallization of attitudes, a resolute stance around certain ideas, and a reconstruction of social solidarity in face of the *anomie*, experienced after the Yom Kippur War."[61] Indeed, while the roots of Gush Emunim can be traced to the late 1950s and 1960s,[62] its acceptance by portions of Israeli society was accelerated by the events surrounding the 1973 war. At a time when the Zionist enterprise seemed to be in decline and under attack in the international community, and the legitimacy of Palestinian nationalism was on the rise, Gush Emunim seemed to offer direction and purpose to many Israelis.

Public Opinion and the West Bank

Although there is little quantitative evidence about the degree of public support for Gush Emunim norms, it seems that over the years, the Gush policies
were in accord with large portions of Israeli public opinion about the West
Bank. Public opinion polls indicate that since 1967 the public's attitudes
toward the territories were more hawkish than those of the government.[63]
But since the Yom Kippur War an interesting trend is distinguished. As
table 6-3 indicates, while the public's response to concessions in the West
Bank was highly negative during the Yom Kippur War, support for the "return nothing" position diminished from 74 percent in 1973 to 31 percent in
January 1975. From that point on, it climbed again and reached 50 percent
in January 1978. If we combine the two hawkish positions—"return nothing" and "return a small part"—we see a similar trend of decline during the
Yom Kippur War and a general increase after 1975. In a survey taken in July
1980, 33 percent replied that they were definitely against returning territories in Judea and Samaria in exchange for peace, and an additional 21
percent were more against than for.[64]

    During 1980, when Israel was debating the question of settlements in
Judea and Samaria, three polls were taken on this issue (see table 6-4). While
support for Gush Emunim-Sharon policies doubled from 14 to 28 percent,
support for those objecting to new settlements during peace negotiations

Table 6-3
Public Attitudes on Concessions in the West Bank
The Question: *As to the West Bank: What concession are you willing to give
in order to reach a peace agreement with the Arab countries?*
(*percentages*)

Survey period		Return everything	Return most	Return a good part	Return a small part	Return nothing	Total
1973	October 7-15	4	2	12	8	74	100
	October 25-29	6	4	13	10	68	100
	October 30-31	5	4	16	11	64	100
	December 3-4	8	8	24	13	47	100
1974	July 1-2	5	9	27	19	40	100
1975	January 5-7	12	17	27	14	31	100
	October 15-19	5	8	31	19	37	100
1976	March 3-6	14	8	29	12	38	100
	September 14-16	5	8	18	12	56	100
1977	January 19-23	5	7	26	21	42	100
	November 21-23	8	7	24	19	42	100
1978	January 2-5	11	7	21	11	50	100

Source: Louis Guttman, "The Israel Public, Peace and Territory: The Impact of the Sadat Initiative" (Jerusalem: Jerusalem Institute for Federal Studies, January 1978), Part 4. Reprinted
with permission.

Table 6-4

Public Attitudes toward Settlements in Judea and Samaria

Question: *Which of the Following Attitudes is the Closest to Yours?* (*percentages*)

Attitude	February-March 1980	August-September 1980	October-November 1980
Gush Emunim-Sharon-Extensive settlement	14	22	28
Ezer Weizman—Controlled settlement in blocs	20	19	15
The position of a portion in the Opposition—only in strategic areas which are not populated	21	20	23
Against new settlements but for strengthening existing settlements	9	11	9
Against new settlements while the peace negotiations are being held	21	14	12
Other opinions	4	1	1
No opinion	11	13	12

Source: Chanoch Smith, "Election Forecast," in *Ma'ariv*, November 28, 1980. Reprinted with permission.

dropped from 21 to 12 percent. At the same time, in the survey taken in July 1980, 41 percent supported large investments in settlements in Judea and Samaria, while 59 percent tended to object.

Gush Emunim as a Vanguard

We have tried to explain the main reasons behind the emergence of Gush Emunim and the support it received from the general public, despite the fact that its core was essentially religious and thus directly representing a minority of Israeli society. This analysis should not be taken to mean that it was supported by a majority of Israeli society or the religious camp. As a matter of fact, the Gush has many opponents in Israel and its emergence was counteracted by other organized groups such as the largely secular Peace Now movement and Oz ve-Shalom (Courage and Peace) in the national religious camp. Yet if we compare the impact all these movements had on government policies, Gush Emunim was the most effective. As we have seen, public-opinion polls indicate that Gush settlement policies received substantial support from the public. The fact that Likud used the settlements it established during its tenure as a principal campaign issue in 1981 and increased its power in those elections is another indication of public support on this issue.

The question regarding the impact of Gush Emunim on Israeli policies toward the territories is addressed in an interesting manner by Ehud Sprinzak in an article entitled "*Gush Emunim:* The Iceberg Model of Political Extremism."[65] In this article the author argues that Gush Emunim is the tip of an iceberg that has grown in Israel since the early years of its independence and with time it became a subculture—the national religious camp—which encompassed a network of institutions, a broad constituency, and defined ideology. The existence of such a reservoir of supporters enabled the Gush to mobilize political, human, and material support to pressure various Israeli governments within a democratic framework. The NRP, which has always been a senior partner of Israeli government, could not ignore the demands of the Gush which spoke in the language of the national religious movement. Gush Emunim, despite its highly ideological nature and messianic features, has always known how to exert pressure through political means in order to accomplish its goals.

While generally accepting Sprinzak's analysis, we contend that Gush Emunim represented more than the iceberg model suggests. Although the motivation, the inner strength, as well as the organizational talent that the Gush has demonstrated derives from the religious nature of this organization, the Gush phenomenon goes beyond religion and messianism. The political strength of Gush Emunim was related to the support it received from nonreligious circles and to the fact that it succeeded in becoming a nationwide movement. By breaking the invisible boundaries that traditionally separated the religious and the nonreligious camps, it went beyond the consociational arrangement that characterized Israeli politics. Within this new framework the Gush succeeded in mobilizing material and political support that enabled it to implement many of its ideas and make an impact on the West Bank.

The ideological roots of Gush Emunim, as well as the consociational framework in which the NRP operated, paved the way for cooperation between religious and nonreligious Jews. Similarly, the decline of normative Zionist socialism created a vacuum which Gush Emunim was qualified to fill. The historic cooperation between Labor and the national religious movements infused the latter with a system of symbols and references which Gush Emunim would use later on in portraying itself as the guardian of the spirit of pioneering—self-attainment and redemption of the Land of Israel.[66] By using these symbols, Gush Emunim was able to legitimize other ideas which might otherwise have had negative associations for the Israeli public. In addition, Israeli society's abandonment of Zionist-Socialism and the embracing of certain traditional Jewish values facilitated the popularization of Gush Emunim. Foreign pressures, to a certain extent, also triggered support for a response that seemed appropriate to both the religious and nonreligious public.

Thus, by the time the Israeli polity was ready for a shift from a Labor partition-oriented government to a right-wing religious coalition, a viable settlement movement was already in existence. This movement was on the rise not only because it was supported by a large section of the NRP—the Youth Circles—but also because it was connected to a large network of institutions: B'nei Akiva *yeshivot*, advanced *yeshivot*, and Hesder *yeshivot*. By May 1977, it had already established a substantial number of settlements in Judea and Samaria. Between 1967 and 1973, the two major settlement projects were Gush Etzion, south of Bethlehem, which was established in 1967; and Kiryat Arba, next to Hebron, established in 1968. Under pressure from Gush Emunim, the Labor government established semiofficial settlements, which later became known as Tekoa, 'Ofra, and Kadum.[67] Without broad public support, Labor leaders would not have given in to these pressures. Future leaders of Gush Emunim like Chanan Porat, Rabbi Levinger, and Benny Katzover came from these settlements. Moreover, Gush Emunim succeeded in mobilizing allies from nonreligious circles. Many of the leaders of Gush Emunim participated originally in the Land of Israel movement which had been founded by secular personalities coming out of the Labor camp, the Revisionists, and even the *Knaanim* (the latter being an antireligious movement).[68] Public figures like Moshe Shamir, an author and a former Shomer ha-Tzair member, and Moshe Tabenkin, also from Labor, became supporters of Gush Emunim. *Chug Ein Vered*, in which many Labor figures participated, was another example of the support the Gush was receiving from nonreligious circles. In May 1977, the transformation seemed complete; not only was there a broad settlement movement but the new government that came into power was an antipartition government which perceived the new territories acquired in June 1967 as an integral part of the State of Israel.

Settlement Patterns in the West Bank

The combination of a nonpartition government and a vigorous movement ready to take the lead in the settlement of Judea and Samaria resulted in new settlement patterns in the West Bank. Gush Emunim had wrested several concessions from the weakened Labor government, and the new government removed the remaining settlement restrictions and provided material support—all of which cleared the way for a broad settlement enterprise. Gush Emunim pressured the government to implement a broader and more intensive settlement policy than it would have done otherwise in light of the economic and foreign pressures the new government faced. Most important however, was the fact that Gush Emunim complemented the new government with an essential element—a settlement movement. As we have indicated previously, the ideology and the consequent establishment of settlement was alien to the Revisionist movement. The national religious component in the new majority provided a tradition of settlement and pioneering which the other partners lacked.

The new settlement drive that started during the first Likud government was implemented by Minister of Agriculture Ariel Sharon. Sharon, who came to politics following a long military career, had a controversial reputation as a hero in all of Israel's wars. He joined the right wing where his hawkish views were more acceptable than in the Labor camp. As agriculture minister and head of the Ministerial Settlement Committee, he launched a broad settlement drive overcoming objections within the government, even though that government was officially committed to the incorporation of Judea and Samaria. In this drive he was assisted by Gush Emunim whom he sometimes encouraged to create facts and thus force the government's hand. At the end of four years, when Likud was facing the electorate for a second term, Sharon presented the voter with forty-four settlements in Judea and Samaria that were founded during his tenure. As part of Sharon's campaign, 300,000 Israelis came to see these settlements. Subsequently, the Likud won a second term in office, Sharon was promoted to defense minister, and Gush Emunim read into the publicity of its settlements proof that the people were with them.[69]

The alliance between Sharon and Gush Emunim started immediately after Sharon took office. In one of his earliest statements as prime minister designate, Menachem Begin promised that there would be many more Elonei More. (Elon More was a controversial settlement group.)[70] In the course of events, it was Sharon who became the champion of the Gush in the government. A few days before taking office, Begin received from Gush Emunim a plan for the establishment of twelve settlements within six months. His reaction was positive.[71] Sharon, on his part, took more direct steps. In the first meeting of the interinstitutional committee for settlements of the government and the Jewish Agency, Elon More, 'Ofra, and Ma'ale Adummim were recognized as official settlements, thus providing them with a status that made them eligible for funds and other help from national institutions.[72] In November 1977, Sharon implied in the Knesset that the government was in favor of granting Gush Emunim the status of an official settlement movement, making the Gush eligible for help from the government and the World Zionist Organization.[73] Following a decision of the Supreme Court which rendered the Elon More settlement illegal and required their removal,[74] Sharon stood behind Gush Emunim and won a decision by the cabinet for a large settlement drive in Judea and Samaria. This decision was seen as an attempt to compensate the Gush for the removal of Elon More. In the confrontation between Sharon and Defense Minister Ezer Weizman, who objected to the settlement strategy of the agriculture minister, it was Sharon's approach that won.[75] The alliance between Sharon and the Gush proved, in retrospect, to be effective in spite of objections from the defense and treasury ministers, and Deputy Prime Minister Yigael Yadin.

Despite this alliance, it would be a mistake to see the two approaches as identical. The patterns of settlement of both approaches were different in certain aspects although they complemented each other and they, in turn, were essentially different from the settlement policy Labor had instituted.

Labor's Pattern of Settlements: The Strategic
Bureaucratic Approach

Labor's West Bank settlement drive took place in three regions: Gush Etzion, Jerusalem, and the Jordan Valley. The prime rationale was strategic; additionally, in the case of Gush Etzion, there had been a Jewish settlement before the War of Independence that was captured by the Arab Legion in 1948. In Jerusalem the idea was to establish a chain of suburbs that would separate the city from the West Bank. Following the reunification of the city the first step was to build residential areas in parts of the city where adverse strategic conditions existed—the region linking the city with Mount Scopus and the Jewish Quarter of the Old City. The next step was the establishment of residential neighborhoods on high ground within the new municipal boundaries in the north (Neve Ya'aqov and Ramot), the south (Gilo), and in the east (East Talpiot). Strategically they cut off the city from its Arab-populated hinterland and defined the dimensions of the city. In this respect Gush Etzion fulfilled the function of separating Jerusalem from the Judea region.[76]

The chain of settlements in the Jordan River Valley were built in accordance with the Allon Plan, and were designed to constitute a defense boundary between the West Bank and Jordan.[77] Another consideration was the fact that this region was not densely populated by Arabs, but was connected in the north with the Bet She'an Valley and could be annexed to Israel in the event of comprehensive settlement.

By May 1976, seventeen settlements had been established along the Jordan Valley Rift; nine in the Gush Etzion, Jerusalem, and Latrun areas. Twenty-five settlements had been established in the Golan Heights, fourteen in the Gaza-Rafah area, and three in the Sinai. The total cost was around $500 million.[78]

There was another element that distinguished Labor's pattern of settlement. The framework for developing Gush Etzion and the Jordan Valley was in accordance with agricultural settlement patterns that had been tried out successfully in Israel prior to 1967. The necessary conditions for success were regional planning, human resources, and initial investment capital.

Though strategic needs were taken into account, the settlements were established near cultivable land and were divided among the various settlement movements that were ready to provide settlers. Early members of these settlements were youth from paramilitary units whose mandatory national service is a combination of military and settlement services. With time these settlements became fully civil settlements either in the form of a kibbutz or moshav. Having invested in the infrastructure, and having provided other advantages, the government expected that in the long run these settlements would become self-sustaining as a result of climatic advantages that would enable them to produce agricultural goods out of season. Industry and tourism were expected to supplement income during slack seasons. Dependence on urban centers within Israel proper was limited to services, not employment. The cluster of villages was designed to become an independent economic and social unit.[79]

Gush Emunim Settlement Patterns: The Ideological Approach

Gush Emunim's approach to settlement could be characterized as the opposite of Labor's. While Labor concentrated its efforts in the relatively unpopulated eastern portion of the West Bank, Gush Emunim pressed for settlements in the heartland of Judea and Samaria, usually in densely populated areas. In accordance with its ideological conception that settling Judea and Samaria was not only a necessity for survival but also a religious obligation, the Gush rejected the notion of justifying settlements in the area for security reasons. Thus, when the legal status of the Elon More settlement came before the Supreme Court in June 1979, Gush Emunim refused to defend the seizure of private land on the grounds of security.[80]

The settlements in which many of the Gush Emunim leaders started off were founded under the Labor government in the Gush Etzion region. The settlement pattern which incorporated Gush Etzion was a product of labor's regional settlement framework—a cluster of self-sustaining units which could be linked to Israel proper. One exception to Labor's approach was Qiryat Arba' near Hebron which was approved by the government in 1970 and established in the heartland of Judea in the vicinity of a heavily populated area.[81] Another exception was the settlement in Qadum which was founded illegally in 1975 and eventually accepted by the Labor government in 1977 because of political pressures. Qadum is in the heart of Samaria and only nine miles west of Nablus, the largest city in the West Bank.[82]

In contrast to the settlements in the Jordan Valley, the settlements in the middle of the Arab population that came into being under the Likud government were established in places without favorable agricultural conditions.

These "spot" settlements, as Elisha Efrat dubbed them,[83] were limited in the amount of land available to them since most of the nearby land was occupied and cultivated by Arab farmers. Consequently, most of the Jewish settlers continued to commute to work in Israel's metropolitan areas. Several of the settlements were deliberately placed far from existing roads and electricity supplies in order to force the government to pave roads and connect them with the Israeli infrastructure. But this was precisely their goal—establishing facts and committing the government to invest in infrastructure and link the whole area to Israel proper. Moreover, it was an aspect of their self-image to establish settlements in remote places where conditions were difficult, thus emulating the pioneer "stockade and tower" settlements of the 1930s.[84] Just as these settlements, which had been founded by the Labor movement against the mandate government's will, ultimately decided Israel's borders of 1949, Gush Emunim argued that their pioneering would define the borders of greater Israel.

The territory-wide aspirations of Gush Emunim toward the whole of the West Bank led to the establishment of spot settlements in Samaria which did not constitute an integrated regional cluster like that established by Labor in the Jordan River Valley. Gush Emunim tried to overcome these difficulties in several ways. One was the development of communal settlements (*yishuv kehilati*) which would be socially of rural nature but urban in terms of employment and economics. This implied the development of local industry without discounting continued commuting to the Tel-Aviv and Jerusalem metropolitan areas. Both sources of employment required the paving of roads and highways that would connect the region with the Israeli economic centers. Gush Emunim also tried to overcome the scattered nature of their settlement through organizational means. The settlements in Judea and Samaria signed a covenant that became the founding document of Gush Emunim: *Amanah* (covenant, in Hebrew). In addition, they formed a Representative Council (Moetzet Yesha) that would voice the collective needs of the settlements in Judea, Samaria, and the Gaza Strip. Each settlement sent two representatives to the council which was designed to articulate the interests of the settlements, voice them before the government, and influence the public in Israel and the diaspora. The settler community started publishing a Hebrew magazine, *Nekuda* (Point), and an English newsletter, *Counterpoint*.[85] Having established three layers of organization—Gush Emunim on the ideological level, Amanah as a settlement organ, and Moetzet Yesha as a political organ—the Gush hoped that its settlements would eventually change the map to such an extent that no Israeli government would be able to withdraw from the West Bank. Regional development was projected to follow the spot settlements.

Sharon's Approach

Sharon's settlement policy differed from Gush Emunim's only in one aspect—the strategic input. While both Gush Emunim and Sharon saw Judea and Samaria as an integral part of Israel's security, Sharon conceptualized the spot settlements into a strategic framework.[86] The Sharon Plan essentially complemented the Allon Plan by adding a chain of settlements in Western Samaria starting from Hinnanit (established in 1981) and Reichan (1979) in the north, both non-Gush Emunim settlements, through Mevo Dotan (1981), Sa Nur (1977), Shave Shomeron (1977), Qedumim (1975), Qarne Shomeron (1977), Yaqqir (1981), and Hallamish (1977), all Gush Emunim settlements (see figure 6-1). This chain of settlements was located on the Samarian Mountains overlooking the coastal plain—the most populated region in Israel. In the Jordan Valley Rift, where the chain of settlements was almost completed during Labor's administration, six settlements were added to the existing seventeen.

Another component in Sharon's strategy was the establishment of settlements along the trans-Samaria road which was designed to cut across Samaria and to connect the Jordan Valley with the coastal plain. Ma'ale Efrayim (established in 1977) was planned to become the urban regional center of the Jordan Valley chain of settlements, and served the additional function of control over the trans-Samaria road. Kefar Tappuah (1978), Ariel (1978), and Elqana (1977) were additional units in the trans-Samaria chain. Elqana was intended to add to the control of the coastal plain together with Ma'ale Shomeron (1979) and Sal'it (1978) to the north. Except for Kefar Tappuah, none of these settlements were Gush Emunim's and all were designed to become urban communities.

The third component in Sharon's strategy was to surround Jerusalem with four clusters of settlements and towns. In addition to the Etzion bloc in the south, three new blocs were established: to the east, the Ma'ale Adummin bloc which included one town, two Gush Emunim settlements, and an industrial center; to the north, the Bet El bloc which included five settlements, three of which were Gush Emunim, and one urban settlement; and to the northwest, the Givon bloc in which two Gush Emunim setlements and one town were founded. These blocs provided a security belt for Jerusalem that complemented the pre-1967 Jewish settlement from the west in the corridor leading from the plain (see figure 6-1).

At the end of his tenure, Sharon had presented the Israeli public with an impressive, though controversial, record of accomplishments. As table 6-5 indicates, fifty settlements were built in the West Bank in four years, in comparison to twenty-seven settlements built during ten years of Labor administration. Out of these, forty-four were established in Judea and Samaria during the Likud administration, compared to ten under Labor's

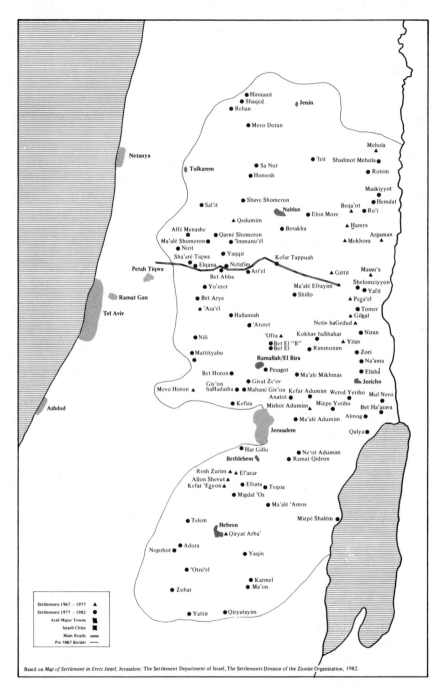

Figure 6-1. Map of Israeli Settlements in the West Bank—1982

Table 6-5
Number of Settlements according to Region and Administration

Region	1967-1977 Labor	1977-1981 Likud	Total
Jordan Valley and the Dead Sea	17	6	23
Judea and Samaria	10	44	54
Total	27	50	77

Source: Adapted from Matityahu Drobles, *The Settlements in Judea and Samaria: Strategy, Policy and Plans* (Jerusalem: World Zionist Organization, Settlement Department, January 1981) (Hebrew).

Note: Labor's ten settlements in Judea and Samaria were distributed as follows: five in the Etzion bloc (to be included within Israel according to the Allon plan); one in the Latrun region (included within the scheme of minor territorial adjustments of the Rogers plan); one in the Jerusalem region (Adummin); one in Qiryat Arba'; and two temporary settlements in Samaria.

administration. Out of Labor's ten, two were temporary Gush Emunim settlements in Samaria: Qadum and Ofra. One of Sharon's earliest decisions was to approve permanent status to these two settlements in Samaria. He also presented a strategic rationale for these settlements: two chains of settlements combined by the trans-Samaria road and a belt of settlement around Jerusalem.

Sharon's pattern of settlement differed from Labor's in the type of settlement established. The predominant model for Labor settlements in the West Bank was the kibbutz or moshav accompanied by a regional center. In contrast, the model advanced by Sharon in cooperation with Gush Emunim was the communal settlement (*yishuv kehilati*)[87] and the urban settlements (see table 6-6). Whereas the communal settlement was designed to become a small-size community (200 to 300 families), the urban settlements were intended to become either towns in their own right or satellite towns. To illustrate this pattern we could use three settlements on the trans-Samaria road: Kefar Tappuah in the east is a communal settlement; Ariel is designated to become a medium-size town; and Elqana will be a satellite community for Tel-Aviv.

This difference between Sharon's and Labor's patterns of settlement bore implications that went beyond strategic interests. Sharon not only expanded the territorial component of his strategic demands but he also broadened the socioeconomic base of the settling population. Labor limited its settlement needs, in accordance with the Allon Plan, to a strip of land eight to twelve miles wide along the Jordan River and to the agricultural sector which involves about 6 percent of the Israeli population. The new types of settlements whose economic base was industry and services opened settlement to the two largest sectors in the Israeli economy. The suburban nature

Table 6-6

Distribution of Settlements in Judea and Samaria according to Settling Movement and Type of Settlement

Settling Movement	Communal Settlement	Urban Settlement (town or regional center)	Kibbutz or Moshav	Industrial Village or Center	Para-military	Total
Gush Emunim[a] -Amanah	21	—	—	—	—	21
NRP Settling[b] Movements	—	—	3	1	—	4
Poalei Agudat[c] Iisrael			1	1		2
Beitar-Herut[d]	3			1	1	5
Other Settling Movements	3			1		4
Nonidentified[e]	1	12		1	4	18
Total	28	12	4	5	5	54

Source: Adapted from Drobles, *The Settlements in Judea and Samaria: Strategy, Policy and Plans* (Jerusalem: World Zionist Organization, Settlement Department, January 1981) (Hebrew)

Notes:

[a]One settlement, Nili, which is nonreligious and appears in Drobles as nonidentified, has since been transferred to Amanah. See *Amanah Settlements, the Settlement Movement of Gush Emunim* (Jerusalem: Amanah, June 1982), p. 7.

[b]Most of these settlements are identified with Gush Emunim. For instance, Chanan Porat, the leader of the Gush lives in Kibbutz Kfar Ezyon.

[c]An ultra-Orthodox movement, identifies with Eretz Israel Movement.

[d]Two out of the five are still in the process of being established.

[e]Out of the twelve nonidentified urban settlements, many are Gush Emunim ideological centers.

of several of the settlements was also designed to attract a large population which aspired to leave the cities only for residential purposes.

The Politics and Ideology of Settlement

The settlement issue was, from the beginning, both a political and ideological question. Labor and Likud shared the view that the West Bank should be strategically controlled by Israel. Where they disagreed was in the details of what strategic control meant. Labor, loyal to its partition orientation aspired to reach a modus vivendi with the Hashemite regime regarding repartition of Palestine. Settlement patterns were therefore limited in their scope to a well-defined area sparse in its Arab population. Likud's nonpartition orientation dictated a new settlement pattern that Ariel Sharon, as agriculture minister, developed and implemented. But while Sharon supplied the strategic framework and the resources, it was Gush Emunim that provided the enthusiasm and the manpower upon which the whole enterprise depended.[88] Without the transformation of the Israeli polity and the legitimacy it received from the Israeli public Gush Emunim might have remained a protest movement with no ability to transform its ideology into a realistic enterprise.[89]

To what extent did Sharon's pattern of settlement render repartition of the West Bank impracticable? Undoubtedly, Likud's goals in establishing as many settlements as possible and the location chosen for those settlements were inspired by domestic political issues and were meant to establish facts which would make it difficult for any government to withdraw from the West Bank. The West Bank was carved up by settlements in such a disparate fashion that it would be impossible to reach a partition agreement with Jordan that would not require the removal of many established settlements. At the same time, the accelerated rate at which these settlements were erected affected their economic base. Many of the settlers resided in temporary housing and continued to find employment within Israel proper. It will be a while until Jewish settlement in the West Bank becomes a significant demographic factor and a substantive economic base emerges. In addition, the Jewish population constitutes only around 3 percent of the total population in the West Bank (excluding the greater Jerusalem metropolitan area). The Likud spoke of 120,000 Jews residing in the West Bank by the year 1985, but even if they reach the projected population they will still constitute a minority of around 15 percent.

The question of the viability of these settlements was the subject of a debate between Labor's Raanan Weitz and Likud's Matityahu Drobles, two heads of the Rural Settlement Department of the Jewish Agency. The two opposing opinions illustrated the differences between the strategic-partition and bureaucratic approach of Labor and the nonpartition, fact-creating approach of Likud. Weitz, while acknowledging that his objection to settlements in Judea and Samaria was motivated by ideological and political considerations, based his pessimism about the viability of these settlements on the lack of regional planning and development and the lack of sufficient resources. His main argument was that settlement activity in Judea and Samaria will divert resources from higher-priority regions like the Golan Heights and the Jordan Rift which are not densely populated by Arabs and are strategically more important. Weitz also maintained that implementation of settlement policy through a "national settlement" organ or through inexperienced movements like Gush Emunim would fail.[90] Drobles, in contrast, defended the settlements in Judea and Samaria and described them as a success story. Recognizing the social, economic, and security problems of commuter settlements and the inability to develop an agricultural base because of the scarcity in water and land, he argued that the economic base of these settlements would be industry and tourism. Nevertheless, he described most of the settlements as prospering socially and self-sufficient economically. The strategic conception that he put forward was based on Israel's need to control the whole West Bank. Consequently, the settlement pattern should be to settle the areas between Arab population centers and to encircle them. Trying to present a regional development framework, Drobles divided the spot settlements of Gush Emunim and the chain settlements of Sharon into clusters. The Settlement Department, according to Drobles, was cooperating with the settlement movements, and was encountering a growing demand for absorption in Judea and Samaria.[91] But as table 6-6 indicates, the settlement movements that played a role in Judea and Samaria were not from the Labor camp. Except for one settlement in northern Samaria (almost on the old border) all the other fifty-three came from either the religious or the civil camps.

In summary, the transformation of the Israeli polity which began following the 1967 war and which was translated into political reality ten years later, produced new realities in the West Bank during the first Likud administration. At the end of four years, the heartland of the West Bank—Judea and Samaria—was spotted with settlements and divided by roads which provided a basis for strategic territorial control of the region and its population. This network of settlements, if they develop and become viable, will make any partition in the future more difficult. The next step of the Likud government is to strengthen political control in the West Bank. This policy started to develop in the second Likud administration, and will be analyzed in the next chapter.

Notes

1. See Roberto Bachi, *The Population of Israel*, pp. 79, 399.

2. The traditional division of the Israeli political and ideological system is into three camps: Labor, Civil, religious. See for instance, Daniel J. Elazar, "Israel's Compound Polity," in Howard R. Penniman, ed., *Israel at the Polls, The Knesset Elections of 1977* (Washington, D.C.: American Enterprise Institute, 1979), pp. 9-16.

3. Moshe Dayan, *Moshe Dyan: Story of My Life* (New York: William Morrow and Co., 1976), pp. 133-134.

4. On these negotiations see Golda Meir, *My Life* (Tel-Aviv: Ma'ariv, 1975), pp. 158-162 (Hebrew).

5. Michael Bar-Zohar, *Ben-Gurion, A Political Biography*, Part II (Tel-Aviv: Am Oved, 1977), p. 852 (Hebrew).

6. Ibid., pp. 853-867.

7. For an examination of the way Ben-Gurion liquidated competing political centers within and outside the military see ibid., pp. 776-843.

8. Michael Brecher, *The Foreign Policy System of Israel* (London: Oxford University Press, 1972), pp. 265-269; and Michael Brecher, *Decisions*

in Israel's Foreign Policy (New Haven: Yale University Press, 1975), pp. 240-243. See also Moshe A. Gilboa, *Six Years—Six Days*, 2d. ed. (Tel-Aviv, Am Oved, 1969), p. 15 (Hebrew).

9. Shlomo Aronson, *Conflict and Bargaining in the Middle East* (Baltimore: The Johns Hopkins University Press, 1978), p. 7.

10. Bar-Zohar, *Ben-Gurion*, p. 866.

11. For a detailed study of Israel's retaliation see Shlomo Aronson and Dan Horowitz, "The Strategy of Controlled Retaliation: The Israeli Example," *Medina u-Mimshal*, vol. 1, no. 1 (Summer 1971):77-100 (Hebrew). See also Dan Horowitz, "The Control of Limited Military Operations: The Israeli Experience," in Yair Evron, ed., *International Violence: Terrorism, Surprise and Control* (Jerusalem: The Hebrew University of Jerusalem, 1979), pp. 258-276; and Ernest Stock, *Israel on the Road to Sinai, 1949-1956* (Ithaca, New York: Cornell University Press, 1967), pp. 67-75.

12. On cooperation regarding Jerusalem, see Michael Brecher, *Decisions in Israel's Foreign Policy*, p. 10. Regarding the Jordan-Yarmuk River system see ibid., p. 224.

13. See Ben-Gurion's speech to the Knesset, *Divrei Ha-Knesset*, October 19, 1958.

14. For further analysis, see Nadav Safran, *From War to War* (New York: Pegasus, 1969), pp. 232-233; and Dan Horowitz, "The Israeli Concept of National Security and the Prospects for Peace in the Middle East," in Gabriel Sheffer, ed., *Dynamics of a Conflict* (Atlantic Highlands; N.J.: Humanities Press, 1975), pp. 244-245.

15. Ben-Gurion expressed his position regarding the electoral system in David Ben-Gurion, *The Restored State of Israel* (Tel-Aviv: Am Oved, 1969), Vol. 2, pp. 575-579 (Hebrew).

16. Bar-Zohar, *Ben-Gurion*, p. 1015.

17. Ben-Gurion, *The Restored State of Israel*, Vol. 1, p. 468. On this development, see particularly the criticism of Moshe Sneh (leader of the Israeli Communist Party) of the two Socialist parties, ibid., p. 472.

18. In 1953, Ben-Gurion published a series of articles in the daily newspaper *Davar*, which were later collected and published in a booklet entitled, *On the Communism and Socialism of Ha-Shomer Ha-Tzair*, under the nom de plume of Saba Shel Yariv (Grandfather of Yariv—Yariv being his grandson's name), published by *Mapai*, Tel-Aviv, 1953.

19. To better understand this relationship see Amitai Etzioni, "The Decline of Neo-Feudalism: The Case of Israel," in Moshe Lissak and Emanuel Gutmann, eds., *Political Institutions and Processes* (Jerusalem: The Hebrew University of Jerusalem, 1971), pp. 70-87.

20. Avraham Avi-Hai, *Ben-Gurion, State Builder, Principles and Pragmatism* (New York: John Wiley and Sons, 1975), p. 273.

21. As a matter of fact, the Labor camp as a whole declined from 63

seats in the Knesset (51.2 percent of the electorate) in the 1965 elections to 56 seats (46.2 percent) in 1969. Source: Central Bureau of Statistics, *Results of Elections to the Eighth Knesset and Local Authorities*, Special Series, no. 461, Jerusalem, 1974.

22. Edward Luttwak and Dan Horowitz, *The Israeli Army* (New York: Harper and Row, 1975), p. 210.

23. The rationale and the ramifications of the Samua reprisal operation are discussed in David Kimche and Dan Bowey, *The Sandstorm* (London: Sacher and Warsburg, 1968), ch. 4.

24. On the impact of the conquest of the West Bank and the new Palestinian consciousness on Israeli Arabs see Rafik Halabi, *The West Bank Story*, ch. 11.

25. For a study of this phenomenon see Rael Jean Issac: *Israel Divided: Ideological Politics in the Jewish State* (Baltimore: The Johns Hopkins University Press, 1978), ch. 3, 5, and 6.

26. Dan Margalit, *Message from the White House* (Tel-Aviv: Otpaz, 1971), p. 13 (Hebrew).

27. The revolution of the youth circles is analyzed in Eliezer Don-Yehiya, "Stability and Change in a Camp Party: The NRP and the Youth Revolution," *State, Government and International Relations*, no. 14 (November 1979):25-52 (Hebrew).

28. The Likud pre-1973 figure is based on the total of the various factions that merged into the Likud, see Shevach Weiss, *The Knesset* (Tel-Aviv, Achiasaf, 1977), pp. 30-31.

29. This conclusion is based on the analysis of the 1979 elections as presented in *The Election Results to the Tenth Kenesset* (Jerusalem: The Central Bureau of Statistics, October 1981).

30. In Hebrew there are two expressions for the concept of settlement: *Hityashvut* and *Hitnachlut. Hitnachlut* is a biblical concept and was used by *Gush Emunim* while *Hityashvut* has a secular connotation. For this and other differences, see Tzvi Ra'anan, *Gush Emunim* (Tel-Aviv: Sifriyat Poalim, 1980), pp. 133-143 (Hebrew).

31. On the ideological and political differences between the Zionist, non-Zionist, and anti-Zionist religious movements, see Eliezer Don-Yehiya, "Origins and Developments of the Agudah and Mafdal Parties," *The Jerusalem Quarterly*, no. 20 (Summer 1981):46-64; and Ilan Greilsammer, "Les Groupes Politiques Marginaux en Israël: Characteristiques et Functions," *Revue Francaise de science politique*, vol. 31, no. 5-6 (October-December 1981):890-921.

32. The two approaches are analyzed in Charles S. Liebman and Eliezer Don-Yehiya, *Civil Religion in Israel: Traditional Judaism and Political Culture in the Jewish State* (Berkeley: University of California Press, forthcoming), ch. 7.

33. On the idea of Torah ve-Avodah see the section on Samuel Hayyim Landau in Arthur Hertzberg, ed., *The Zionist Idea* (New York: Atheneum, 1981), pp. 433-439. On the two sections Mizrachi and Ha-Poel ha-Mizrachi see Gary S. Schiff, *Tradition and Politics, The Religious Parties of Israel* (Detroit: Wayne State University Press, 1977).

34. The best application of the consociational model in explaining religion and state in Israel is Eliezer Don-Yehiya, "Religion and Coalition: The National Religious Party and Coalition Formation," in Asher Arian, ed., *The Elections in Israel—1973* (Jerusalem: Jerusalem Academic Press, 1975), pp. 260-264. For a more elaborate and empirical study of this issue see Eliezer Don-Yehiya, *Cooperation and Conflict between Political Camps: The Religious Camp and the Labor Movement and the Education Crisis in Israel*, a dissertation submitted to the Hebrew University of Jerusalem (September 1977) (Hebrew with an abstract in English).

35. Besides Don-Yehiya's detailed analysis of the education crisis in *Co-operation and Conflict between Political Camps,* see also Emanuel Gutmann, "Religion and Its Role in National Integration in Israel," *Middle East Review,* vol. 12, no. 1 (Fall 1979):31-36. For the impact of the national religious education system on the emergence of Gush Emunim see Lawrence Kaplan, "Education and Ideology in Religious Zionism Today," *Forum,* no. 36 (Fall/Winter 1979):25-34; and Eliezer Goldman, "Simplistic Messianism," *B'tfutzot HaGolah,* no. 79/80 (Winter 1977), pp. 112-113 (Hebrew).

36. See Ehud Sprinzak, "Gush Emunim: The Iceberg Model of Political Extremism," in *State, Government and International Relations,* no. 17 (Spring 1981):29-30 (Hebrew).

37. Arend Lijphart, *Democracy in Plural Societies,* p. 53.

38. Interview with Uriel Simon, in *The Jerusalem Post,* magazine section, March 12, 1982, p. 3. Simon is one of the heads of Oz ve-Shalom—a small group in the national religious camp.

39. Ibid. See also Don-Yehiya, "Stability and Change," pp. 37-38.

40. Dan Horowitz, "The Impact of Structural Processes and Conjectural Phenomena on the Election Results," *B'tfutzot HaGolah,* no. 81/82 (Summer 1977):169-170.

41. Charles S. Liebman, "Myth, Tradition and Values in Israeli Society," *Midstream* (January 1978):44.

42. Charles S. Liebman and Eliezer Don-Yehiya, "Israel's Civil Religion," *The Jerusalem Quarterly,* no. 23 (Spring 1982):60. See also Charles S. Liebman and Eliezer Don-Yehiya, *Civil Religion in Israel: Traditional Judaism and Political Culture in the Jewish State,* especially the concluding chapter.

43. Amnon Rubinstein, *From Herzl to Gush Emunim and Back* (Tel-Aviv: Schocken, 1980) (Hebrew).

44. Ibid., pp. 104-110. Quote from p. 106.

45. Ze'ev Shternhal, "The Basic Problems of the Political System," *B'tfutzot HaGolah*, no. 81/82 (Summer 1977):171-172 (Hebrew).

46. Ben-Gurion often repeated three principal goals of Zionism: the in-gathering of the exiles, security, and Hebrew labor, which was later on transformed to settlement of the land. See for instance, David Ben-Gurion, *Vision and Road* (Tel-Aviv: Mapai, 1957), Vol. 1, pp. 8-9, and Vol. 3, pp. 20-21; David Ben-Gurion, *In the Battle* (Tel-Aviv: Mapai, 1957, sixth edition), Vol. 1, pp. 53-54. For an interpretation of Ben-Gurion's value system see Shmuel Sandler, "Ben-Gurion's Attitude toward the Soviet Union," *The Jewish Journal of Sociology*, vol. 21, no. 2 (December 1979):154-156.

47. Daniel J. Elazar, *Israel: From Ideological to Territorial Democracy*, Jerusalem Institute for Federal Studies, Occasional Papers (January 1978) p. 2.

48. Ibid.

49. Liebman and Don-Yehiya, *Civil Religion in Israel*, ch. 4.

50. Gush Emunim leaders legitimized this claim on Rabbi Kook's teachings. See for instance an interview with Rabbi Yohanan Fried in Ra'anan, *Gush Emunim*, pp. 177-178; and an interview with Rabbi Eliezer Waldman, ibid., p. 195.

51. Benny Katzover in an interview, Israel Television's special program on the fifteenth anniversary of the Six Day War, June 3, 1982. See also an interview with Rabbi Fried in Ra'anan, *Gush Emunim*, pp. 187-188.

52. See an interview with Rabbi Waldman in Ra'anan, *Gush Emunim*, pp. 195-197. See also Mordechai Nisan, "A Herzlian Zionist Model for Judea and Samaria," in *Forum*, no. 41 (Spring/Summer 1981):85-90; and by the same author, "Gush Emunim: A Rational Perspective," *Forum*, no. 36 (Fall/Winter 1979):15-23.

53. Mordechai Nisan, "*Gush Emunim* and Israel's National Interest," *Jerusalem Letter* (January 1980):5-6. (Jerusalem: Jerusalem Center for Public Affairs.) Reprinted with permission.

54. Quoted in Sprinzak, "Gush Emunim: The Iceberg Model," p. 45, fn. 43.

55. The notion that Gush Emunim is a deviation from traditional Zionism can be detected in such books as Ra'anan, *Guish Emunim*, see especially chs. 5 and 6; and Rubinstein's *From Herzl to Gush Emunim*, especially ch. 8.

56. Nisan, "Gush Emunim and Israel's National Interest," p. 2.

57. This phrase is taken from Balaam's prophecy (Numbers, 23:9).

58. Rabbi Waldman provides a philosophical interpretation of this prophecy as it relates to the destiny of the Jewish people. See Ra'anan, *Gush Emunim*, pp. 205-206 and 210-211.

59. Rubinstein, From *Herzl to Gush Emunim*, ch. 7.

60. Janet O'Dea, "Gush Emunim: Roots and Ambiguities, The Per-

spective of the Sociology of Religion," *Forum,* No. 2 (25), 1976:39-50. For a criticism of this interpretation see Shulamit Hareven, Natan Rotenstreich, and Eliezer Goldman in *B'tfutzot HaGolah,* 79/80 (Winter 1977):104-113 (Hebrew).

61. Quotes taken from O'Dea, "Gush Emunim: Roots and Ambiguities," pp. 39 and 45.

62. Goldman, "Simplistic Messianism," p. 112.

63. See Louis Guttman, "The Israel Public, Peace and Territory: The Impact of the Sadat Initiative," (The Jerusalem Institute for Federal Studies, Paper JR 1, Part 1, table 1, January 1978, Jerusalem). This data is based on a continuing survey by the Israel Institute of Applied Social Research and the Communications Institute of the Hebrew University.

64. Pesach Adi, "The Likud and the Alignment in the Eyes of the Voter, in the Context of Domestic and External Policies and the Evaluation of Their Leadership," The Israel Institute of Applied Social Research, *Yedion,* no. 54 (February 1981):19 (Hebrew). For another poll indicating hawkish attitudes, see Hanoch Smith, "Election Forecast," *Ma'ariv,* November 28, 1980.

65. Sprinzak, "Gush Emunim, The Iceberg Model," pp. 22-49.

66. Amnon Rubinstein argued that the explanation for Gush Emunim support from many in the labor camp was its representing the continuation of pioneering settlement tradition, in Rubinstein, *From Herzl to Gush Emunim,* p. 115. See also an interview with Ephrayim Ben-Hayim, a member of the Kibbutz ha-Meuhad movement traditional *Ahdut ha-Avodah*—a supporter of *Gush Emunim,* in Ra'anan, *Gush Emunim,* pp. 212-221.

67. Rubinstein, *From Herzl to Gush Emunim,* p. 126.

68. For the alliance between these different groups in the Land of Israel movement, see Rael Jean Issac, *Israel Divided,* ch. 3.

69. See *Nekudah,* no. 31 (July 17, 1981):2 (Hebrew). *Nekudah* is the bulletin of the settlements in Judea, Samaria, and the Gaza Strip.

70. The story of the Elon More group is summarized by Aharon Dolav in *Ma'ariv,* October 26, 1979.

71. *Ma'ariv,* July 27, 1977.

72. Ibid.

73. *The Jerusalem Post,* November 10, 1977.

74. For a legal analysis of the Elon More case, see Moshe Drori, "Land and Israeli Settlements in Judea and Samaria," *Law and Legislation in Israel,* Part 2, pp. 3-7. New York: American Jewish Congress, Commission on International Affairs, n.d.

75. On the controversy surrounding the Elon More issue see Yosef Harif's articles in *Ma'ariv,* November 2, 1979, and November 9, 1979. See also, *The Jerusalem Post,* November 12, 1979.

76. This analysis is based on Elisha Efrat, "Spatial Patterns of Jewish

and Arab Settlements in Judea and Samaria," in Daniel J. Elazar, ed., *Judea, Samaria and Gaza: Views on Present and Future*, pp. 25-27.

77. On the rationale of this approach, see Yigal Allon, "The West Bank and Gaza within the Framework of a Middle East Settlement," *Middle East Review*, vol. 12, no. 2, (Winter 1979/80):15-18. See also an interview with Yisrael Galili, chairman of the settlement ministerial committee, *Ma'ariv*, May 14, 1976.

78. *Herald Tribune*, May 13, 1976.

79. Efrat, "Spatial Patterns of Jewish and Arab Settlements," pp. 21-23.

80. See Moshe Drori, "Land and Israeli Settlements," Part 2, p. 6. See also the courts decision in *Ma'ariv*, Oct. 20, pp. 17-20.

81. On Qiryat Arba' see *Ha'aretz*, weekend magazine, May 18, 1979, pp. 7-9.

82. On Qadum, see *The Jerusalem Post*, magazine section, May 14, 1976, pp. 10-11. On the meaning of Qadum in Labor settlement policies, see *Herald Tribune*, May 13, 1976.

83. Efrat, "Spatial Patterns of Jewish and Arab Settlements," pp. 23-25. See also an article by Efrat in *Ha'aretz*, February 16, 1982.

84. Efrat, "Spatial Patterns of Jewish and Arab Settlements," p. 28.

85. Nisan, "A Herzlian Zionist Model," p. 89. See also Sprinzak, "Gush Emunim: The Iceberg Model," p. 28.

86. On Sharon's strategic approach see an interview with him in *Ma'ariv*, January 26, 1979; and an article by Aharon Priel in *Ma'ariv*, October 17, 1980. The analysis is also based on a lecture given by Sharon's advisor on settlement affairs, Uri Bar-On, at Tel-Aviv University, on April 17, 1980.

87. For a full explanation of the *yishuv kehilati*, see Raanan Weitz, *The New Settlements* (Jerusalem, September 1979), pp. 12-13.

88. See interview with Sharon, *Ma'ariv*, January 26, 1979.

89. See Sprinzak, "Gush Emunim: The Iceberg Model," p. 27.

90. Weitz, *The New Settlements*, pp. 15-19; and Raanan Weitz, "Should Settlement of the West Bank be Continued?" (Jerusalem: The World Zionist Organization, September 1980) (Hebrew). See also the debate between Weitz and Drobles in *Ma'ariv*, September 21, 1979.

91. See Matityahu Drobles, *The Settlement in Judea and Samaria— Strategy, Policy and Plans* (Jerusalem: World Zionist Organization, Settlement Department, January 1981).

7

Israel and the Palestinian Communal Structure: The Struggle in the West Bank and Lebanon

The evolution of the Arab-Israeli conflict from a primarily interstate conflict to a conflict with intercommunal aspects following the Six Day War, was accompanied by a transformation of both the Palestinian and the Israeli communities. While the Palestinian communal structure evolved into a diaspora center with a territorial periphery, Israel's partition elite was replaced by a leadership and a settlement movement committed to the manifest integrity of the Land of Israel. By definition, these developments were bound to bring the two opposing centers—the Israeli and the Palestinian—into direct conflict. This confrontation took place in both the territorial periphery, the West Bank, and the diaspora center, Lebanon. The clash involved military and political confrontations, and in essence represented a new development in the history of the Arab-Israeli conflict.

Up until the war in Lebanon, one of the outstanding features of the Arab-Israeli conflict was that although the Palestinians were the principal victims of the conflict, the protagonists were Israel and the Arab states. This point was observed by Israeli sociologist Baruch Kimmerling who has described the June 1982 war in Lebanon as the most important war since 1948.[1] In all the previous wars Israel fought for its existence, it never fought the only entity that claimed the right to replace Israel. Following the collapse of their sociopolitical structure, the Palestinian community, according to Kimmerling, transferred the mandate of the war against Israel to the Arab states. Only in 1982 did the two entities claiming the right over *Eretz Yisrael*-Palestine clash again. Indeed up until 1982, the Jewish and Palestinian communities had never encountered each other on the battlefield directly in an organized and comprehensive fashion. The 1982 showdown was only the military expression of a direct political struggle that had reached a new stage with the transformation of both polities. It emanated from the new realities in the Palestinian communal structure which the new Israeli elite that had come into power in 1977 had to face. The clash, however, started in the fall of 1981 and it took place in the West Bank.

The Attack on the West Bank

Ten years after the beginning of the Israeli occupation the heretofore implied struggle between Israel and the Palestinians over the West Bank came out into the open. It was a struggle between a national-religious coalition in Israel and a diaspora center with its territorial periphery.

On the Palestinian side, the period of the first Likud administration represented a tightening of the diaspora center's control over the Palestinians in the West Bank through domination over institutions and coordination of political activity via West Bank pro-PLO leaders. On the Israeli side, the new Likud government penetrated the heartland of the West Bank through broad settlement. It soon became clear that Prime Minister Begin considered the subject of the autonomy plan, which became a part of the Camp David Accords, to be limited to self-rule for the population. The Autonomy Committee headed by the prime minister demanded Israeli authority over land, water, internal security, and other crucial functions. A more liberal interpretation of Israel's perception of the future autonomy forwarded by the Defense Ministry was rejected by Begin and his cabinet in early May 1979.[2]

West Bank demonstrations in protest of new settlements and the autonomy plan, directed and organized by the diaspora center and its territorial extension, indicated the growing power of the new Palestinian communal structure, as well as the new pattern of the conflict. The struggle was now over the West Bank.

Israel's response to the new Palestinian communal structure during the first Likud administration was relatively moderate. Prime Minister Begin, himself absorbed in the peace negotiations with President Sadat, was also surrounded by two ministers who perceived their main objective as promoting peace.[3] Thus Ezer Weizman, who was responsible in his capacity as defense minister for the West Bank, enacted a policy of moderation.[4] He had anticipated that the Palestinians in the West Bank and the Gaza Strip would eventually join the autonomy negotiations, or abide by them once a framework was agreed upon between Israel and Egypt. Foreign Minister Moshe Dayan, more pessimistic than Weizman in this regard, tried to promote Palestinian cooperation through direct meetings with Palestinian leaders in the West Bank.[5] Another route that Dayan tried unsuccessfully to advance was unilateral autonomy. According to this approach, once Israel unilaterally implemented the autonomy, the West Bank leaders would have to assume responsibility for self-rule functions.[6] The replacement of both ministers by two hawks—the newly appointed Foreign Minister Yitzchak Shamir who abstained in the Knesset during the vote on the Camp David Accords, and the new Defense Minister Ariel Sharon whose approach to the West Bank was demonstrated during his tenure as minister of agriculture—

facilitated the development of another stage in the struggle over the West Bank.

The assault on the Palestinian communal structure was directed at both the charismatic center and its extension in the territorial periphery. It was a concentrated effort, taking place within the span of a year and beginning after the victory of the Likud in the 1981 elections. Since the first target of the new approach was the West Bank, we shall first analyze the attack on this periphery. It will become evident further on in the chapter that the later action in Lebanon was part of the same campaign.

The man who was appointed by Sharon to administer the West Bank was Menahem Milson, whose ideas on the Palestinian problem had been articulated on various occasions prior to his nomination as head of the Civil Administration in the West Bank. Milson served as advisor on Arab Affairs to the Military Government from July 1976 to September 1978. In an article appearing in May 1981, Milson argued that the PLO's political domination of the West Bank was the major obstacle to implementation of the Camp David peace plan. Arguing that previous Israeli policies were responsible to a large extent for the strengthening of PLO influence in the West Bank, he then concluded: "Continued political domination of the territories by the PLO will guarantee that organization's continued legitimacy within the Arab world, not to mention its power to veto any Arab move in the direction of Camp David."[7] His operational conclusion was therefore that "Israel will have to engage in a persistent political campaign against PLO domination in the territories." On a previous occasion when he had been asked how this goal should be implemented, Milson replied, "Regarding the details of the ways and means of the struggle against the PLO's domination in the territories, it is not a matter for public debate. Just as we don't publicize operational plans and tactics in the course of a military struggle, we should not publicize the ways of a political struggle."[8] The analogy between the two domains, however, was an indication of what Milson had in mind.

Indeed, Milson approached his administrative assignment as if it was a military operation. He started with an attempt to outflank the PLO power centers by promoting alternative routes of authority, and then launched a frontal attack. This coordinated strategy, adopted by Sharon and Milson, was composed of three elements: the promotion of the village leagues as a potential alternative leadership to the mayors; the dismissal of pro-PLO mayors; and the application of pressures on other national institutions in the West Bank.

The Village Leagues (Rawbit al-kura)

The attempt to build up the village leagues started in 1978 during Milson's first tenure in the West Bank. The military government, faced with the growing power of pro-PLO mayors, discovered that side by side with the towns in the West Bank there existed a population which had lived in underdeveloped villages, constituting around 70 percent of the inhabitants. Although the Jordanian administrative structure was left untouched under Israeli rule the mayors of the cities and towns in effect became representatives of and responsible for the villages of the district. Each village head (*mukhtar*) in every district was thus under the authority of the mayor who represented them all before the government.[9] Gabriel Baer, in a study of the village *mukhtar* in Palestine, noted that the *mukhtar* held great power in his hands because all official documents, permissions, and personal requests had to be channeled through him.[10] The significance of this power became increasingly important even before 1967. At the same time, Baer argued, the integration of villages into the central administration complemented other developments of political modernization in reducing the status of the *mukhtar*. It was this structure, maintained by Israel for more than a decade of rule, that the military government now wanted to change.

The promotion of the village leagues started to gain momentum with the appointment of Milson as head of the Civil Administration in November 1981. In addition to the already extant Hebron-district village league (the first one to be founded and the most powerful), six more leagues emerged in the districts of Bethlehem, Ramallah, Jenin, Nablus, and Qabatiya and in the village of Habla.[11] Excluding the Jordan Valley, they constitute a geographic network which includes almost all the West Bank Arab villages. Following their establishment, funds for village development became available. Requests for family reunions received special treatment if presented through the leagues. Identification cards seized during demonstrations were returned through the leagues. Licenses for summer visits from Arab countries to the West Bank, which had been previously submitted through the municipalities, were now handled by the leagues.[12] It has been observed that the role given to the leagues and their geographical location around major cities could indicate that the municipal structures on the West Bank are slated to be phased out.[13]

The PLO's reaction was clear and dramatic. Yusuf al-Khatib, the head of the Ramallah village league, was assassinated on November 17, 1981, and several attempts were made against his colleagues. Jordan reacted by announcing, on March 9, 1982, that those who supported the village leagues were collaborating with Israel. Jordan's Prime Minister Mudar Badran issued a military order giving them one month to withdraw or face either the possible confiscation of their property or the death penalty.[14] Israel's response to both challenges was unprecedented since occupation of the West Bank: members of the village leagues were armed and trained in self-defense.[15] Following Badran's announcement, Sharon warned that the statement put Jordan in the same camp as that of terrorists and that Israel would treat Jordan accordingly.[16] Receiving strong and explicit support from the Israelis, the village-league leaders threatened Jordan with retaliation against its supporters. Before the month was over, Mustafa Dudein, the Hebron-area leader considered to be the head of the other village-league leaders, professed his loyalty to King Hussein. While stressing his loyalty to the Palestinian cause, in a meeting with Israeli professors and journalists, he added that it was only in order to secure practical aid for roads, schools, and medical care that the village leagues cooperated with the Israelis at all.[17] His principal message at that meeting was to appeal to the Israeli media not to portray him as a collaborator. A few days later, threats and acts of violence were executed against the Bethlehem Municipality, the Bethlehem University, and East Jerusalem newspapers. Indications pointed to the village leagues (and more directly to the Kumsia family heading the Bethlehem village league) as the perpetrators of the violence.[18]

The promotion of the village leagues raises a question regarding Israel's ultimate goals for the West Bank. What did Israel hope to achieve by promoting a rural leadership whose widespread support by the West Bank population had yet to be proven? Amnon Cohen, who had served as adviser for Arab Affairs to the military government in the West Bank, criticized Milson's policies in promoting the village leagues on the basis that he did not see in them a potential alternative to the PLO's political influence.[19] In Cohen's opinion, the only group within the West Bank that could mount a successful campaign against PLO influence was the supporters of King Hussein. Instead of increasing the rivalry between Hussein and the PLO, Israel offered them both a common enemy in the form of the village leagues. Jordan objected to the leagues because they served to weaken its already weakened status.

Milson's ultimate aim, if we judge from his public statements, was an agreement with Jordan. According to Milson: "Any agreement on the permanent solution of the Palestinian problem must ultimately be struck between Israel and that political entity whose center is Amman."[20] Jordan's proclamation of a death sentence on the supporters of the village leagues, he agreed during an Israeli television interview, represented a serious threat.[21] Unlike Cohen, Milson perceived the destruction of PLO influence in the West Bank as a precondition for either autonomy or a settlement with Jordan. The village leagues were one instrument in achieving that goal.

In this regard one can distinguish between Milson and Sharon. Sharon, in conjunction with Begin, has seen the West Bank as an integral part of Israel. For Sharon, village leagues have served as a means to divide and rule in order to control the population. Since the Likud coalition did not perceive Jordan as a potential legitimate contender for the West Bank, Sharon preferred to support the leagues over pro-Jordanian elites who could probably counterbalance PLO influence more effectively. If we also consider Sharon's settlement initiatives and his objection to the support given to Hussein in September 1970, Sharon's intentions may become clearer. In any event, whatever the differences between Sharon and Milson may have been, their common denominator in terms of policy has been the destruction of the new Palestinian communal structure.

The Municipalities

The move to dismiss pro-PLO West Bank mayors which began in March 1982, was in the making for a long time. The institution of the Civil Administration, which was designed to separate military and civilian functions in the West Bank, could in retrospect be seen as the first move in this direction. Though this new structure could be viewed as a step in preparing the way for autonomy, it could also be interpreted as an attempt to remove PLO representatives from the West Bank. Even if the Civil Administration was simply a device to prepare for autonomy, it was still a direct challenge to the PLO's political status in the region. For the mayors, however, this administration also implied a shift from military occupation, under which they could justify instrumental cooperation with Israel, to a more permanent situation where cooperation would have meant granting some legitimacy to Israel's presence. In any event, the mayors boycotted Milson's administration.

Sharon's direct attack began on March 11, 1982, with the outlawing of the National Guidance Committee which had already suffered various acts of the military government.[22] On March 18, Ibrahim a-Tawil, the mayor of Al-Bireh, was dismissed and his municipal council was disbanded because the mayor had refused to meet with the head of the Civil Administration. Milson declared that "The Council was dismissed because, for several months, it had proclaimed, both verbally and in writing a boycott of not only the head of the civil administration, but of the very fact of its existence."[23] The municipalities of Nablus, Ramallah, and Al-Bireh called immediately for a three-day strike and were joined by other municipalities, but none of the mayors resigned. On March 25, Bassam Shak'a of Nablus and Karim Khalaf of Ramallah were dismissed despite their contention that they continued to see themselves as mayors duly elected by their people.[24]

In the following months, five more mayors were fired, the most important being the mayor of Jenin where an appointed council of local citizens agreed to take over the municipality. (The others were the mayors of Anabta, Dura, Qalqilya, and Deir Dibwan).[25] In Nablus, Ramallah, and Al-Bireh, Israeli officials took over municipal affairs when local citizens refused to serve on municipal committees. But this refusal and a month of demonstrations in which nine Arabs and two Jews were killed, were the only manifestations of resistance against the Israeli moves. The PLO call for mass resistance was the only clear policy that came out of Beirut.[26] With its hands tied in Lebanon because of a July 1981 cease-fire agreement, the PLO's options were very limited. The limitations of the PLO as an external center providing leadership and direction for its territorial periphery in time of crisis were manifest in the behavior of the leading West Bank mayors. Karim Khalaf, for instance, announced at first that he was resigning as a reaction to Tawil's dismissal, and then refused to submit his resignation. In an Israeli television interview on March 21, he proclaimed loyalty to both Amman and Beirut (meaning the PLO). Bassam Shak'a, before being ousted, followed the line of Mayor Elias Freij of Bethlehem, a moderate, and refused to resign.[27] One Israeli journalist summarizing the reaction in the West Bank noted that despite recent events, 80,000 workers were still crossing into Israel each day to work in Israel's private sector, and thousands were employed in building Jewish settlements in the territories.[28]

The establishment of the Civil Administration and the removal of the mayors involved a certain added cost for Israel. The new structure effectively negated what was perceived by Israel as an accomplishment; holding free elections despite its role as occupier. Begin himself, in February 1981, described the 1976 elections as an indication of Israel's policy of noninterference in the territory's local affairs.[29] Within this system, a tacit agreement was reached in which functions were divided between the various parties. High-policy matters were decided by Israel, and local affairs decided by elected officials. The new policy involved more direct intervention by the Civil Administration. Instead of communicating with the local inhabitants through their elected officials, the new structure required a process of managing the towns through Israeli officials. The move by Sharon and Milson against the municipalities was described by Amnon Cohen as "Israel's re-conquest of Judea and Samaria."[30]

But as we have indicated, the strategic goal of the second Likud administration was the destruction of the relationship between the West Bank and their diaspora center. In order to accomplish this goal, Israel also struck at other power centers of the PLO in the West Bank.

Other Power Centers

In November 1981, Nadim Zaro, the former mayor of Ramallah, returned to the West Bank following twelve years of exile in Jordan. Zaro returned in response to Sharon's early signals indicating a new liberal approach to the West Bank. By this time, the struggle against PLO power centers had already started. Following two days of rioting, Bir-Zeit University was closed on November 4, 1981, for two months. This came in the wake of several other measures which included the temporary closure of *Al-Fajr*, restrictions on the movement of several leaders suspected of instigating disruptions, and the ban of monetary transfers from the PLO to institutions and individuals in the West Bank. Israel's persistence in pressuring these institutions in the ensuing period indicated that the second Likud administration, and especially its new defense minister, had decided to eradicate the PLO's power centers in the West Bank.

The clash between the Civil Administration and Bir-Zeit University illustrates the struggle that took place in the West Bank. The first closure came in response to demonstrations at the university against the new Civil Administration. One of the innovations of the administration was the inclusion of institutions of higher learning under the authority of its own education department. Following the reopening of Bir-Zeit, an official of the education department came for an appointment with Dr. Baramki, acting president of the college. When he came for a second meeting on February 15, the official was beaten up by rioting students after being abandoned by Baramki. In retaliation, Bir-Zeit was closed for another two months. On April 19, the university reopened amid an atmosphere of pessimism. Indeed, steps like the confinement of members of the student council to town limits and occasional arrests of students suspected of holding explosive material, rendered it unlikely that the university would finish the academic year. On July 8, following several days of clashes between students and troops, the university was closed for another three months. It reopened on October 2, with the next academic year due to start on October 11. Even though the students were well aware that their demonstrations would bring about closure and the loss of the academic year, they apparently could not stay silent when Israel was attacking their charismatic center in Beirut.[31]

Relations with the Arab press also deteriorated during the second Likud administration. In the previous years, the Weizman rule guided censorship. According to this rule, whatever had been published in the Hebrew press was publishable in the Arab press. Consequently, Arab editors would tip Israeli journalists to West Bank news items and then rewrite the stories they had inspired. This policy was changed in the summer of 1981 by the new defense minister and in the subsequent period censorship became increasingly rigorous.[32] Before Sharon's new measures, the censor would have looked the other way or given the publication in question some warning if they published material which they had not submitted for censorship. During the winter of 1982, the Israeli authorities started to take action. On several occasions, publication of *Al-Fajr* and *Al-Sha'ab* was suspended or circulation in the West Bank was banned. Following expiration of their annual distribution licenses in March 1981, editors Hanna Siniora of *Al-Fajr* and Mahmoud Yáish of *Al-Sha'ab* refused to sign applications for new licenses. Their objection was that the forms included new restrictions. While denying these charges the spokesman for the Civil Administration did admit that the licenses were being issued for a shorter period of time. *Al-Quds*'s editor, however, picked up his license. In June 1982, the editors of the two more-radical newspapers were called in to Yigal Karmon, Milson's advisor for Arab affairs, and were warned that if they continued to publish items that were not submitted for censorship, they would be banned. When the newspapers ignored this warning, Israel again banned circulation, and the case went before the High Court of Justice.[33] The censor seemed to ban accounts of disorders which might have contributed to the rebellious mood of the territory. According to the editor of *Al-Fajr*'s English edition, Saman Khoury, the censor's new policy was to remove almost all news stories about the territories. Abu Zuluf, the editor of *Al-Quds* also complained in March 1982, about an unprecedented crackdown by the censor. The censor also rejected publication notices from people announcing withdrawals from the village leagues.[34]

Another significant change that surfaced in the summer of 1981 was the cutoff of money transfers from the PLO to the West Bank. One of the PLO's sources of influence was its ability to pour money into municipalities and probably to universities as well. Despite the constant flow of money, and the source of that money, Defense Minister Weizman had ordered that as long as the imported money was not used for making explosives, the transfers should not be stopped.[35] Following Weizman's departure this policy started to change, but the real crackdown came when Sharon took office as defense minister. Sharon forbade any transfer of money that originated in the PLO, thus effectively blocking the Joint Jordan-PLO Committee which distributed the funds. The effect of this order was felt a year later. With a small budget allocated to the territories by Israel and priority given to villages over cities, the municipalities started living off their savings.[36] At the same time, the Civil Administration started inspecting the universities' budget to track down PLO money.[37]

Despite the severance of funds, it seemed that a total cutoff of PLO resources was impossible. Some money was being smuggled in through the allowance of 1,000 Jordanian Dinar permitted to each person coming into Israel through the bridges.[38] In addition, other PLO assets were tapped in Western Europe and the United States. For example, a United Palestine Appeal (UPA) was founded in the United States. Its founder, according to Jack Anderson, was Paul Ajlouny, publisher of *Al-Fajr*; thus indicating a PLO orientation.[39] It was easier for Israel to seal off funds from the Joint Jordan-PLO Committee than to control money transfers from abroad.

Finally, the military government and the Civil Administration decided to regulate other lines of communication between West Bank leadership and external influences. In the summer of 1981, the military government of the

West Bank decided to implement an order existing since 1968 which forbade any encounters between a West Bank inhabitant who was abroad and an organization hostile to Israel. With this came an end to the policy of disregarding direct meetings between public figures from the West Bank and PLO leaders.[40] Toward the summer of 1982, Israeli journalists reported that the policy of open bridges between Israel and Jordan was being reviewed by the Civil Administration and officers of the military government.[41] One result of this review was that starting in June the procedure for crossing the bridges into Jordan was prolonged, giving the Civil Administration more control. Similarly, the procedure for summer visits to Israel was changed; instead of the municipalities controlling the requests, authority was transferred to the village leagues.

As the end of the first year of the second Likud administration approached, it seemed clear that there was a decided effort to stop the PLO's political influence in the territories. This assault complemented the settlements drive in Judea and Samaria which had been launched during the first Likud administration. Following a visit in April 1982, William B. Quandt, the former director of the Middle East office of the National Security Council, perceived the settlements issue to be foremost in the minds of West Bank residents. Other issues which aroused discontent involved Israeli intervention in the municipal councils, educational councils, and newspapers.[42]

The campaign against these modernizing institutions was a result of the realization that they had become PLO power centers. A former coordinator of activities in the territories indicated on the eve of the war in Lebanon that Israel had decided to eradicate the PLO's political influence in the West Bank and the Gaza Strip, as it had done to their military base in the territories.[43] Apparently, incoming Defense Minister Sharon had reached the conclusion that in order to achieve that goal, a crackdown on the PLO power base in the West Bank would not be sufficient. In order to accomplish the destruction of the new Palestinian communal structure it was necessary to attack not only the territorial periphery but the diaspora center as well.

The Attack on the Diaspora Center

The Peace for the Galilee operation that started on June 6, 1982, must be understood in the context of the Likud's policies toward the West Bank. The pretext for the war was the threat in the north originating from a PLO military buildup in Lebanon. This base served as a center for terrorist activities, not only against settlements in the Galilee but also against Jewish targets all over the world. Nevertheless, it became clear immediately that Israel's strategic goals went beyond the forty-kilometer *cordon sanitaire* that was initially declared to be the goal of the campaign. The real aim of the war was the PLO center in Beirut which radiated authority far beyond Lebanon and especially into the West Bank where the government's concerns lay.[44]

The real goals of the operation in Lebanon were unique in the history of Israeli wars. In a lecture to the National Defense College held in early August, Prime Minister Begin compared the war to the Sinai Campaign and the Six Day War by distinguishing between a war of no alternative and a war of choice. Whereas the 1948 war and the Yom Kippur War belonged to the first category, the others, including Peace for the Galilee, were wars of choice that prevented later wars where Israel would have to fight under worse circumstances.[45] However, the accepted classification in Israeli national defense literature is between a preventive war and a preemptive attack. The Sinai Campaign in 1956 was generally defined as a preventive war, in light of the growing military strength of Egypt which might have tipped the balance of power; and the Six Day War was defined as a preemptive attack designed to strike before the Arabs attacked Israel.[46] In both cases, Israel acted out of the fear that inaction might endanger its existence, whether in the future or in the short term. In 1982, the PLO did not present an immediate threat to Israel's existence; neither did it present a potential threat to the balance of power.

The war in Lebanon could not be classified as an extended retaliation operation along the lines of previous Israeli actions following terrorist activities from across the border.[47] The order of battle employed in this operation and the duration of the war went far beyond any criteria for a retaliatory operation. More important, the traditional goal of such operations had always been to force the host government to control terrorist activities originating in its territory. In 1982, it was clear that the Lebanese government had no means of controlling the PLO. Moreover, a traditional by-product of retaliation policy was the satisfaction of domestic demands for revenge, as was the case throughout the 1950s and in 1978 following the massacre on the road to Tel-Aviv. In order to accomplish such a goal, there was no need to extend the war to Beirut. Finally, if the goal was to provide security to Israeli northern settlements, there was no need to go beyond the initial stage of clearing a forty-kilometer strip.

As we observed at the outset of the chapter, this was the first war in which Israel clashed directly, though not exclusively, with Palestinian armed forces. It was also the first time that Israel was engaged in a war with political goals that went beyond security and national existence. The real aim of the war was to destroy the military and political infrastructure of the PLO in Lebanon in anticipation that this accomplishment would have an impact on the other components of the Palestinian communal structure. In order to accomplish this goal, Israel for the first time in her history besieged an Arab capital for over two months. The siege generated a great deal of negative public opinion as a result of heavy civilian losses. In timing the operation, Israel took into account the presidential elections in Lebanon scheduled for the end of August.[48] This calculation is another new aspect of the Israeli strategy. Military force thus became a means of influencing internal affairs in a neighboring Arab country in order to help establish a leadership with whom Israel had previous contacts.[49] Bashir Jemayel, the president elected in 1982, was expected by Israel to not only restore order in Lebanon but also to ensure that the PLO would not reestablish itself in Lebanon. All these newly developed goals and by-products reverberated within Israel when opposition to the war was voiced in the streets as the war was still being fought.

The attack on the PLO in Lebanon must also be placed in the context of the conceptual framework that had started to unfold several years earlier. It was another stage in the Likud's campaign not to relinquish any part of Judea and Samaria. It was directly linked to the new settlements policy adopted during the first Likud administration and to the attempt to destroy PLO influence in the West Bank which was launched during the second Likud administration. Sharon's repeated warnings, during his first year as defense minister, about the threat in the north, and the evidence that the operation was planned during the summer of 1981 further indicate that the operation was an integral part of a broad political framework adopted by the new ruling elite.

How was the expulsion of the PLO from Beirut expected to influence the West Bank? First, it was assumed that by dealing a blow to the PLO in Beirut, its status in the West Bank would decline. The increasing PLO influence in the West Bank was linked to its success in establishing a political and military base in Lebanon after its expulsion from Jordan in 1970 and 1971. Therefore, Israeli decision makers may have assumed that the destruction of that center would have a corresponding negative impact on regard for the PLO by Palestinians in the West Bank. Second, the government must have assumed that the destruction of the military, economic, and political infrastructure in Lebanon would curtail the PLO's ability to influence the leadership of the West Bank. A crippled PLO with a new order of priorities would find it more difficult to divert resources to the territorial Palestinians, and would no longer be in a position to intimidate Arab governments into financially supporting the Palestinian diaspora organ. Similarly, the destruction of the organization in Beirut was anticipated to spill over to their organization offshoot in the territories which had already been shaken by Sharon and Milson. Thirdly, Lebanon was the only Arab country in the Middle East where the PLO could establish a relatively independent base—a state within a state. It was anticipated that the expulsion of the PLO from Lebanon to other Arab states would destroy its freedom to rebuild such an elaborate operation and would place it under the close scrutiny of other Arab regimes. The authoritarian nature of those Arab regimes, subject to Israeli retaliation, would compel them to confine activities against Israel and restrict PLO organization growth. Finally, Israel hoped that the expulsion of the PLO from Beirut would also strike a blow to Fatah's hegemony and Yassir Arafat's leadership in the organization, thus bringing out ideological and political rivalries among the eight groups making up the PLO. Such a development would effect the PLO's ability to lead the West Bank.

The relationship between the Peace for the Galilee operation and government West Bank policies was clear from an Israeli perspective, but the connection between these two components on another level was not as obvious. How does one explain the fact that while their diaspora center was being destroyed, the population and the leadership in the territories remained calm and did not react violently to Israel's assaults? Throughout the siege of Beirut, workers from the territories continued to work in Israel, the stores were open, and matriculation exams were held on schedule. Scattered demonstrations that were held at Al-Najah and Bir-Zeit universities followed demonstrations by Israelis in Tel-Aviv.[50] Other small demonstrations in Nablus, Bethlehem University, and Gaza[51] did not approach the scale of the territory-wide demonstrations held during the institution of the Civil Administration in November 1981, or during the crackdown on West Bank mayors in March and April 1982. The West Bank in general was quieter from June to August 1982 than it was during the expulsion of the PLO from Jordan in 1970.

One possible explanation of this phenomenon was the diffusion of PLO power centers that took place in the period preceding the operation in Lebanon. The removal from office of the central figures in the PLO establishment in the West Bank, accompanied by tight measures against the universities and the press, reduced the capability of the PLO to mobilize the masses into disorder. While continuing to claim the PLO as their sole representative, West Bank leaders were no longer in a position to act on their own convictions.

More important was the reality that the PLO was not the sole center that radiated authority in the West Bank. As we indicated earlier, Jordan and Israel had their own channels of influence over public life in the West Bank. Taking their cue from Jordan, who stayed on the sidelines while the operation was going on, the pro-Jordanian elites also abstained from leading pro-PLO demonstrations. Continued financial interests and investments in Jordan and the Gulf oil states, and family connections in the East Bank also influenced the behavior of the West Bankers. Similarly, the economic dependence of the West Bank on employment in Israel, Israel's capability of closing the Jordan bridges and institutions of higher learning, in addition to administrative and physical measures, apparently deterred the population from initiating public disturbances. Moreover, the emergence of the PLO as a national center to the West Bank deprived them of leadership. Consequently, when their charismatic center was under siege, they were unable to take independent action. Essentially, they were waiting to see the outcome of the Israeli attack on the PLO in Beirut.

The low profile kept by the Arab states during the war in Lebanon was at least as remarkable as that of the Palestinian Arabs in the West Bank. Despite constant Arab claims that the Palestinian problem constituted the core of the Arab-Israeli conflict, the Arab governments barely went beyond verbal support during the Israeli-Palestinian confrontation. Even Syria, which was involved militarily, acted only when its own presence in Lebanon was endangered. Also evident was the lack of Arab unity—a phenomenon in sharp contrast to the usual upsurge of Arab solidarity during an interstate war with Israel.

Undoubtedly the Arab states' behavior was influenced by the military balance of power. The buildup of Israeli military power following the Yom Kippur War was not paralleled in Egypt or any other Arab confrontation state. Israel's air superiority was demonstrated during the bombing of the Iraqi nuclear reactor in the summer of 1981, and again in the early days of the war in Lebanon when Syria lost scores of planes in air fights and when Syrian missiles in the southern Bekaa were knocked out. The abundantly clear strength of the Israeli air force apparently had an impact on the Arab states' decisions. With Egypt and Israel involved in a peace treaty, Iraq involved in a war with Iran, and Israel threatening Damascus on two fronts (the Golan Heights and Lebanon), the decision to stay out of a military confrontation was rational in military terms.

Inter-Arab rivalries also played a role.[52] Syria's policies in the preceding period alienated many Arab states. Syria's sabotage of Prince Fahad's plan for a Middle East settlement in November 1981 which recognized Israel's existence indirectly in exchange for a Palestinian state, its indirect support for the Soviet invasion of Afghanistan, and Syrian support for Iran in the war against Iraq antagonized Saudi Arabia, the Gulf states, and other Arab states. The only exception was the rejection front which included Libya, Algeria, South Yemen, and the PLO. The latter's close, but cautious, relations with Syria and its participation in the radical rejection front did not promote the PLO's popularity among the more moderate Arab states. Syria, on its part, may have reckoned that a blow to the PLO would render the Palestinian organization weaker and therefore make it more dependent on Syria. Jordan, perceiving the PLO as its main competition in the West Bank and aware of continued subversive attempts by the PLO on the East

Bank, was also not ready to risk a military confrontation with Israel for the sake of serving the Palestinian revolutionary center.

As we have suggested throughout this book, the coalescence of the Jewish and Palestinian communities following the 1967 war within one governmental framework created an intercommunal reality. This new reality was strengthened by Egypt's behavior in the following years. Egypt's limited goals during the 1973 war, the handing over of the territories' representation to the PLO in Rabat in 1974, and the separate peace between Egypt and Israel, all represent a new configuration of relationships in the Middle East. The emergence of a Palestinian communal structure with inter-Arab and international status relieved the Arab states of some of their responsibilities. This new situation was reflected by Arab inaction during the Israeli-Palestinian confrontation in the West Bank and in Lebanon. Arab solidarity with the Palestinian cause was limited to verbal protests on the world scene and their agreement to accept groups of unarmed PLO fighters in eight Arab countries, thus preventing a total annihilation of the organization.

This new pattern, which came to a climax in the Lebanon crisis, was a direct reversal of the process that took place in the period following the Arab revolt in Palestine, from 1936 to 1939. During that period, the conflict was being transformed from a communal to an interstate conflict. The interstate paradigm that was dominant from 1948 to 1967, gave way to a new framework for the post-1967 period. In subsequent years the intercommunal pattern began to influence the behavior of the actors involved.

In summary, the 1982 war in Lebanon represented the new realities that emerged in the region in the fifteen years that elapsed since the June 1967 war. The emergence of a new Palestinian communal structure and a parallel transformation of the Israeli polity, which now laid claims in no uncertain terms over Judea and Samaria, created a direct struggle between the Jewish polity and the Palestinian community. This struggle took place in both domains of the Palestinian communal structure—the West Bank and Lebanon; that is, their territorial periphery and the locus of their diaspora center. The Israeli campaign on the West Bank was fought largely through administrative means. In Lebanon, military means came to the fore and were used to uproot the concentrated Palestinian diaspora center. Thus the war in Lebanon, although it required the crossing of interstate borders, was not an interstate war (except for the clashes with Syria) but rather an intercommunal war, and as such an extension of the Jewish-Palestinian struggle over Eretz Yisrael-Palestine. This direct confrontation which had lain dormant since 1948 when the Yishuv overwhelmed the Palestinians, was almost unavoidable because of the nature of the new situations in both the Jewish and the Palestinian communities.

Notes

1. Baruch Kimmerling, "The Most Important War since the War of Liberation," *Ha'aretz*, August 1, 1982.

2. See Yosef Harif's report in *Ma'ariv*, May 11, 1979.

3. On the attitudes of Weizman and Dayan toward the peace process, see Uzi Benziman, *A Prime Minister Under Siege* (Tel-Aviv: Dvir, 1981) (Hebrew).

4. Defense Minister Weizman, in one of his first meetings with officers of the military government in Judea and Samaria, called for a liberal approach. See *Ma'ariv*, July 7, 1977. This policy came to be known as the "soft hand" approach.

5. Moshe Dayan, *Shall the Sword Devour Forever?* (Jerusalem: Edanim, 1981), pp. 126-130 (Hebrew).

6. Interview with Yair Kotler in *Ma'ariv*, June 26, 1981.

7. Menahem Milson, "How to Make Peace with the Palestinians," p. 35. Reprinted from *Commentary*, May 1981, by permission; all rights reserved.

8. Menahem Milson, "The PLO, Jordan, and the Palestinians: Why Are They Not Ready to Participate in the Peace Process?" in Alouph Hareven, ed., *Is There a Solution to the Palestinian Problem?* (Jerusalem: The Van Leer Jerusalem Foundation, 1982), p. 43 (Hebrew).

9. David Richardson, "Leagues Out of Their Depth," *The Jerusalem Post*, magazine section, March 19, 1982, pp. 3-4; and Yosef Tzuriel's report on the village leagues in *Ma'ariv*, August 28, 1981.

10. Gabriel Baer, "The Economic and Social Position of the Village Mukhtar in Palestine," in Gabriel Ben-Dor, ed., *The Palestinians and the Middle East Conflict*, p. 112.

11. Based on information provided by Civil Administration spokesman Michael Oren on August 15, 1982.

12. See Zvi Barel's article in *Ha'aretz*, August 2, 1982.

13. Richardson, "Leagues Out of Their Depth," p. 4.

14. See Oded Zarai's analysis of the Jordanian move in *Ha'aretz*, March 14, 1982.

15. By March 1982, it was estimated that 170 villages received arms and following the Jordanian warning, Israeli security sources promised to intensify and broaden these programs. See *Ma'ariv*, March 11, 1982; p. 1.

16. *Ma'ariv*, March 11, 1982, p. 3.

17. *The Jerusalem Post*, April 4, 1982.

18. *The Jerusalem Post*, editorial, April 9, 1982.

19. Amnon Cohen in *Ma'ariv*, April 7, 1982. For other criticisms see Yehuda Litani in *Ha'aretz*, March 22, 1982; David Landau in *The Jerusalem Post*, March 31, 1982; and Binyamin Ben Eliezer, previous military governor of the West Bank, in *Ma'ariv*, March 22, 1982.

20. Milson, "How to Make Peace with the Palestinians," p. 35. Reprinted from *Commentary*, May 1981, by permission; all rights reserved.

21. Israeli Television, March 24, 1982. The interview was published by the Israel Ministry of Foreign Affairs, Information Division, *Briefing* 184/28.3.82/3.08.01.

22. *Yediot Aharonot*, March 12, 1982; and Yosef Tzuriel in *Ma'ariv*, March 29, 1982.

23. Menachem Milson on Israeli Television, March 24, 1982.

24. *Yediot Aharonot*, March 26, 1982.

25. Based on information provided by Michael Oren, spokesman of the Civil Administration, August 15, 1982.

26. *Ha'aretz*, March 21, 1982.

27. Report by Y. Litani in ibid.

28. David Richardson in *The Jerusalem Post*, March 26, 1982.

29. Begin's statement is quoted by David Landau in *The Jerusalem Post*, March 31, 1982.

30. *Ma'ariv*, April 7, 1982.

31. On the linkage between the events in Beirut and Bir-Zeit, see Akiva Eldar in *Ha'aretz*, July 16, 1982.

32. See Milton Viorst, "Report from the West Bank," *Columbia Journalism Review* (November/December 1982):43-44.

33. This information is based on reports in *The Jerusalem Post* from March 30, April 2, April 6, April 7, 1982; and interviews with Hanna Siniora, editor of *Al-Fajr*, July 7, 1982, Michael Oren, spokesman of the Civil Administration, and Shlomo Amar, officer in charge of interior affairs in the Civil Administration.

34. *The Jerusalem Post*, March 30, 1982. Regarding the items that were censored see Zvi Barel's article in *Ha'aretz*, May 16, 1982. Since March 1982, the English-language edition of *Al-Fajr* has started releasing weekly censorship reports.

35. Yosef Tzuriel in *Ma'ariv*, July 31, 1981.

36. Yosef Tzuriel in *Ma'ariv*, July 23, 1982; and Shmuel Segev in *Ma'ariv*, May 14, 1982.

37. *Ma'ariv*, February 18, 1982.

38. Interview with Michael Oren, August 15, 1982.

39. *The Jerusalem Post*, April 19, 1982.

40. Tzuriel in *Ma'ariv*, July 31, 1981. See also *The Jerusalem Post*, September 19, 1979.

41. Shmuel Segev in *Ma'ariv*, May 15, 1982.

42. *The New York Times*, May 9, 1982.

43. Interview with Danni Mat, a former coordinator of activities in the territories, June 1, 1982.

44. Chanoch Bar-Tov in *Ma'ariv*, June 18, 1982. On the relationship between the war in Lebanon and the West Bank, see Alouph Hareven in *The Jerusalem Post*, July 13, 1982.

45. Excerpts from Prime Minister Begin's lecture were published in *Ma'ariv* and *The Jerusalem Post*, August 20, 1982.

46. Ernest Stock, *Israel on the Road to Sinai 1949-1956, with a Sequel on the Six Day War*, ch. 7 and pp. 224-234; and Shimon Peres's reply to Begin in *Ma'ariv* and *The Jerusalem Post*, August 27, 1982.

47. Aronson and Horowitz, "The Strategy of Controlled Retaliation,"; and Stock, *Israel on the Road to Sinai*, pp. 110-116.

48. Wolf Blitzer, *The Jerusalem Post*, August 30, 1982.

49. On these encounters, see Shmuel Segev in *Ma'ariv*, August 27, 1982.

50. Interview with Menahem Milson, *Ma'ariv*, July 9, 1982.

51. *The Jerusalem Post*, June 10, 1982.

52. For an analysis of inter-Arab rivalries as an explanation of their behavior during the war in Lebanon see Daniel Dishon, "A Chain of Non-Reaction," *The Jerusalem Post*, magazine section, June 18, 1982.

8　Conclusions

The conflict over Palestine-Eretz Yisrael has always been contested in two settings—the interstate and the communal. What has been subject to change has been the salience of either of the two settings. In Mandate Palestine the conflict was essentially communal. Between 1948 and 1967, the interstate setting became prominent, and after 1967 the conflict was once again marked by the rise of the communal dimension. The basis for the reappearance of the communal element was the physical remunification of Mandate Palestine and the gathering of the two contesting communities under one governmental framework.

The changes that took place in the attitudes of the parties toward the conflict further contributed to this transformation. In Israel, an elite dedicated to partition and the interstate framework was replaced by a government dedicated to the integration of the historic Land of Israel. This government proposed solving the Palestinian problem within a communal framework, which was reflected in the autonomy proposals. Among the Arab states there was a change of behavior; some of the Arab states began detaching themselves from the conflict, refusing to play out their traditional roles. A comparison of the behavior of these Arab states before and during the 1948 war with their behavior in 1982 indicates the magnitude of this change. In the first war, the Arab League took upon itself the liberation of Palestine to the extent that they deliberately limited the autonomous freedom of action of the Arab Palestinian community. Seven Arab armies participated in the struggle against the fledgling Jewish state. By contrast, in 1982 in Lebanon, only Syria participated militarily alongside the Palestinians, and did so only halfheartedly.

The transformations that took place within the Palestinian national movement also contributed to intensification of the intercommunal conflict. The emergence of an organized disapora center that penetrated the political fabric of the West Bank raised the conflict from a Jordanian-Israeli bilateral issue to a complicated contest among states and communities. The extensive Jewish settlement enterprise, escalating since 1977 in the heartland of the Arab population, finally brought the two communities into direct conflict over Judea and Samaria.

Although the conflict encompasses broader issues—the PLO charter calls for the liquidation of the Jewish state, and Israel refuses to accept an independent Palestinian state in any part of Eretz Yisrael—the focus of intercommunal rivalry has been on the West Bank. It was in the West Bank that an intercommunal conflict took place between Jordanians and Palestinians even before 1967. It was here, and to a lesser degree in the Gaza Strip, that the opposing parties met face to face for the first time since 1948. The West Bank became the target of PLO attempts to establish a territorial periphery. It was Judea and Samaria that inspired the integrationist doctrine within Israel which has been translated into political realities since 1977. It was over this region that Israelis and Palestinians fought directly in Lebanon.

Beyond the intercommunal aspect, the West Bank conflict relates to the Palestinian national movement in and of itself. The emergence of a diaspora-center-territorial-periphery structure in the Palestinian national movement was limited in its ability to advance Palestinian goals. The diaspora center may succeed if it deals with a colonial power that does not need to hold the territory in order to ensure its survival. Neither Israel nor Jordan would fall into this category. However, the disapora setting itself exposes the national movement to pressures and vulnerability, as the ordeals in 1970, 1976, and 1982 demonstrate. Thus, despite the impressive accomplishments of the PLO on the international scene, its standing within the region suffered serious setbacks. It failed to territorialize along the lines of the Zionist model.

The shortcomings of the Palestinian communal structure are even more apparent within the West Bank. A solid argument could be made that the Palestinian cause could have been better served had the PLO never emerged. Had the diaspora center not developed and won the support of the Arab world and the international community, the Palestinians might have concentrated on the creation of political and instrumental organs in the West Bank. Under Israeli rule, they might have had the opportunity of reversing the process of peripheralization which began under Jordanian rule when Arab Palestinian aspirations were divided between Arab nationalism and Amman. In contrast to the situation under Jordanian control, they had an opportunity to develop an infrastructure in the West Bank during the first ten years of the Israeli administration. The development of such institutions as the municipalities, the universities, and the press are indicative of the latitude they enjoyed. The clear dividing lines between the Arab Palestinians and the Jewish society provided for a degree of potential that had not existed under Jordanian occupation. Capital for the creation of instrumental organs was available from the Arab world, and even from within the West Bank as a result of contacts with the Israeli economy. To be sure, they had to contend with two neighboring centers, Jordan and Israel. But the rivalry between the two states could have been exploited for the creation of independent power bases. Instead, the creation of a diaspora center only drained authority and resources from the West Bank, thus contributing to peripheralization and the existence of total control by exogenous forces. Instead of reversing the process of territorial peripheralization, the PLO's development reinforced historical patterns of weakening territorial Arab Palestinians.

One could argue that concentrating on developing institutions and leadership in the diaspora weakened the PLO's hold over the periphery. The weakness of local mobilizing institutions made the local leadership vulnerable to Israeli countermeasures. Exile or removal from office of local pro-PLO leaders sufficiently obstructed the intensification of the PLO's control over the West Bank. The reaction within the West Bank during the June-September 1982 war reinforces this argument.

The ascendance of the communal aspect in the Arab-Israeli conflict and the failures of the Palestinian movement have not relieved Israel's problem of achieving stability and a peaceful settlement. Interstate realities in the Middle East have not been changed to such an extent that Israel could absorb the West Bank without threatening future peace agreements with its neighbors. Intercommunal realities may have complicated the network of Israel-Arab relations. As long as the conflict was primarily an interstate struggle, there was always a possibility that it could be resolved by existing interstate mechanisms. The addition of an intercommunal conflict to interstate rivalry has produced a situation in which mechanisms of communal conflict resolution do not apply.

Moreover, Israel cannot absorb the West Bank because of internal factors. Even peripheralized communities like the West Bank and the Gaza Strip would place a heavy demographic burden on Israeli society and political institutions. This is especially true in light of the fact that the peripheralization is a product of linkage with three external centers. Israeli annexation could transform that situation and the stagnation of that community may disappear. In addition, the Israeli-Arab segment could cause a rift in Israeli society, which we have deliberately avoided analyzing. Israeli rule over the West Bank, and the new Palestinian communal structure have influenced the Israeli-Arab sector in the direction of a Palestinian identity. Intensification of this trend would further complicate communalism in Israel proper.

Israel paid a price in the intercommunal struggle against the Palestinians—a price beyond that paid in world public opinion. Israeli policies on the West Bank settlements and the crackdown against PLO support have split Israeli society. Despite the broad public support the government enjoys, the war in Lebanon brought to the surface strong opposition to intercommunal war. The traditional consensus that existed in time of war was nonexistent once the war was expanded beyond the original declared aim of Peace for the Galilee. The split in Israeli society over the issue of the territories, which was reflected to a certain extent in the 1981 elections (when Labor and Likud received almost the same number of votes), corresponded also with attitudes over the war in Lebanon. Demonstrations for and against the war took place while the war was still being fought. As the IDF is a popular army, the divisiveness cut across all military ranks.

It would not have been inappropriate for the Likud government to show some degree of magnanimity toward the Palestinians after Israel's victory in Lebanon and the subsequent dispersion of the PLO. This could conceivably have taken the form of an offer of shared rule of the territories. But the ideological commitment of the ruling elite dictates the course of action the government will take. The fact of the diffusion of the settlements throughout the West Bank puts serious constraints on the possibilities of territorial autonomy or territorial repartition.

Under such circumstances, and unless drastic changes take place in both the Israeli and Palestinian communities, one could expect that intercommunal conflict would continue to afflict their relationship. At this point none of the traditional resolutions to communal conflict—integration, power-sharing, or partition—seems realistic. Relative stability may be maintained through mechanisms outlined by Horowitz and Lustick in their respective studies of dual-authority polities and control, but these mechanisms are not oriented toward solutions.

Looking at the conflict from a territorialization perspective, we may witness two developments in the future. On the Israeli side we may see a territorialization process in Judea and Samaria. Israel has diverted considerable resources to its settlement enterprise in this region. Gush Emunim conceives of its mission as a continuation of that of the Yishuv period; Judea and Samaria are the heartland of the Land of Israel, as they are geographically and as they were historically. The organization and the leadership of the Gush is already based in Judea and Samaria. Mass settlement in Judea and Samaria has begun recently. The new families are moving not only for ideological reasons but also because the region offers attractive and inexpensive suburban and exurban housing. If the trend continues, a pattern of territorialization may be in the making.

On the Palestinian side, a parallel pattern of territorialization may take place. The vulnerability of the Palestinian diaspora center demonstrated in the summer of 1982, and the limitations of relying on Arab states for the attainment of Palestinian goals may force the Arab Palestinians to territorialize in a different manner. One alternative would be to shift the emphasis to the West Bank through the transfer of resources and concede partial leadership to territorial Palestinians. Another possibility would be closer cooperation with Jordan, where Palestinians comprise almost half of the population. Hussein, being aware of this potential internal threat and being aware of the Likud's claim that Jordan is Palestine, will probably make sure that cooperation with the PLO would entail safeguards and concessions from the PLO. From the West Bank's point of view, such cooperation would involve closer cooperation between pro-Hussein and pro-PLO elites. In any event, each option would require PLO concessions. These concessions would have to be on the ideological and the political levels. The question remains whether the PLO would be able to make such hard decisions.

Should both developments take place—Israeli territorialization in Judea and Samaria and a new pattern of Palestinian territorialization—we may witness an intensified intercommunal conflict over territorialization in the West Bank. Israel must realize that even if it prevails in the contest, it will still be faced with a hostile indigenous community. The Palestinians must realize that time is working against them and they may lose their territorial base if they continue to be misled by external entities. The ramifications of such a reality hopefully will influence both sides to reach a compromise either in terms of territorial repartition or power sharing.

Selected Bibliography

Books

Aronson, Shlomo. *Conflict and Bargaining in the Middle East*. Baltimore: The Johns Hopkins University Press, 1978.

Aruri, Naseer H. *Jordan: A Study in Political Development (1921-1965)*. The Hague: Martinus Nijhoff, 1972.

Avi-Hai, Avraham. *Ben-Gurion, State Builder, Principles and Pragmatism*. New York: John Wiley and Sons, 1974.

Bachi, Roberto. *The Population of Israel*. Jerusalem: The Institute of Contemporary Jewry, The Hebrew University of Jerusalem, 1974.

Bailey, Clinton. "The Participation of Palestinians in the Politics of Jordan." Ph.D. diss., Columbia University, 1966.

Bar-Zohar, Michael. *Ben Gurion: A Political Biography*. Tel-Aviv: Am Oved, 1977 (Hebrew).

Ben-Dor, Gabriel, ed. *The Palestinians and the Middle East Conflict*. Ramat-Gan, Israel: Turtledove Publishing, 1978.

Ben-Gurion, David. *In the Battle*. Tel-Aviv: Mapai, 1957 (Hebrew).

———. *Vision and Road*. Tel-Aviv: Mapai, 1957 (Hebrew).

———. *The Restored State of Israel*. Tel-Aviv: Am Oved, 1969 (Hebrew).

Ben-Porath, Y., and Marx, E. *Some Sociological and Economic Aspects of Refugee Camps on the West Bank*. Report R-835-FE. Santa Monica, Cal.: Rand Corporation, August 1971.

Ben-Shahar, Haim; Berglas, Eitan; Mundlak, Yair; and Sadan, Ezra. *Economic Structure and Development: Prospects of the West Bank and the Gaza Strip*. Report R-839-FF. Santa Monica, Cal.: Rand Corporation, 1971.

Bhagwatis, Jagdish N., ed. *Economics and World Order*. New York: The Free Press, 1972.

Brecher, Michael. *The Foreign Policy System of Israel*. London: Oxford University Press, 1972.

Brecher, Michael. *Decisions in Israel's Foreign Policy*. New Haven: Yale University Press, 1975.

Bregman, Arye. *The Economy of the Administered Territories, 1974 and 1975*. Jerusalem: Bank of Israel Research Department, 1976.

Brown, Baratt Michael. *The Economics of Imperialism*. New York: Penguin Books, 1974.

Bull, Vivian. *The West Bank: Is It Viable?* Lexington, Mass.: Lexington Books, D.C. Heath and Co., 1975.

Claude, Inis L. *Power and International Relations*. New York: Random House, 1962.

Cohen, Amnon. *Political Parties in the West Bank under the Hashemite Regime.* Jerusalem: The Magnes Press, The Hebrew University, 1980 (Hebrew).

A Conversation with the Exiled West Bank Mayors. Washington, D.C.: American Enterprise Institute, 1981.

Dayan, Moshe. *Moshe Dayan: The Story of My Life.* New York: William, Morrow and Co., 1976.

Dayan, Moshe. *Shall the Sword Devour Forever.* Jerusalem: Edanim, 1981 (Hebrew).

Deutsch, Karl W., and Foltz, William, eds. *Nation Building.* Chicago: Aldine Atherton, 1966.

Deutsch, Karl W. *The Analysis of International Relations.* Englewood Cliffs, N.J.: Prentice-Hall, 1972.

Don-Yehiya, Eliezer. "Cooperation and Conflict between Political Camps: The Religious Camp and the Labor Movement and the Education Crisis in Israel." Diss., Hebrew University of Jerusalem, September 1977 (Hebrew).

Drobles, Matityahu. "The Settlement in Judea and Samaria—Strategy, Policy, and Plans." Pamphlet. Jerusalem: World Zionist Organization, Settlement Department, January 1981 (Hebrew).

Drori, Moshe. *Local Government, Democracy, and Elections in Judea and Samaria: Legal Aspects.* Jerusalem: Jerusalem Institute for Federal Studies, Bar-Ilan University Institute of Local Government, 1980 (Hebrew).

Efrat, Elisha. *Spatial Patterns for the Implementation of Autonomy in Judea and Samaria.* Tel-Aviv: The Tel-Aviv University Project on Peace, 1980.

Eisenstadt, S.N. *Traditional Patrimonialism and Neopatrimonialism.* Beverly Hills, Cal.: Sage Publications, 1973.

_____ . *Revolution and the Transformation of Societies.* New York: The Free Press, 1978.

Elazar, Daniel J., ed. *Self Rule/Shared Rule: Federal Solutions to the Middle East Conflict.* Ramat-Gan, Israel: Turtledove Publishing, 1979.

_____ . *Judea, Samaria, and Gaza: Views on the Present and Future.* Washington, D.C.: American Enterprise Institute, 1982.

_____ . *Governing Peoples and Territories.* Philadelphia: Institute for the Study of Human Issues, 1982.

Eliav, Binyamin, ed. *The Jewish National Home.* Jerusalem: Keter, 1976.

Elpeleg, Zvi. *King Hussein's Federation Plan: Genesis and Reaction.* Tel-Aviv: The Tel-Aviv University, 1977 (Hebrew).

Field, Michael, ed. *The Middle East Annual Review, 1978.* London: The Middle East Review Co., 1977.

Finger, Nahum. *The Impact of Government Subsidies on Industrial Management.* New York: Praeger Publishers, 1971.

Friedrich, Carl. J. *Trends of Federalism in Theory and Practice.* New York: Praeger Publishers, 1968.

Furnivall, J.S. *Colonial Policy and Practice: A Comparative Study of Burma and Netherland India.* Cambridge, Eng.: Cambridge University Press, 1948.

Gilboa, Moshe A. *Six Years—Six Days.* 2d ed. Tel-Aviv: Am Oved, 1969 (Hebrew).

Halabi, Rafik. *The West Bank Story.* New York: Harcourt Brace Jovanovich, 1981.

Hansen, N.M., ed. *Growth Centers in Regional Economic Development.* New York: The Free Press, 1972.

Harkabi, Yehoshafat. *On the Guerrilla.* Tel-Aviv: Ma'arachot, 1971 (Hebrew).

_____ . *The Palestinian Covenant and Its Meaning.* London: Vallentine, Mitchell, 1979.

Hertzberg, Arthur. *The Zionist Idea.* New York: Atheneum, 1981.

Hirschman, A.O. *The Strategy of Economic Development.* New Haven: Yale University Press, 1958.

Horowitz, Dan, and Lissak, Moshe. *MiYishuv LeMedina* (The Origins of the Israeli Polity). Tel-Aviv: Am Oved, 1977.

Hilal, Jamil. *The West Bank: Its Social and Economic Structure, 1948-1973.* Beirut: Palestine Liberation Organization and Research Center, 1975.

Hurewitz, J.C. *The Struggle for Palestine.* New York: Greenwood Press, 1968.

International Bank for Reconstruction and Development. *The Economic Development of Jordan.* Baltimore: The Johns Hopkins University Press, 1965.

Isaac, Rael Jean. *Israel Divided: Ideological Politics in the Jewish State.* Baltimore: The Johns Hopkins University Press, 1978.

Israel National Section of the International Commission of Jurists. *The Rule of Law in the Areas Administered by Israel.* Tel-Aviv: Israel National Section of the International Commission of Jurists, 1981.

Jacob, Philip E., and Toscano, James V., eds. *The Integration of Political Communities.* Philadelphia: Lippincott, 1964.

John, Robert, and Hadawi, Sami. *The Palestine Diary.* New York: New World Press, 1972.

Johnson, E.A. *The Organization of Space in Developing Countries.* Cambridge, Mass.: Harvard University Press, 1970.

Kanovsky, Elyahu. *Economic Development of Jordan.* Tel-Aviv: University Publishing Projects, 1976.

Karmon, Yigal. *Eretz Yisrael.* Tel-Aviv: Yavneh Publishing, 1978 (Hebrew).

Keohane, Robert O., and Nye, Joseph S., Jr., eds. *Transnational Relations and World Politics.* Cambridge, Mass.: Harvard University Press, 1970.

_____. *Power and Interdependence: World Politics in Transition.* Boston: Little, Brown, 1977.

Kimche, David, and Bowey, Dan. *The Sandstorm.* London: Sacher and Warsburg, 1968.

Konikoff, A. *Transjordan: An Economic Survey.* Jerusalem: Economic Research Institute of the Jewish Agency for Palestine, 1946.

Kuper, Leo, and Smith, M.G., eds. *Pluralism in Africa.* Berkeley: University of California Press, 1969.

Laqueur, Walter. *A History of Zionism.* New York: Schocken Books, 1976.

Lesch, Ann Mosely. *Israel's Occupation of the West Bank: The First Two Years.* Report RM-6295-ARPA. Santa Monica, Cal.: Rand Corporation, August 1970.

Liebman, Charles, and Don-Yehiya, Eliezer. *Civil Religion in Israel: Traditional Judaism and Political Culture in the Jewish State.* Berkeley: University of California Press, forthcoming.

Lifshitz, Ya'acov. *Structural Changes and Economic Growth in the Administered Territories, 1922-1972.* Research Report no. 6. Tel-Aviv: David Horowitz Institute for the Research of Developing Countries, 1974 (Hebrew).

Lijphart, Arend. *Democracy in Plural Societies.* New Haven: Yale University Press, 1977.

Litwin, Uri. *The Economy of the Administered Territories, 1976-1977.* Jerusalem: Bank of Israel Research Department, 1980.

Lucas, Noah. *The Modern History of Israel.* London: Weidenfeld and Nicholson, 1974.

Lustick, Ian. *Arabs in the Jewish State: Israel's Control of a National Minority.* Austin: University of Texas Press, 1980.

Luttwak, Edward, and Horowitz, Dan. *The Israeli Army.* New York: Harper and Row, 1975.

Mahmoud, Amin Abdullah. "King Abdullah and Palestine." Diss., Georgetown University, Washington, D.C., 1972.

Margalit, Dan. *Message from the White House.* Tel-Aviv: Ot Paz, 1971 (Hebrew).

Mazur, Michael P. *Economic Growth and Development of Jordan.* Boulder, Col.: Westview Press, 1979.

McRae, Kenneth, ed. *Consociational Democracy.* Toronto: McClelland and Stewart, 1974.

Meir, Golda. *My Life.* Tel-Aviv: Ma'ariv, 1975 (Hebrew).

Merritt, Richard L., and Rokkan, Stein, eds. *Comparing Nations: The Use of Quantitative Data in Cross-National Research.* New Haven: Yale University Press, 1966.

Migdal, Joel S., et al. *Palestinian Society and Politics.* Princeton, N.J.: Princeton University Press, 1980.

Mishal, Shaul. *The conflict between the West Bank and the East Bank under Jordanian Rule and Its Impact on the Governmental and Administrative Patterns in the West Bank, 1949-1967.* Jerusalem: The Hebrew University of Jerusalem, 1974 (Hebrew).

––––––. *West Bank/East Bank: The Palestinians in Jordan 1949-1967.* New Haven: Yale University Press, 1978.

Nakhleh, Emile A., ed. *A Palestinian Agenda for the West Bank and Gaza.* Washington, D.C.: American Enterprise Institute, 1980.

Nisan, Mordechai. *Israel and the Territories: A Study in Control 1967-1977.* Ramat-Gan, Israel: Turtledove Publishing, 1978.

Myrdal, Gunnar. *Rich Lands and Poor.* New York: Harper and Row, 1957.

Nordlinger, Eric. *Conflict Regulation in Divided Societies.* Cambridge, Mass.: Harvard University Center for International Affairs, 1972.

Quandt, William B.; Jabber, Fuad; and Lesch, Ann Mosely. *The Politics of Palestinian Nationalism.* Berkeley: University of California Press, 1973.

Palestine Government. *A Survey of Palestine.* Jerusalem: Government Printer, 1946.

Pentland, Charles. *International Theory and European Integration.* London: Faber and Faber, 1973.

Porat, Yehoshua. *The Emergence of the Palestinian Arab National Movement, 1918-1929.* London: Frank Cass, 1974.

––––––. *The Palestinian Arab National Movement 1929-1939.* London: Frank Cass, 1978.

Pye, Lucian W. *Aspects of Political Development.* Boston: Little, Brown, 1966.

Ra'anan, Tzvi. *Gush Emunim.* Tel-Aviv: Sifriyat Poalim, 1980 (Hebrew).

Rabushka, Alvin, and Shepsle, Kenneth A. *Politics in Plural Societies: A Theory of Democratic Instability.* Columbus, Ohio: Charles E. Merril, 1972.

Rosen, Stephen J.; Kurth, James R.; and Deutsch, Karl W., eds. *Testing Theories of Economic Imperialism.* Lexington, Mass.: Lexington Books, D.C. Heath and Co., 1974.

Rosenau, James N., ed. *Linkage Politics: Essays on the Convergence of National and International Systems.* New York: The Free Press, 1969.

Rubinstein, Amnon. *From Herzl to Gush Emunim and Back.* Tel-Aviv: Shokhen, 1980 (Hebrew).

Safran, Nadav. *From War to War.* New York: Pegasus, 1969.

Shamir, Shimon, et al. *The Professional Elite in Samaria.* Tel-Aviv: Shiloach Center, Tel-Aviv University, 1975 (Hebrew).

Schiff, Gary S. *Tradition and Politics, The Religious Parties of Israel.* Detroit: Wayne State University Press, 1977.

Shalev, Arieh. *The Autonomy: Problems and Possible Solutions.* Tel-Aviv: Center for Strategic Studies, Tel-Aviv University, 1979 (Hebrew).

Shapiro, Yonathan. *The Formative Years of the Israeli Labour Party: The Organization of Power 1919-1930.* London: Sage Publications, 1976.

Shils, Edward. *Center and Periphery: Essays in Macrosociology.* Chicago: University of Chicago Press, 1978.

Sinai, Anne, and Pollack, Allen, eds. *The Hashemite Kingdom of Jordan and the West Bank.* New York: American Academic Association for Peace in the Middle East, 1977.

State of Israel, Prime Minister's Office, Economic Planning Authority. *Israel Economic Development, Past Progress and Plan for the Future.* Jerusalem: Israel Program for Scientific Translations, 1968.

State of Israel, Central Bureau of Statistics. *Results of Elections to the Eighth Knesset and Local Authorities.* Special Series no. 461. Jerusalem, 1974.

State of Israel Central Bureau of Statistics. *Statistical Abstract of Israel 1978.* Jerusalem, 1978.

State of Israel, Ministry of Defense, Coordinator of Government Operations in Judea and Samaria, Gaza District, Sinai and Golan Heights. *A Thirteen Year Survey (1967-1980).* Mimeographed report, 1981.

Stock, Ernest. *Israel on the Road to Sinai 1949-1956.* Ithaca, N.Y.: Cornell University Press, 1967.

Sykes, Christopher. *Cross Roads to Israel.* London: The New English Library, 1965.

U.S. Department of State, Agency of International Development. *Regional Cooperation in the Middle East.* Mimeographed report, 1979.

Van Arkadie, Brian. *Benefits and Burdens: A Report on the West Bank and Gaza Strip Economics since 1967.* New York: Carnegie Endowment for International Peace, 1977.

Vatikiotis, D.J. *Politics and the Military in Jordan, A Study of the Arab Legion 1921-1957.* London: Frank Cass, 1967.

Weitz, Raanan. *The New Settlements.* Jerusalem, September 1979.

_____ . "Should the Settlements of the West Bank Be Continued?" Jerusalem: The World Zionist Organization, September 1980 (Hebrew).

Wilkenfeld, Jonathan, ed. *Conflict Behavior and Linkage Politics.* New York: McKay, 1973.

Yaniv, A. *PLO—A Profile.* Haifa: Israel Universities Study Group for Middle Eastern Affairs, 1974.

Yariv, S.S. (David Ben-Gurion). *On the Communism and Socialism of HaShomer HaTzair.* Tel-Aviv: Mapai, 1953 (Hebrew).

Articles

Adi, Pesach. "The Likud and the Alignment in the Eyes of the Voter, in the Context of Domestic and External Policies and the Evaluation of Their Leadership." The Israel Institute of Applied Social Research, *Yedion,* no. 54 (February 1981):17-20 (Hebrew).

Allon, Yigal. "Israel: The Case for Defensible Borders." *Foreign Affairs,* vol. 55, no. 1 (October 1976):38-53.

————. "The West Bank and Gaza Strip within the Framework of a Middle East Settlement." *Middle East Review,* vol. 12, no. 2 (Winter 1979/80):15-18.

Aronson, Shlomo, and Horowitz, Dan. "The Strategy of Controlled Retaliation: The Israeli Example." *Medina U'Memshal,* vol. 1, no. 1 (Summer 1971):77-100 (Hebrew).

Badran, Nabil. A. "The Means of Survival: Education and the Palestine Community, 1948-1967." *Journal of Palestine Studies,* vol. 9, no. 4 (Summer 1980):57-61.

Baily, Clinton. "Changing Attitudes toward Jordan in the West Bank." *The Middle East Journal,* vol. 32, no. 8 (1978):155-166.

Baily, Yitzchak. "The Palestinians and Jordan between the Six Day War and the Yom Kippur War." In Eytan Gilboa and Mordechai Naor, eds., *The Arab-Israeli Conflict.* Tel-Aviv: Israel Defense Ministry, 1981.

Budeiri, Musa. "The Universities of the West Bank." *Middle East International,* no. 110 (October 1979).

Daadler, Hans. "The Consociational Democracy Theme." *World Politics,* vol. 26, no. 4 (July 1974):604-621.

Dann, Uriel. "Regime and Opposition in Jordan since 1949." In Menachem Milson, ed., *Society and Structure: Political Structure in the Arab World.* New York: The Van Leer Foundation Series, The Humanities Press, 1973.

Davies, Phillip E. "The Educated West Bank Palestinians." *Journal of Palestine Studies,* no. 31 (Spring 1979):65-81.

Deutsch, Karl. "National Integration: Some Concepts and Research Approaches." *The Jerusalem Journal of International Relations,* vol. 2, no. 4 (Summer 1977):1-29.

Don-Yehiya, Eliezer. "Religion and Coalition: The National Religious Party and Coalition Formation." In Asher Arian, ed., *The Elections in Israel—1973.* Jerusalem: Jerusalem Academic Press, 1975.

_____ . "Stability and Change in a Camp Party: The NRP and the Youth Revolution." *State, Government and International Relations.* no. 14 (November 1979):25-52 (Hebrew).

Don-Yehiya, Eliezer. "Origins and Developments of the Agudah and Mafdal Parties." *The Jerusalem Quarterly,* no. 20 (Summer 1981):46-64.

Drori, Moshe. "Land and Israeli Settlements in Judea and Samaria." *Law and Legislation in Israel.* New York: American Jewish Congress Commission on International Affairs, n.d.

Duchacek, Ivo D. "Antagonistic Cooperation: Territorial and Ethnic Communities." *Publius,* vol. 7, no. 4 (Fall 1977):3-29.

_____ . "Federalist Responses to Ethnic Demands." In Daniel J. Elazar, ed., *Federalism and Political Integration.* Ramat-Gan, Israel: Turtledove Publishing, 1979.

Elazar, Daniel J. "Israel from Ideological to Territorial Democracy." Jerusalem Institute for Federal Studies, Occasional Papers (January 1978).

_____ . "Israel's Compound Polity." In Howard R. Penniman, ed., *Israel at the Polls, The Knesset Elections of 1977.* Washington, D.C.: American Enterprise Institute, 1979.

_____ . "The Role of Federalism in Political Integration." In Daniel J. Elazar, ed., *Federalism and Political Integration.* Ramat-Gan, Israel: Turtledove Publishing, 1979.

Enloe, Cynthia H. "Internal Colonialism, Federalism, and Alternative State Development Strategies." *Publius,* vol. 7, no. 4 (Fall 1977):145-175.

Esman, Milton. "The Management of Communal Conflict." *Public Policy,* vol. 21 (Winter 1973):49-78.

Etzioni, Amitai. "The Decline of Neo-Feudalism: The Case of Israel." In Moshe Lissak and Emanuel Gutmann, eds., *Political Institutions and Processes.* Jerusalem: The Hebrew University of Jerusalem, 1971.

Farchi, David, "Political Attitudes in Judea and Samaria, 1972-1973," *Ma'arachot* no. 231 (July 1973):9-14.

Farchi, David. "Society and Politics in Judea and Samaria." In Raphael Israeli, ed., *Ten Years of Israeli Rule in Judea and Samaria.* Jerusalem: The Magnes Press, The Hebrew University of Jerusalem, 1980 (Hebrew).

Foreign and Commonwealth Office, London. "Palestine Liberation Organization." Background Brief, November 1979.

Galtung, Johan. "A Structural Theory of Imperialism." *Journal of Peace Research,* vol. 13, no. 2 (1971):81-118.

Goldman, Eliezer. "Simplistic Messianism." *B'tfutzot HaGolah*, no. 79/80 (Winter 1977):112-113 (Hebrew).

Guttman, Louis. "The Israel Public, Peace and Territory: The Impact of the Sadat Initiative." Paper JR1. Jerusalem: The Jerusalem Institute for Federal Studies, January 1978.

Gutmann, Emanuel. "Religion and Its Role in National Integration in Israel." *Middle East Review*, vol. 12, no. 1 (Fall 1979):31-36.

Haas, Ernest B. "The Balance of Power: Prescription, Concept, or Propaganda?" *World Politics*, vol. 5, no. 4 (July 1953):442-477.

Hamid, Rashid. "What Is the PLO?" *Journal of Palestine Studies,* vol. 4, no. 4 (Summer 1975):90-109.

Heller, Mark. "Politics and Social Change in the West Bank." In Joel Migdal et al., *Palestinian Society and Politics.* Princeton, N.J.: Princeton University Press, 1980.

Horowitz, Dan, and Mishal, Shaul. "The Political Elite in the West Bank." Department of Sociology/Department of Political Science, The Hebrew University of Jersualem. Jerusalem, 1972.

Horowitz, Dan. "The Israeli Concept of National Security and the Prospects for Peace in the Middle East." In Gabriel Sheffer, ed., *Dynamics of a Conflict.* Atlantic Highlands, N.J.: Humanities Press, 1975.

_____ . "The Impact of Structural Processes and Conjectural Phenomenon on the Election Results." *B'tfutzot HaGolah*, no. 81/82 (Summer 1977):168-170 (Hebrew).

_____ . "The Control of Limited Military Operations: The Israeli Experience." In Yair Evron, ed., *International Violence: Terrorism, Surprise, and Control.* Jerusalem: The Hebrew University of Jerusalem, 1979.

_____ . "Dual Authority Polities," *Comparative Politics,* vol. 14, no. 3 (April 1982):329-349.

Israel Information Center. "Institutions of Higher Learning in Judea and Samaria." Information Briefing. Jerusalem: Israel Information Center, 1981, 361/30.8.81/8.08/2.

_____ . "How the Abuse of Academic Freedom Led to the Temporary Closure of Bir-Zeit University." Jerusalem: Israel Information Center, 1981, IIC/423/22.11.81/3/3.08/12.

Kaplan, Lawrence. "Education and Ideology in Religious Zionism Today." *Forum*, no. 36 (Fall/Winter 1979):25-34.

Karsel, Gideon M. "Consumption Patterns in the Administered Territories after Ten Years of Israeli Rule." In Raphael Israeli, ed., *Ten Years of Israeli Rule in Judea and Samaria.* Jerusalem: The Magnes Press, The Hebrew University, 1980 (Hebrew).

Klieman, Aaron S. "Israel, Jordan, Palestine: The Search for a Durable Peace." *The Washington Papers,* vol. 9, no. 83, 1981.

Lesch, Ann Mosely. "Israeli Settlements in the Occupied Territories." *Journal of Palestine Studies,* vol. 8, no. 1 (Autumn 1978):103-105.

Levy, Sasson. "Local Government in the Administered Territories." In Daniel J. Elazar, ed., *Judea, Samaria, and Gaza: Views on the Present and Future.* Washington, D.C.: American Enterprise Institute, 1982.

Liebman, Charles S. "Myth, Tradition, and Values in Israeli Society." *Midstream*, vol. 24, no. 7 (January 1978):44-52.

Lijphart, Arend. "Federal, Confederal, and Consociational Options for the South African Plural Society." In Nic Rhoodie, ed., *Intergroup Accommodation in Plural Societies.* London: St. Martin's Press, 1979.

Litani, Yehuda. "Leadership in the West Bank and Gaza." *The Jerusalem Quarterly*, no. 14 (Winter 1980):100-109.

Lustick, Ian. "Stability in Deeply Divided Societies: Consociationalism vs. Control." *World Politics,* vol. 31, no. 3 (April 1979):325-344.

Metzer, Jacob. "Fiscal Incidence and Resource Transfer between Jews and Arabs in Mandatory Palestine." The Falk Institute for Economic Research in Israel, Discussion Paper no. 8014. Jerusalem: September 1980.

Milson, Menahem. "How to Make Peace with the Palestinians." *Commentary* (May 1981):25-35.

_____ . "The PLO, Jordan, and the Palestinians: Why are They not Ready to Participate in the Peace Process?" In Alouph Hareven, ed., *Is There a Solution to the Palestinian Problem? Israeli Positions.* Jerusalem: The Van Leer Jerusalem Foundation, 1982.

Mishal, Shaul. "Judea and Samaria: An Anatomy of Municipal Elections." *HaMizrach HeHadash,* vol. 24, no. 1-2 (93-94) (1974):63-67 (Hebrew).

_____ . "The Palestinian West Bank Political Elite—A Behavioral Portrait." In Asher Arian, ed., *Israel—A Developing Society.* Assen, The Netherlands: Van Gorcum, 1980.

"The Mood of the West Bank: Interviews with Three West Bank Mayors." *Journal of Palestine Studies*, vol. 9, no. 1 (Autumn 1979):114-116.

Nisan, Mordechai. "Gush Emunim: A Rational Perspective." *Forum,* no. 36 (Fall/Winter 1979):15-23.

_____ . "Gush Emunim and Israel's National Interest." *Jerusalem Letter* (January 1980):1-6.

_____ . "A Herzlian Zionist Model for Judea and Samaria." *Forum,* no. 41 (Spring/Summer 1981):85-89.

O'Dea, Janet. "Gush Emunim: Roots and Ambiguities, The Perspective of the Sociology of Religion." *Forum,* no. 2 (25) (1976):39-50.

Rejwan, Nissim. "The Palestinian Press under Israeli Administration." *Midstream*, vol. 14, no. 9 (November 1973):15-23.

Rubenstein, Daniel. "The Jerusalem Municipality under the Ottomans, British, and Jordanians." In Joel L. Kramer, ed., *Jerusalem: Problems and Prospects.* New York: Praeger Publishers, 1980.

Sandler, Shmuel. "Ben-Gurion's Attitude toward the Soviet Union." *The Jewish Journal of Sociology,* vol. 21, no. 2 (December 1979):145-160.

Sela, Abraham. "The PLO, the West Bank, and Gaza Strip." *The Jerusalem Quarterly,* no. 8 (Summer 1978):66-77.

Shternhal, Ze'ev. "The Basic Problems of the Political System." *B'tfutzot HaGolah,* no. 81/82 (Summer 1977):171-174 (Hebrew).

Smith, Tony. "The Underdevelopment of Development Literature: The Case of Dependency Theory." *World Politics,* vol. 13, no. 2 (January 1979):247-280.

Smooha, Sammy. "Control of Minorities in Israel and Northern Ireland." *Comparative Studies in Society and History,* vol. 22, no. 4 (April 1980):256-280.

Sprinzak, Ehud. "Gush Emunim: The Iceberg Model of Political Extremism." *State, Government and International Relations,* no. 17 (Spring 1981):22-49 (Hebrew).

"Statement by the West Bank Municipalities and Nationalist and Professional Institutions on the Egypt-Israel Peace." *Journal of Palestine Studies,* vol. 8, no. 2 (Winter 1979):163.

State of Israel, Ministry for Foreign Affairs, Department of Information. "Excerpts from the Statements Submitted to the Supreme Court on Behalf of the Attorney General." (January 11, 1981) 119/1.11.061.

Stock, Ernest. "The Reconstitution of the Jewish Agency: A Political Analysis." *American Jewish Year Book, 1972.* Philadelphia and New York: American Jewish Committee and Jewish Publication Society, 1973.

Sutcliffe, Claude R. "The East Ghor Canal Project: A Case Study of Refugee Resettlement, 1961-1966." *The Middle East Journal,* vol. 27, no. 4 (Autumn 1973):471-482.

Tennenbaum, Michael. "Struggling with Autonomy, Voices of the West Bank and Gaza." *New Leader* (March 26, 1979):7-9.

Viorst, Milton. "Report from the West Bank." *Columbia Journalism Review* (November/December 1981):43-44.

Newspapers and Periodicals

Hebrew
Al-HaMishmar
Davar
Ha'aretz
Ma'ariv
Yediot Aharonot
Nekudah

Arabic
Al-Fajr
Al-Quds
Al-Sha'ab
Shu'un Filastiniya (a periodical published by PLO Research Center in Beirut)

English
The Jerusalem Post
Herald Tribune

Index

About the Authors

Shmuel Sandler is a senior lecturer at the Department of Political Studies—Bar-Ilan University, and a Fellow at The Jerusalem Center for Public Affairs. Dr. Sandler completed the M.A. at the Hebrew University of Jerusalem and the Ph.D. in political science at The Johns Hopkins University in 1977. He has published various articles in journals and books on American foreign policy, Israeli politics, and the West Bank.

Hillel Frisch is a research associate at The Jerusalem Center for Public Affairs. He completed his undergraduate work in history and Middle Eastern studies at Tel-Aviv University and received the M.A. in international affairs from Columbia University.